Palestine Is Our Home

Palestine Is Our Home

Voices of Loss, Courage, and Steadfastness

Nahida Halaby Gordon, editor

Foreword by Mitri Raheb

Palestine Books
www.palestinebooks.com

First Edition published by Palestine Books

Edited by Nahida Halaby Gordon
Foreword by Mitri Raheb

ISBN 978-0-9972635-0-3
Printed in the United States of America

Contents

Foreword

Nahida Halaby Gordon is a Palestinian Arab Christian. I met her the first time at a General Assembly of the Presbyterian Church (U.S.A.) where she is a member. At first I thought she must be a lawyer. She was actively defending Palestinian rights and lobbying for ending the Israeli Occupation. But as it turned out, she was a professor of mathematics and biostatistics. During the course of years I was able to follow her writings and passion for Palestine. Through this book, I came to know Nahida much better. Born in Jerusalem in 1939 and raised as child in Jaffa, Nahida and her family had to leave Jaffa, the place of her childhood memories and her safe haven. Nahida and her family became refugees overnight, scattered together with 750,000 other Palestinian refugees all over the world. In 1951, Nahida came to the United States and had a successful career at a prestigious American university. Yet the land of opportunity with all its wealth and endless possibilities could not make Nahida forget the land of promise, Palestine, that she was forced to leave behind as a child. Nahida and her family were not economic refugees that came to the US; her father was a successful businessman in Jaffa, a flourishing city that was nicknamed as "The Bride of the Sea". Nahida' s family had their home just steps away from the Mediterranean shore. For them, Palestine was the land of promise and Jaffa was the land of endless opportunities.

The dream of Nahida and her family turned in 1948 into a nightmare, and a catastrophe. The Nakba was not a natural catastrophe; it was rather part of a European colonialism of Palestine using western European Jews as their imperial tool. No wonder that this whole book focuses on the Nakba. In this book, Nahida invites 22 eyewitnesses to tell their stories and includes two chapters on Palestinian art and costume. Through these stories, the reader is invited to feel the "hopes and fears of all the years". Behind these collected stories lies a lot of hard work and rich research by Nahida that cannot be underestimated. Nahida chose the eyewitnesses carefully; she wanted to make sure that they are reliable and credible sources. Then, she was able to knit these multiple Palestinian voices into one colorful tapestry depicting the Palestinian narrative surrounding the Nakba.

Since 1948 and while living in the United States, Nahida never gave up her hope to be able to return one day to the Promised Land, Palestine. With the Psalmist, Nahida kept praying day and night: "How shall we sing the Lord's song in a foreign land? If I forget you, O Jerusalem, let my right hand forget its skill! Let my tongue stick to the roof of my mouth, if I do not remember you, if I do not set Jerusalem above my highest joy!"

And yet, life in exile took longer than expected. Almost seventy years have passed and Nahida is still longing to the promise and right of return. Slowly she started doubting if she will live long to see that date. She writes: "I am getting old now and will probably never live long enough to see my dream of returning to my home in Palestine…With passing time, it is now difficult to see how we can live our dreams of return, but we can hold unto wonderful memories of home and family." In this book, Nahida wants to capture those stories and memories; to collect them in an album and pass them on to the next generation, to her grandchildren and to the next generation of Palestinians so that they will not forget and instead hold to the dream of return to the land of their forefathers and foremothers, to Palestine. Put in the words of Laura Baramki Khoury: "We will never forget; our stories will continue to be passed on from one generation to the next, and someday justice will prevail." In that sense, this book is a kind of testimony that Nahida leaves to us, asking us not to forget, but to hold up the light of right in spite of the prevailing power of might.

But this book is more than that; it is one of the best and most creative guides to Palestine, to its history, geography, and rich culture. Through it, Nahida invites the readers to cross the river with her to the Promised Land. She leads the readers to Jerusalem, Yafa (Jaffa), Jericho, Ramallah, Nablus, Gaza, Acre, al-Ramla, and Tulkarem. Here, they get a glimpse of the pluralistic history of Palestine, where Christians, Jews, Muslims, and Samaritans were sharing land, culture, and neighborhood. Nahida is not interested in showing the invitees the "dead stones" and the different layers of archaeology; rather, she invites them to meet the "living stones", the survivors of the Nakba, with some still living in Palestine while others are scattered in the USA, Kuwait, Jordan, Egypt, Lebanon, and the United Kingdom. The readers are invited to see the human side of the story; through the pages they meet Palestinian artists, architects, teachers, musicians, intellectuals, and business people. The readers recognize that these are the promise of Palestine.

The book is an open invitation by Nahida to the readers to visit her home, the home where she grew up but is now occupied by strangers. During these seventy years, her house is no longer the same. It was remodeled several times and turned upside down. Its character was changed. Still, Nahida can identify her home; her home in Jaffa, and her home Palestine. Even if she is denied entrance to her home, her home lives in her in Exile. She has the deed to her home. She takes her children and grandchildren with her to see their grandma's home, and she invites the readers to come visit her homeland, Palestine. And for those traveling to Palestine as pilgrims, or studying the land of the Bible in churches, this book offers a unique guide to the land and people of Palestine, and a window to a paradise lost, and justice waiting to be restored.

Those acquainted with the Bible will realize the Palestinian Nakba of 1948 is a mirror of the Babylonian exile in 587 BC. Palestine continues to be an occupied land, occupied by powers and empires, its people (today Palestinians) scattered all over the world, waiting for their return home. While they lament the loss of their land, they keep living on the promise that one day a highway will be prepared for them so that they can return home. The readers of this book are challenged to listen to this story of loss, courage and steadfastness, and to get engaged so that Nahida can experience the fulfillment of the promise and can exercise her right of return before it is too late.

Rev. Dr. Mitri Raheb
Bethlehem
1st Advent 2015
www.mitriraheb.org

Acknowledgments

I express heartfelt thanks to all Palestinians who contributed narratives. You are activists, administrative detainees, artists, authors, businessmen, editors, engineers, housewives, pastors, physicians, prisoners, professors, refugees, researchers, students, teachers, and university administrators living either in Palestine, refugee camps, or exile. This project would not have been possible without the generous contribution of your personal narratives during the ongoing Nakba.

Also thanks go to Gail Farrell whose reading of the manuscript was of invaluable help and to Amgad Beblawi, Coordinator of the Middle East and Europe World Mission Program of the Presbyterian Church (U.S.A.) whose positive encouragement was indeed appreciated. Of particular note is the role of the Palestine Israel Mission Network of the Presbyterian Church (U.S.A.) in encouraging this work through its Education Committee. A special thanks goes to John Anderson, Pauline Coffman, Walt Davis, and Noushin Framke who were readers of the early drafts of the work. Other readers were Beth Coetzee, Donald Gordon, Sami Halaby and especially my sister, Samia Halaby, who encouraged me at every stage of the project and contributed the Kafr Qasem narrative and the chapter on Liberation Art of Palestine. This work would not have been complete without the addition of its last chapter on The Origins of Traditional Palestinian Costume contributed by Hanan Munayyer.

I am grateful to contributors Jen Marlowe, author of the narrative of the Awajah family in Gaza; John Halaka who contributed the narrative of Umm Aziz; and the Addameer Prisoner Support and Human Rights Association, which contributed the Majeda Akram Fidda narrative.

Last and most importantly, I thank my husband, Donald Gordon, without whose continuing comments and encouragement this project would not have been possible.

Palestine District Map

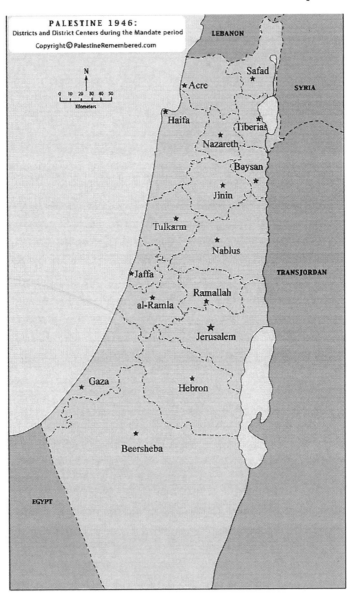

PALESTINE 1946:
Districts and District Centers during the Mandate period
Copyright © PalestineRemembered.com

LEBANON

SYRIA

TRANSJORDAN

EGYPT

Safad

Acre

Haifa

Tiberias

Nazareth

Baysan

Jinin

Tulkarm

Nablus

Jaffa

Ramallah

al-Ramla

Jerusalem

Gaza

Hebron

Beersheba

N

0 10 20 30 40 50
Kilometers

Introduction

Within these pages are the memories of Palestinians who have suffered loss and yet have kept their identity as Palestinians and through perseverance have kept their culture vibrant and alive. It is hoped that in meeting these people, the reader will understand at the human level the personal suffering and loss of Palestinians; see the Palestinian longing for freedom and peace; and join in supporting their struggle for justice.

Before the creation of Israel in 1948, Palestine was a multicultural society that accepted religious refugees. In one of the narratives, the reader will meet an Armenian-Palestinian-American, some of whose family survived the Armenian genocide. The Armenians came to Palestine to seek refuge with a wish to live, raise their families, and contribute to the culture of their new home. They embraced the culture, learned the language, and most importantly, contributed to the rich diversity of Palestinian society. Deep friendships and lasting family connections were common among the newly arrived Armenians and the indigenous Palestinians.

At the beginning of the twentieth century, there was a small Jewish presence in Palestine. Jewish Palestinians spoke Arabic, lived peacefully on the land with Christian and Muslim Palestinians, and enjoyed life in Palestine, as did their Christian and Muslim neighbors. Remarkable among them were the Samaritan Jews who lived side by side with Muslims and conducted business with them in the City of Nablus and elsewhere. They too were part of a multicultural Palestine. Friendships between Jewish Palestinians and their Christian and Muslim neighbors were common.

So why did things change? They changed with the mass immigration of Jewish refugees, primarily from Europe to Palestine, facilitated by Great Britain, which was granted the mandatory power over Palestine in 1922 by the League of Nations. These newly arrived immigrant Jews, rather than integrating into the existing Palestinian society as the Armenians had done earlier, came instead with a leadership that intended to displace Christian and Muslim Palestinians. They initially purchased land, but when this land was not sufficient for their purposes, they took the land of Palestine from a majority of its inhabitants by a relentless campaign of terror and expulsion that continues unabated to this day. This campaign created an ever-growing refugee population that mostly lives in ghettos throughout historic Palestine, in refugee camps in its immediate surroundings, or in the diaspora.

Western countries contributed to the establishment of Israel perhaps wishing for atonement for their contribution to the Jewish holocaust; and by their mostly unconditional support, they enabled the continuing dispossession of Palestinians by successive Israeli governments. The creation of the state of Israel, whether or not it was in atonement for the suffering of one people, has created another suffering and dispossessed people. The continuing dispossession of the Palestinians and the violation of their human rights, including the right to political self-determination, is a blight on the collective international community. A major obstacle to restitution of justice for the Palestinian people is the ongoing and unconditional support of Israel by Western nations, especially the United States, which allow Israel to act with impunity.

Who are the people of Palestine?

A question frequently asked is, "What is Palestine, and when did the area take that name?" The question is immaterial and its answer is not informative, as this question deals with nomenclature rather than the heart of the matter – the people of Palestine. A better question is, "Who are the people of Palestine?"

Historically, Palestine was part of a larger geographic region known as the land of the ancient Canaanites. Ancient Canaan covered the area now known as modern Palestine/Israel, Jordan, Lebanon, coastal Syria, and southern inland Syria. Jonathan Tubb[1] demonstrates through careful examination of the archaeological evidence that "there was population continuity through successive millennia" in the land of Canaan. Archaeological evidence of human habitation dates from the twelfth millennium BC to the present, constituting fourteen millennia. The estimated existence of the geographic entities of the ancient kingdoms of Israel and Judah constitutes but a small sliver of time – less than five hundred years. An enduring contribution of Canaanite culture is the invention of an alphabet using 24 symbols for consonants with vowel sounds understood – much like Arabic of today. This revolutionized the way language was written, and through the Phoenicians, who were also Canaanites, this language was spread throughout the West.[2] Another enduring contribution of the Canaanites is that their land was the birthplace of two of the world's great religions – Judaism and Christianity.

There is no reason to doubt that Palestinians are descendants of the original inhabitants of Canaan. For example, Palestinian weaving and embroidery, a language of art and culture, expresses belonging to the land. The chapter on "The Origins of Traditional Palestinian Costume," contributed by Hanan Karaman Munayyer, demonstrates through its careful research the connection of today's Palestinians to their ancient land of Canaan.

To Palestinians, especially those who were exiled from their homes and communities in 1948, in 1967, and continuing until the present time, keeping memories of Palestine alive is central to who they are. As part of keeping these memories alive, Palestinian homes frequently have table runners, table clothes, and pillows embroidered with traditional Palestinian themes. Wearing dresses, skirts, shawls, vests, and jackets embroidered with traditional Palestinian designs also keeps these memories alive. By showing and having Palestinian embroidered clothes and cloths one sends a message to friends and acquaintances that is captured by the first line of the Palestinian poet Mahmoud Darwish's poem, "I am from there:" "I am from there and I have memories." Palestinians use embroidery to show pride in their ethnic heritage and to tell people that they are "from there." Embroidery helps them remember who they are in positive and happier terms. It is a piece of Palestine that they can keep close to their hearts and homes.

Many friends of Palestinians who visit Palestine and see for themselves the ongoing suffering and courageous perseverance of Palestinians return home with embroidered vests, jackets, dresses, and handbags. They wear them in public to show their solidarity with Palestinians in their struggle and demonstrate that the Palestinian culture is alive and thriving.

From the time of the ancient Canaanites to contemporary times, Palestine has been invaded and occupied by empires and their surrogates from the South, the East, and the North, and a very few from the West – the Mediterranean Sea. Throughout time, the people of the land of Palestine have learned to overcome adversity and hold on. There is no archaeological evidence whatsoever for a complete disappearance of a people from Palestine and their replacement by outsiders. The one exception is the attempt (though only partially successful) by the Government of Israel to transplant a Jewish majority from abroad into Palestine in an attempt to replace its indigenous people and their culture.

The history of Palestine in the 20th century is unique in that the latest invaders, as mentioned above, are attempting to replace the indigenous population and have mounted an intensive propaganda campaign to demonize the Palestinians and erase their culture. As can be seen from these pages, Palestinians, in spite of their suffering and against extreme odds, are carrying on with life and are building their communities. They will overcome, persevere, and ultimately prevail because they know that justice is on their side.

Ever since the time of the creation of Mandate Palestine and the United States' recognition of the state of Israel on 78 percent of Mandate Palestine, the people of Palestine, even though they shared and continue to share in the cultural, religious, and linguistic characteristics of what was known as Greater Syria, which was part of the Ottoman Empire, considered themselves and continue to consider themselves as Palestinians.

With the Nakba (Catastrophe) of 1948, when more than 750,000 Palestinians were driven from their homes by the forces of the nascent state of Israel, and the continued policies of occupation and expulsion by the state of Israel, some believe the Palestinian people and their culture are suffering from the imposition of a campaign of sociocide! This work will demonstrate that Palestinians, as a people, even though they live under Israeli occupation throughout Mandate Palestine, and in several Arab countries in its immediate surroundings, are still a people with a unique culture. Their rich cultural experience and their shared sense of injustice imbue them with the will to survive and flourish. This is *Sumud*, steadfastness in the face of suffering and dispossession.

In these pages, you will read about their experiences and see their will to survive as a people. Even though those of the old generation who directly experienced the Nakba of 1948 are slowly diminishing, their spirit and will to have justice with peace lives on in the younger generation. The letter to Teta (grandmother) is an example (see Narratives, Jaffa District).

Where is the Palestinian Gandhi?

Frequently Palestinians are asked, "Where is the Palestinian Gandhi?" The answer is that he is everywhere. You can see him in these pages: the young man who risks life and limb to climb high on a minaret or church steeple to place the Palestinian flag, proclaiming to the Israelis, "I am here, and do not intend to leave my homeland." You will see Gandhi in those who mortgage their homes to be able to preserve the heritage of Palestinian embroidery. You will see him in the artist who spends years to earn the trust of a village that has undergone a massacre by the Israeli border guards, and who tells the world of this massacre in compelling art, and in the personal narratives of those who lost family in this massacre. You see Gandhi in the university administrator who refuses to buckle down under Israeli pressure to close his university. You see him in the staff and faculty of Birzeit University, who risked imprisonment and torture and yet continued their efforts to provide quality education to their young students.

Among the graffiti on the apartheid wall that imprisons Bethlehem, there is one that proclaims: "To Exist Is to Resist." This graffiti tells only part of the story. Palestinians are doing more than existing. They are building, and they remain a cohesive culture. We hear their voice: "We are Palestine – our culture and our existence as a People will continue in spite of all hardships."

Here is another example of a Gandhi! In a Huffington Post article by Yasmine Hafiz, we read about a young boy who was denied access to the Al-Aqsa mosque for Friday prayers.[3] In an act of defiance, he put his prayer rug on the street and prayed (Fig. 1). This boy knows well his vulnerability! He knows that the Israelis break into houses after midnight when families are asleep, and take pictures and the names and ages of those in the house. At a later date they may come again during the night to arrest young boys, put them in jail for indefinite periods of time under administrative detention without charges, and subject them to torture - as can be seen from Iyad Burnat's narrative (see Narratives, Ramallah District). The boy knows all this because maybe an older brother, a friend, or a neighbor has suffered this mistreatment at the hands of the occupying Israeli forces. In spite of all these vulnerabilities, this boy is brave enough to, in effect, say to the occupiers and torturers: "You can decide where and when I can or cannot go, you can break my bones, but you cannot break my spirit." This is resistance! This is Palestinian *sumud*!

The work by Rana Bishara, an installation artist who lives in the Galilee, depicts a leaf of the cactus plant, called *saber* in Arabic. The artist took a saber leaf and dipped the lower part in chocolate (Fig. 2). Rana Bishara is telling us that "Palestine is sweet but it is difficult to enjoy it." *Saber* also means patience in Arabic. The *saber* plant is easy to destroy with a bulldozer, but its roots are tenacious in their hold on the land. This plant is often used as a fence between Palestinian homes. When Israel destroyed entire villages with bulldozers, the *saber* plants grew back, showing the fence lines of houses in the village. The sweet, fragile interior of the *saber* fruit is wrapped in a tough prickly exterior. Palestinians dream of having such qualities as they steadfastly confront Israeli terrorism. Another interpretation of this work is that Palestinians in their hospitality and warmth may seem sweet and gentle, but they are tenacious and difficult to eradicate. The *saber* plant is also a symbol of *sumud* – the steadfastness and persistence of the Palestinian people in refusing to be denied their land, identity, and culture.

Figure 1. Samia A. Halaby. *Denied Prayer at Al-Aqsa Mosque*. Pencil on paper, 14 x 11 in, 35 x 28 cm.

Figure 2. Rana Bishara. *Sweetie.*

Questions for Reflection

1. Is the conversion of the multiethnic society in Palestine prior to May 15, 1948, to a *Jewish* State, as the present Israeli Government officials insist that Israel should be acknowledged, in step with modern twenty-first century sensibilities?

2. Do the Christian communities in the West need to atone for the Jewish holocaust? If so, why and how?

3. Does the Jewish holocaust justify the expulsion of the Palestinians from their lands?

4. What role does the international community have in the perpetuation of the Israeli occupation of Palestine?

5. Do you see the Palestinians' *sumud* as a viable reaction to occupation, and does it have a chance of ending the occupation?

I. Brief Contemporary History of Palestine

During the first two decades of the twentieth century, the land of Canaan, also known as Greater Syria in contemporary times, was part of the Ottoman Empire. After the First World War, when the Ottoman Empire was dismantled, England and France divided the Middle East into separate mandates. On January 25, 1919, the League of Nations was created, and shortly thereafter on June 22, 1922, it issued the Mandate for Palestine[1] to be administered by Great Britain. Palestine was considered a class A mandate territory,[2] which legally meant that it has the rights and privileges of a country.

The mandate document for Palestine begins with the statement that the purpose of the mandate is to give "effect to the provisions of Article 22 of the Covenant of the League of Nations." Article 22 concerns territories and communities formerly part of the Ottoman (Turkish) Empire, such as Palestine, and states clearly in paragraph one the responsibilities of the mandatory power that,

> "...there should be applied the principle that the well-being and development of such peoples form a sacred trust of civilization and that securities for the performance of this trust should be embodied in this Covenant."[3]

Further, paragraph four of Article 22 states that,

> "Certain communities formerly belonging to the Turkish Empire have reached a stage of development where their existence as independent nations can be provisionally recognized subject to the rendering of administrative advice and assistance by a Mandatory until such time as they are able to stand alone. *The wishes of these communities must be a principal consideration in the selection of the Mandatory* [emphasis added]."[4]

However, England had other plans for Palestine that were contrary to its responsibilities. In 1917, the British government issued the Balfour Declaration, in which

> "His Majesty's Government view with favour the establishment in Palestine of a national home for the Jewish people, and will use their best endeavours to facilitate the achievement of this object, it being clearly understood that nothing shall be done which may prejudice the civil and religious rights of existing non-Jewish communities in Palestine."[5]

In this declaration, "the Palestinians were never once cited by name, whether as Palestinians or as Arabs, and were referred to only as 'non-Jewish communities,' possessing solely civil and religious rights; their national and political rights were mentioned in neither. By contrast, national rights were ascribed to the 'Jewish people,' and the Mandate made it a solemn responsibility of Great Britain to help the Jews create national institutions. The mandatory power was specifically called upon to extend all possible assistance to the growth and development of this national entity, notably by encouraging Jewish immigration."[6] At this time, the census of Palestine[7] showed that Jews constituted 7.9% of the population. The incongruence between the League of Nations charter and the actions of Great Britain as a mandatory power was ignored.

"Starting soon after the British occupation, Palestinians repeatedly pressed Great Britain to grant them their national rights of self-determination and representative government."[8] They claimed these rights on the basis of the American president Woodrow Wilson's Fourteen Points,[9] specifically point V, which states that "A free, open-minded, and absolutely impartial adjustment of all colonial claims, based upon a strict observance of the principle that in determining all such questions of sovereignty the interests of the populations concerned must have equal weight with the equitable claims of the government whose title is to be determined."[10]

Therefore, rather than being a liberator, Great Britain became a conqueror as it disposed of Palestine according to its wishes, thus ignoring the human rights of the Palestinian people and their rights as the majority population of a class A mandate. Great Britain facilitated the mass immigration of Jews from Europe into Palestine thus changing its ethnic composition dramatically. By 1946, the population consisted of 608,225 (32.96 percent) Jews and 1,237,334 (67.04 percent) Muslims and Christians.[11] Therefore, in spite of the great influx of European Jews into Palestine, the Jewish population continued to be a minority population.

Palestinians objected to the Balfour Declaration and launched uprisings, the most notable being from 1936 to 1939 (which can be characterized as the first Intifada) to protest the mass immigration of Jews into Palestine. This uprising ended with a brutal suppression by the British and the execution or exile of the uprising's leadership.[12] It is estimated that "violence left 5,000 Palestinians dead, 15,000 wounded, and 5,600 incarcerated".[13] The uprising was against the British form of occupation[14] and the mass immigration of Jews into Palestine.

Many years of lobbying by prominent Jewish citizens of the United States, and months of cajoling and threats by United States officials in the Truman Administration,[15] preceded the United Nations General Assembly vote to recommend partition. Therefore Great Britain, in issuing and enforcing the Balfour Declaration, violated Article 22 of the League of Nations and point V of Woodrow Wilson's League of Nations fourteen points. And the United States, in imposing[16] its will on the UN General assembly to recommend the partition of Palestine, violated both the United Nations Charter, articles 1 (paragraph 2), 55, and 73,[17] and the General Assembly's Declaration on the Principles of International Law concerning the Friendly Relations and Cooperation among States. These violations infringed on the Palestinian human right of self determination.[18]

According to Curtis Doebbler, an international human rights lawyer, this right of self-determinations provides all peoples, including the Palestinian people, the right to determine their own future. "It is a right that Israelis [because of their minority status] did not enjoy in the Palestinian territory when they unilaterally declared their state in violation of the Palestinians' right to self-determination. The Palestinians' right to self-determination preexisted any effort by Israel to occupy Palestinian lands. It is a right that all Palestinians are entitled to exercise according to international law from the very beginning of the British mandate in the 1920s. It is thus a right that is enjoyed over all of mandate Palestine."[19] The occupation of Palestine by the British began in 1922, continued by Israel on May 14, 1948 when it unilaterally declared itself a state, and continues to the present time.

The Dismemberment of Palestine

On November 29, 1947, the United Nations General Assembly (Resolution 181) voted to *recommend* partition[20] of Palestine into two states, one Jewish and the other Palestinian. The territories designated to the Jewish and Palestinian states would be 56 percent and 43 percent of Palestine, respectively. Jerusalem and Bethlehem were to become an international zone.[21] At the end of 1946, Jews had acquired by purchase 6 to 8 percent of the total land area of Palestine and comprised approximately one third of its population. In other words, the recommended plan in effect took land owned by Palestinians and proposed to give it to the Zionists. Palestinians, who were never consulted in promulgating the proposed partition, objected to the plan, (Fig. 3). Israeli propaganda uses UN GA resolution 181 as a justification for the right of Israel to exist as a country when in fact the United Nations does not have the legal right to partition a country. Israel as a state was won at the point of a gun, and its recognition by the Truman Administration[22] gave it instant "legitimacy."

Between November 19, 1947, and May 14, 1948, both sides engaged in violence. The Israelis were better trained and equipped than the Palestinians. It is estimated that before May 1948, 442,000 Palestinians were expelled from Palestine and became refugees in the West Bank, Gaza, and the surrounding Arab countries, principally Lebanon, Syria, Jordan, and to a lesser extent Egypt. It is also estimated that 225 villages were depopulated and or destroyed.[23] The Israelis called it the war of independence, but the Palestinians called it the Nakba (the catastrophe). The Israelis say that the Palestinians left of their own free will,[24] urged on by their leaders, while the Palestinians say they were terrorized into leaving, thinking that they would be able to return to their homes once the violence abated. Most historians[25] now agree that the expulsion of the

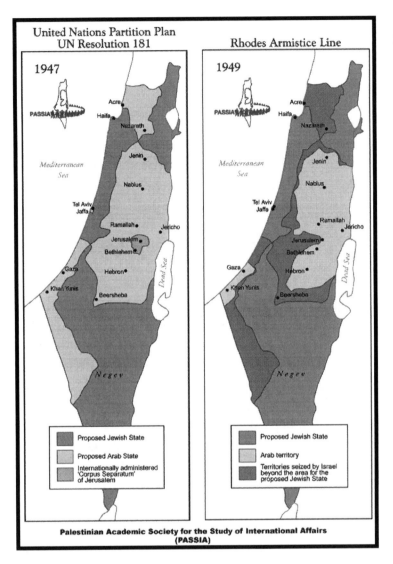

Figure 3. Proposed partition plans.

Palestinians occurred against their free will, and an Israeli historian, Ilan Pappe,[26] uses the term 'ethnic cleansing' to characterize what happened to the Palestinians.

It was only after May 14, 1948, that Lebanon, Syria, Jordan, and Egypt sent a portion of their armed forces into Palestine to protect the Palestinian populace. The Israeli forces were better trained and equipped. By July 20, 1949, armistice agreements[27] with these four countries and Israel were signed. By the end of this war, Israel had gained more territory and was in control of 78 percent of Palestine. Also at this time it is estimated that more than 750,000 Palestinians were expelled from their homes and more than 500 villages were depopulated or destroyed.[28] A few evicted Palestinians were able to return; however, most were shot on sight as they tried to return to their homes and lands.

The Nakba

The campaign of expulsion of the Palestinians from their homes and communities in Palestine began in 1947 and continues to the present day. However, there were two major periods of expulsion. The first period began in 1947 and ended in 1949, and the second period was during the 1967 war and its aftermath.

The forced expulsion and murder of Palestinians began in all the districts of Palestine where there was a measurable Jewish population: Jaffa, Al-Ramla, Beersheba, Gaza, Haifa, Jenin, Jerusalem, Tiberias, and Tulkarm. The campaign began in 1947 and continued to mid-May, when Israel declared itself a state.

Salman Abu Sitta, in his book *Atlas of Palestine, 1917-1966*, describes in detail war crimes perpetrated by the Zionist forces against the Palestinian civilian population. In a table labeled "War Crimes (Atrocities, Massacres, Destruction, Plunder and Looting) between 1947 and 1956," Abu Sitta compiled 232 incidents.[29] "Almost every one of the 30-odd Zionist/Israeli military operations was accompanied by one or two massacres of civilians. There were at least 77 reported massacres, two-thirds of which took place before any Arab regular soldier set foot in Palestine."[30] Abu Sitta used 105 citations to justify the information presented about these incidents.[31]

Abu Sitta also describes the tactics used in the military operations of the Yishuv/ Israeli military forces, listing by date, locality, and battalion executing the operation.

"The pattern of expulsion was consistent throughout regardless of the region the date or the particular battalion which attacked the village . . . Most serious research and all oral testimonies given at different times by refugees from different regions in Palestine confirmed the same pattern.

"After the village is attacked and conquered whether it resisted or surrendered, a curfew is imposed. Sometime later, probably the following morning, the villagers where gathered in the main square or a nearby field into separate groups: the men from the age of 15 to 50 and the women, children and very old men. The village was surrounded from three directions leaving the fourth open for escape or expulsion. The gap left open was pointing towards Lebanon and Syria in the Galilee region, towards the West Bank and Jordan in central Palestine, and towards Gaza and Egypt in the south.[32]

"The women were stripped of their jewelry and valuables in order to walk towards the gap or open gate, without looking back. Shots were fired over their heads to encourage their flight. There have been cases of rape, enslavement and murder. The men were lined up by a hooded man for review. Very frequently selected young men were taken in groups of four, ordered to dig their graves, and then they were shot and thrown in the dug pits. "

Abu Sitta further describes the tactics used in the case of a massacre:

"The soldiers separated the men and the women depositing them at different locations around 50 yards from the killing pits. The soldiers divested their victims of whatever valuables they possessed. [One witness] recalled vividly the picture of these people most of whom were undressed to the waist lying for hours in the sun and getting severely sunburnt. For, after undressing, they had to lie prostrate in a confined area and we were not permitted to move. When the killing was finally ready to commence, the soldiers formed a gauntlet running between the staging ground for the killing and the killing site itself. Successive groups of 15 to 20 were forced to run to the killing site's pit, to run the gauntlet with the soldiers shouting at them and beating them with rifle butts as they passed by.

"In some instances, "the men were led to forced labor camps. They were tortured, shot and killed at the first sign of disobedience and made to work on the Israeli military effort such as digging trenches, carrying ammunition and making war items such as camouflage nets. They were also used in carrying the looted material from Arab homes, burying the dead, and removing the debris from demolished Arab houses."

"In January 1949, the International Committee of the Red Cross [ICRC] found 6,360 prisoners of whom 5,013 where Palestinians. The Palestinians were mostly ordinary farmers from Galilee villages. [. . .] Testimonies by several survivors indicated that Palestinian civilians were detained and forced to work in 17 other camps and locations never visited by ICRC. It is estimated that almost 25,000 Palestinian civilians were rounded up, detained and put into forced labor camps for periods from 10 months to two years. They have received no appreciable compensation or publicity about their plight."[33]

The Zionist Israeli leadership wanted to have the land of Palestine without a people – free of all non-Jewish Palestinians whether Christian or Muslim. This wish has been expressed in various forms early from the founding of Zionism to this day. Nur Masalha in his book *The Politics of Denial: Israel and the Palestinian Refugee Problem*,[34] describes in detail the theme of "population transfer" or "ethnic cleansing" in the thinking and action of the Zionist movement in Palestine-Israel. His work is largely based on Hebrew and Israeli archival sources; it represents some of the most original work in this area and is frequently cited by later authors.

For example, Masalha writes that Israel Zangwill, a prominent Anglo-Jewish writer, was an early advocate of the transfer solution and worked relentlessly to propagate the slogan "a land without a people for a people without a land."[35] Zionists knew that in fact that the land had people; however they viewed the Palestinians as people not worth considering. The view of Palestinians by most Zionists has not changed over the past century! As early as 1891, a leading liberal Russian Jewish thinker, Ahad Ha'Am (Asher Zvi Ginsberg) observed that the Zionist "pioneers" believed that:

"... the only language that the Arabs understand is that of force. ... [The Zionist 'pioneers'] behave towards the Arabs with hostility and cruelty, trespass unjustly upon their boundaries, beat them shamefully without reason and even brag about it, and nobody stands to check this contemptible and dangerous tendency."[36]

Masalha documents with meticulous detail the Zionist elites' early plans that the "transfer" of the Palestinian people was a necessary prelude to the founding of the state of Israel. Tactics for such a transfer evolved with time. In the beginning there was hope through negotiations with colonial powers such as Italy, England, and Turkey that these powers would co-operate with the voluntary or forced transfer of the Palestinian population. When these tactics failed, then purchase of land was the attempted device; however by late 1947, the Jewish National Fund and others had acquired by purchase only 6 to 8 percent of the land (see 'The Dismemberment of Palestine" above). Clearly other tactics were necessary if the Zionist leaders were to achieve their goal of taking possession of a 'land without people.' After the United Nations General Assembly voted to recommend partition of Palestine in 1947, civil war erupted. The Yishuv (the Jewish community in Palestine) armed forces, the Hagana, Irgun Tzavi Leumi, and Lehi groups, were fully armed and on the offensive against largely unarmed, disorganized, and powerless Palestinian groups. Both force and psychological intimidation were tactics used to initiate and implement the mass exodus of 750,000 to 800,000 Palestinians. After the cessation of hostilities and successful takeover of many villages by the Yishuv armed forces, the massacre of villagers was used as a successful device of intimidation that resulted in the mass exodus.[37] For the Christian and Muslim Palestinians, the tragedy of the Nakba was one of violent dispossession following decades of suffering during and after the First World War.

Figure 4. John Halaka (www.johnhalaka.com). *Stripped of Their Identity and Driven from Their Land. From the series: Forgotten Survivors*, 1993/1997/2003. Rubber-stamped ink and acrylic on canvas, 87 x 272 in, 221 x 691 cm..

The 1967 War

In June 1967, Israel attacked Egypt, Jordan, and Syria. At the end of six days, Israel had taken the Gaza strip and the Sinai from Egypt, East Jerusalem and the West Bank from Jordan, and the Golan from Syria. The United Nations Security Council passed resolution 242,[38] which requested the withdrawal of Israeli armed forces from territories occupied in the 1967 war and emphasized the inadmissibility of the acquisition of territory by war and the need to work for a just and lasting peace in which every State in the area can live in security. At this time, the Golan Heights, the West Bank, East Jerusalem, and the Gaza strip are still under total Israeli control.

Palestinian Diaspora

Palestinians who remained in Israel but were driven from their villages became "internally displaced persons." Indeed, rather than allowing these displaced Palestinians to return to their lands and villages, the Israeli government declared them to be "present absentees" under the Absentee Property Law and proceeded to confiscate their lands.[39]

Obtaining accurate estimates of the worldwide numbers of Palestinians is difficult; however, estimates exist. Since 2008, the Palestine Central Bureau of Statistics has periodically published data and estimates that there are 10.3 million Palestinians worldwide.[40] Of these Palestinians, the United Nations Relief and Works Agency (UNRWA) estimates that 4.7 million are registered refugees. The definition of a registered refugee is a person "whose normal place of residence was Palestine between June 1946 and May 1948, who lost both their homes and means of livelihood as a result of the 1948 Arab-Israeli conflict. To be eligible for UNRWA's services a refugee must be registered."[41] UNRWA estimates that it responded to the needs of approximately 750,000 refugees when it began operation in 1950. Furthermore, after the 1967 war, UNRWA estimates that another 140,000 persons became refugees in Jordan and an additional 240,000 citizens of the West Bank were "displaced persons."

Right of Return

The right of return of refugees to their countries of origin is a customary right and has origins in several sources. First, in Leviticus, Chapter 25[42]; second, the Universal Declaration of Human Rights, articles 9, 13, and 15, address the individual's right of return[43]; third, the UN GA passed Resolution 194(III) concerning the progress report of the United Nations Mediator for Palestine, which specifically addresses the issue of the right of return of refugees;[44] and fourth, article 12, section 4, of the International Covenant on Civil and Political Rights[45], issued by the Office of the

United Nations High Commissioner for Human Rights. Clearly, then, the Right of Return of refugees is granted under accepted practices and is firmly anchored in international law.

Salman Abu Sitta, a researcher on the land and people of Palestine; the founder and president of the Palestine Land Society, London; a member of the Palestine National Council; and general coordinator of the Right of Return Congress; claims:

". . . . the essence of the struggle has not changed: It is the expulsion of the people of Palestine from their homes and the confiscation of their land. Since then the Palestinian refugees have been dispersed all over the world, many of them living in deplorable conditions in exile, others suffering under occupation or virtual siege, harassed by friend and foe alike. The implementation of their inalienable rights is the key to a permanent peace."[46]

John Quigley, Professor of Law at The Ohio State University, expresses another view about the right of return in his article "Displaced Palestinians and a Right of Return."[47] He methodically examines all international laws and argues for or against the right of return depending upon whether the refugees were expelled by Israel or whether they left of their own accord. His conclusion is that they have the right of return irrespective of the reasons for fleeing their homes in Palestine and stresses that;

"[i]f the final status negotiations are to produce a settlement that enjoys the respect of the parties, and of the people who make up their constituencies, the issue of the displaced Palestinians must be resolved in a way that satisfies legitimate expectations. The parties would do well to recall the 1948 advice . . . of the U.N. mediator, Count Bernadotte, who thought that 'it would be an offence against the principles of elemental justice if these innocent victims of the conflict were denied the right to return to their homes.'"[48]

A Palestinian artist's view of the issue of right of return is depicted in a work of sculptor Ahmad Canaan, who

Figure 5. Ahmad Canaan. *What About Coexistence?* Installation art erected in the Negev desert, 1995.

created and erected it in the Negev Desert in 1995 as part of an international event sponsored by Poland.[49] The sculpture is made up of two standing crosses facing each other on either side of one grave. Each cross represents a victim: one is Palestinian and the other Israeli, yet they are identical and unmarked. The key of return hangs on a rope, strung between them, over the shared grave – a shared death. When the strong winds of Al Nakab (Negev) desert blow, the crosses move, and the rope between them tightens and slackens, thus making the key bounce (Fig. 5). It is as though the bouncing key, the Palestinian symbol of the right of return, is begging the question of co-existence in the face of Israeli expropriation of Palestinian homes and lands. Canaan said, "This key represents the reality that is always going to be hanging in the air, regardless of diplomacy and propaganda."[50] This work suggests that the Palestinians and Israelis share a common fate unless the issue of the right of return is resolved justly. Ahmad Canaan is a Palestinian Arab living in the Galilee and a member of the substantial Palestinian communities that Israel could not exile.

Questions for Reflection

1. At the end of World War I, the large majority of the people living in Palestine were Christian or Muslim. How do you view their wish for their national rights for self-determination?

2. Put yourself in the place of Palestinians who saw the demographic makeup of Palestine dramatically change as a result of Jewish immigration facilitated by Britain. If you were living in a state that had a massive influx of immigrants who came to take over and wanted to expel you from your home and community, how would you react? Are there any circumstances in which the immigrants would be justified?

3. How do you view the role of the United Nations in the question of Palestine? Do you see its role as being effective?

4. How do you view the role of the United States government in quickly recognizing the state of Israel, and how has this contributed to the present day conflict?

5. Of the three major actors in the creation of Israel, Great Britain, the United States, and the United Nations, which do you think has the major responsibility for the present impasse in Palestine-Israel?

6. The Israeli government claims that any Jew living anywhere in the world has a right to move to Israel and become a citizen. They claim that all Jews have a right to "return" because Palestine was once the home of Ancient Israel in the first millennium BC, but they deny the Palestinians, who were born and lived for millennia in Palestine, the right to return. Keeping in mind the history of the Canaanites, from whom both Semitic Jews (who are only a portion of modern Jews) and Palestinians are descended, do you think it reasonable that one group of descendants has a right to residency on the land and deny residency to another group?

II. The Narratives

Jerusalem District

Thirty-nine villages in the Jerusalem District were depopulated and or destroyed.[1] The most notable and widely known of the villages is Dayr Yasin. Dayr Yasin was destroyed and more than 100 of its people massacred in an Israeli campaign to intimidate and strike terror in the heart of all Palestinians – as can be seen by the mention of the Dayr Yasin massacre in several of the narratives. As a result, more has been written about Dayr Yasin than any other destroyed village. What follows is a brief description of Dayr Yasin before and after 1948; greater detail can be found in the book edited by Walid Khalidi, *All that Remains: The Palestinian Villages Occupied and Depopulated by Israel in 1948.*

The village of Dayr Yasin, located about one kilometer west of Jerusalem, was situated on a high hill providing a panoramic view of the countryside, including Jerusalem. The United Nations, in its partition plan, recommended an international zone, which included Jerusalem and the surrounding countryside. Dayr Yasin was within this international zone; its population was estimated at 610 people, and the village had 91 houses and buildings.[2]

"In 1948, Dayr Yasin was a prosperous, expanding village at relative peace with its Jewish neighbors with whom much business was done."[3] In the early hours of April 9, 1948, approximately 130 Irgun Zva'I Leumi (IZL or the Irgun) and Lohamei Herut Yisrael (LHI or Stern Gang) members attacked Dayr Yasin from the northeast and southeast.[4] "The attack was chaotic, as the IZL and LHI units converged from the east, south, and north. The villagers, armed with 'only some old guns and pistols,' put up effective resistance and inflicted casualties. After a brief Hagana [precursor of the Israeli Defense Forces] intervention, the town ceased resisting about late morning. It appears that atrocities which began during the attack spread and were sustained over the ensuing hours and even days."[5] There are various estimates of the numbers killed. The Hagana first published the figure of 254 killed but later recanted and said that this number was inflated to strike terror into the Palestinian populace.[6] Later estimates by Walid Khalidi[7] claim that the number was probably closer to 110.

The gruesome slaughter, sexual molestation and rape of victims, and mutilation to obtain jewelry from victims are crimes detailed briefly in a publication by the Institute of Jerusalem Studies and Badil Resource Center.[8]

"Survivors of the massacre were paraded and (their) hands forced above their heads through the streets of Jewish-held Jerusalem, said Eliyahu Arieli, the commander of the Hagana force, which moved into Dayr Yasin following the Massacre.[9] Meir Pail, the Hagana 'observer,' recounted that, after parading a group of twenty-five men, Irgun and Lehi members 'put them in a line in some kind of quarry, and shot them.'[10] According to Arieli, 'All of the killed, with very few exceptions, were old men, women and children […] the dead we found were all unjust victims and none of them had died with a weapon in their hands.'[11] After the massacre, Zionist forces took the bodies of the victims to Dayr Yasin's rock quarry, poured gasoline on them and set them alight."[12]

This attack occurred in spite of a non-belligerency agreement that Dayr Yasin had, as did several other villages in the area, with the Hagana.[13]

Twice a Refugee
Lucy Janjigian

I am the first-born child (December 1932) of Mary and Haroutune Boyadjian, both survivors of the Armenian genocide of 1915. In July of that year, news of the atrocities befalling the Armenians in the interior of what became the nation of Turkey reached those who lived in the Cilicia region. Clerics and civil leaders organized the inhabitants of eight villages to take refuge in the densely vegetated Musa Dagh (literally, Mountain of Moses). Women, children, and old men with their animals carried bedding, gardening equipment, and food and climbed up the mountain. No dogs or roosters were to be taken with them, as their noises would reveal their position. Men aged 18-45 years of age were absent, as they had been conscripted into labor camps or murdered and thrown into mass graves. My father, Haroutune, and my mother's two brothers, Paul and Sarkis Karakashian, were among those that took refuge up the mountain.

After 60 days of isolation and hiding, a scout on watch duty standing at the edge of a cliff noticed a ship. Charles Diran Tekeian, who was of Armenian descent and an officer of the French Destroyer "Le Guichen," helped organize the mass evacuation of about five thousand exhausted yet exhilarated people who had taken refuge up the mountain in Musa Dagh. The refugees were transported in six battleships to the Lazaret refugee camp near Port Said, Egypt

At this time, England was at war with the Ottoman Empire (Turkey), which controlled Palestine. Due to the war (World War I), Mr. Reynolds, headmaster of the Anglican St. George's School in Jerusalem, left Jerusalem for Egypt, which was territory controlled by Britain. In Egypt, Reynolds volunteered to teach scouting, soccer, and English at the Lazaret refugee camp. At the end of the First World War, when England took Palestine as a Mandate, he decided to return to Jerusalem and chose five boys from Lazaret refugee camp who excelled in their academic work to go with him to Jerusalem. My father, Haroutune, and my mother's brothers were among the five boys. After Haroutune graduated from St. George's School in 1925, he was invited to join the faculty and eventually became the first non-British headmaster of the school.

My mother, Sima Karakashian, was born in a village in the Cilicia region of the Ottoman Empire and was orphaned as a young child. During the Armenian genocide there were righteous Muslims who hid Christian children. My mother's aunt found a home for her with Rafaat Bey's wealthy family, who were Muslim Arabs holding Turkish citizenship. They changed her name to "Nariman." After several years with this family who treated her very kindly, her aunt brought Nariman to the Franciscan nuns' convent in Lebanon. The nuns gave her a new Christian name, Mary, which was the one she went by the rest of her life.

When Mary's two brothers graduated from St. George's School they asked Zarouhi, Mary's sister, who was also placed with the nuns at the convent, and Mary to join them in Jerusalem, Palestine. The sisters spoke Armenian, French, and Turkish but did not speak Arabic or English. Haroutune, who was a friend of Mary's brothers, volunteered to teach her English. They fell in love and were married at St. George's Cathedral on September 29, 1930. This is how my parents escaped extermination and survived the horrors that were inflicted upon the Armenians in what Winston Churchill later called the first holocaust of the 20th Century,[14] only to be made refugees once again.

As a child, I attended an English Anglican School with Palestinian (Muslim and Christian), Jewish, Armenian, and other girls of many nationalities. Our home was in an international quarter where Abyssinian, Arab, Armenian, Assyrian, English, French, Jewish, Polish, and Russian families lived in harmony and within proximity of each other.

In 1946, militant Zionists were blowing up British police and military targets. On July 22, 1946, the Zionist Irgun terrorists blew up the King David Hotel that housed the British Mandate Government, killing 92 Arab, Armenian, British, Greek, and Jewish personnel, including my aunt Eugenie, and a Greek girl I knew who was a recent graduate from our school. Others were children of friends of our family. Hotel Semiramis, whose owners were friends of my parents, was blown up January 5, 1948, killing 26 innocent people. Both of these barbarous, horrific acts, now infamous for being acts of Zionist terrorism, touched us personally.

One Saturday night British police caught Zionist terrorists planting a bomb to be detonated when the British High Commissioner would be coming to St George's Cathedral for worship on Sunday morning. Had they not been caught many of us children would have died along with him and his motorcade, as we would stand by the Cathedral gate to see him arrive in his escorted car.

We lived on the second floor of a two-family house in a multi-ethnic quarter on Nabi Samuel [Prophet Samuel] Road, across the street from St. George's School, where my father taught and my two brothers attended. With terrorism rampant, a curfew was declared after dark. Soldiers were stationed on the street beneath our balcony. Many of our neighbors had left their homes and gone to live with relatives or in convents in the security of the Old City. Our movements were confined. There were no more parties, gatherings, or activities. Our street officially became No Man's Land.

Whenever fighting erupted bullets would fly through our kitchen window and through the house. Jerusalem had taken on a dark, scary mood. In spite of the growing doom, we remained in our home, and every night we closed the curtains in case of shattering glass.

On November 29, 1947, the United Nations General Assembly recommended the partition of Palestine. It was a momentous day that changed the course of our lives. One night, Zionist Israeli forces blew up the four-story Mandelbaum Apartment Building, which was behind our house and whose Jewish residents had been evacuated that day. This blast also turned out to be momentous. The blast terrified us and shook us out of bed. Our windowpanes shattered, dogs barked, pictures and dishes crashed to the tiled floor. Shards of glass and china flew everywhere that night, like an omen of the pieces our lives were to become.

It was a long night, and when morning finally came, Bishop Stewart from St. George's Cathedral sent word that we could no longer live in our home because it was precariously located in the middle of the fighting. So we had to leave. Since my father had taught both Palestinian and Jewish students who were now fighting each other, in deference to him, both sides declared a two-hour "no shooting" truce so our family could leave. The scene outside our house was surreal, and we were not given permission to use the main outside stairs that overlooked the demolished Mandelbaum building. The few suitcases we had packed in a rush with some random clothes were lowered to the street from a balcony, and we carried them to St. George's school nearby with the help of a young Armenian man. None of our Arab friends were allowed to help us since our house was in No Man's Land.

We locked the house doors and walked out. We were never able to go back home! The street, Nabi Samuel, which was beneath our balcony, became known as the Mandelbaum gate (Fig. 6), named after the demolished apartments. They divided our city into two parts – West Jerusalem fell under Israeli control and East Jerusalem under Jordanian control. Our street became a concrete barbed wire barrier, operated by United Nations personnel, separating East and West Jerusalem.

Figure 6. The Mandelbaum gate - a check point.

I didn't realize it at the time, but I was witness to events about which volumes have been written. The Swedish Count Folke Bernadotte, the United Nations Security Council mediator, helped bring about the June 11, 1948, ceasefire which was signed in our adopted living room at the Saint Mary's section of St. George's School. A team of United Nations observers and high-ranking Israeli and Jordanian military and civilian officials accompanied Count Folke Bernadotte. This first truce lasted 28 days. Both sides took advantage of that time to arm and improve strategic positions.

The battles continued all summer, and in September, the shocking news came that the Count had been assassinated by what turned out to be later known as the Stern Gang, a Zionist terrorist group that had as a member the future prime minister of Israel, Yitzhak Shamir. But before his assassination, the Count had laid the groundwork for the United Nations Relief and Works Agency for Palestine Refugees, now known as UNRWA, without which the millions of today's Palestinian refugees could not survive. In 1950, I worked at one of the UNRWA refugee camps among the thousands of refugees who were living in tents. I saw and learned a lot in those camps that I cannot forget. Even though my family was not living in the tents, we were all exiles who had been forced to leave home.

In that fateful summer of 1948, as the fighting got worse, we had to move yet again to safety. This time we moved to another building of St George's School where the basement walls were three feet thick. It was where we retreated at night, especially when fighting erupted. In bed, hearing the bullets and bombs above, I was comforted by the hymn that I would recite in my mind over and over, which lulled me to sleep.

"Oh God our help in ages past,
Our hope for years to come,
Our shelter from the stormy blast
And our eternal home."

Lucy Janjigian is a Palestinian-American born of Armenian descent in Jerusalem. She has served as a short-term volunteer with the Armenian Missionary Association of

America and is an elder at Westside Presbyterian Church in Ridgewood, New Jersey. Lucy is an artist and world traveler.

Stranded in No Man's Land:[15] You Can Never Go Home Again
Raouf J. Halaby

On January 10, 2013, snow fell in abundance in Jerusalem, Palestine. The six inches of snow that fell in Jerusalem and environs was the heaviest snowfall in thirty years, and some parts of the Galilee and the West Bank had as much as twelve inches of snow.

Israelis and Palestinians enjoyed this blanket of white by throwing snowballs and making snow sculptures. Images of snow-covered landscapes, historic landmarks, snowmen, and a first, a Palestinian snowwoman, were posted on blogs and printed on the front pages of newspapers around the world. One of the most iconic images was that of the radiant gilded cupola of the Dome of the Rock mosque with its brilliant golden hues boldly juxtaposed against a placid blanket of fluffy white eiderdown of repose on the Temple Mount and Mosque plaza surrounding Islam's oldest monument, and in close proximity to Judaism's Wailing Wall. For me after seeing these images, two recollections immediately came to mind.

One's tendency to associate current events with personal past experiences prompted me to revisit my personal repertoire of memories associated with snow in the Jerusalem of my childhood, and I travelled back in time to January 1949, when my family and I were stranded in the snow at the Mandelbaum Gate crossing because the Israelis had refused to allow us to go to our home in West Jerusalem. Soon after the United Nations recommended Partition Plan for Palestine was announced in New York on November 29, 1947, tension between the indigenous Palestinians and recently arrived, mostly European Jewish immigrants increased, and attacks and counter attacks reached a crescendo in early 1948, with Jewish paramilitary groups gaining the upper hand.

Organized Jewish terrorist attacks by the Irgun and Stern gangs struck terror in the hearts of a mostly agrarian Palestinian population, the culmination of which was the massacre of Palestinians in the village of Dayr Yasin (Monastery of Yasin). Over 100 women, children, and old men were brutally butchered in a massacre that has been likened to the Babi Yar Nazi massacre of Jews in Kiev, Ukraine.

Most refugees fled on foot, and to this day, almost 65 years later, descendants of these refugees live in the disquietude of refugee camp enclosures in Gaza, the West Bank, Israel, Jordan, Syria, and Lebanon, where the welcome mats are increasingly pulled out from under their feet, while hundreds of thousands live in diaspora around the globe. Had it not been for a sequence of fortunate turns, my family might well have been residing in one of these camps.

In most cases fathers, holding out for international mediation, initially sent their wives and children into flight, grandparents and the elderly followed, and finally, when it was obvious that the Israelis were getting the upper hand, the fathers fled, not knowing where their loved ones were. And in the process parents were separated from their children, and husbands from their wives.

While some family members headed for Gaza and Jordan, others headed for Syria or Lebanon. The search for lost family members took weeks and months, and in numerous instances years, before families were reunified. Caught up in the post-Dayr Yassin Massacre maelstrom of violence and counter-violence, and fearing for his widowed sister and her five children, my childless maternal uncle and his wife advised my mother to take her five children to Jordan "until the violence is over." Thus it was that, like the majority of Palestinians, my family, composed of my mother and my four siblings, the oldest of whom, an only sister, was ten years old, and the youngest, twin boys two-and-a-half years old, left Jerusalem with several suitcases and a handful of personal belongings and drove to Salt, Jordan, in early April of 1948.

When the harsh winter set in the remote Jordanian town, and because we did not have warm winter clothes (our sojourn, after all, was to have been brief), we moved to Jericho and rented a house in the middle of a banana and citrus *bayyara* (grove). Some 1,200 feet below sea level, Jericho's temperate climate was ideal, and for a playground we had the entire bayyara with its rich canopy of lush greenery, a virtual Avatar landscape. My only vivid memories of that brief sojourn are images of the shallow water aqueducts that meandered through and dissected the landscape's lush green vegetation, a serene world – an embryonic heaven on earth worlds away from the eddying whirlpool that was engulfing the region. I especially remember sitting in these aqueducts for what seemed like hours at a time, as well as watching my older siblings and cousins race their sailboats in the circumrotation of the pristine gushing waters diverted from the Jordan River. What I would give to be baptized, yet again, in these waters. With tree bark for hulls and banana leaves for mainsails, the boats sailed away into the distance. The sailing exploits were reserved for the older siblings and cousins, and we, the younger kids, were accorded the privilege of serving as spectators and cheerleaders.

By late November of 1948 it became clear that Israel had no intentions of allowing any displaced Palestinian refugees to return to Palestine, and the International Red Cross, under the auspices of the United Nations, launched a Reunification of Displaced People effort to help reunite displaced and separated family members. Utilizing radio broadcasts as a medium, radio stations in East Jerusalem, Amman, Damascus, and Beirut began to announce daily programs that went something like this:

"This is Nawal Awad, the wife of Elias Awad. Except for Fouad, the children and I are living in tent #329 at the Yarmook Refugee Camp. During the flight Fouad couldn't keep up, and my father and mother-in-law carried him and stopped to rest. We thought that they would catch up with us. Their names are Salem and Muna Awad. If anyone hears this message, please tell Kareem Awad, my husband, from the town of Safad, and my in-laws, where they can find us. Please hurry, conditions are horrible and we want to go back home. *Allah Maakum* (God be with you)!"

With money running out and the paucity of proper schooling, Katrina Halaby, my mother, took matters into her own hands. She contacted the Red Cross and requested that the following be broadcast on an East Jerusalem (by now occupied by Jordan) radio station, "This message is for my brother Naim Halaby of Upper Baka'a in West Jerusalem. Your sister Katrina and her children are in Jericho and wish to go back home. Anyone hearing this message please contact Naim Halaby and relay this urgent message."

This desperate appeal, one of thousands such voices crying out from the wilderness of diaspora, resonated with someone on the other side of the Green Line (which would eventually become the Armistice Line), and somehow my uncle received the message. He immediately went into action. Soon after my father's death in 1947, Naim Halaby and his wife left a successful business in New York and moved to Jerusalem; eventually, he become our guardian and ran my father's business, responsibilities he undertook with the utmost gravity.

On the Jordanian side, Abdallah al Tal, a Jordanian Colonel and the chief Jordanian negotiator in the Armistice Talks between Jordan and Israel, was asked to "allow the widow Katrina Halaby and her five children to cross the border and go back to their home in West Jerusalem." On the Israeli side, uncle Naim Halaby contacted two Jewish men, a Mr. Bassan and a Mr. Simon. The first was a Jewish attorney in Mandate Palestine and had served as my father's legal counsel, and the second was a well-to-do businessman with whom my father had numerous business dealings. If memory serves me correctly, I was told Simon became the Military Governor of Jerusalem soon after the 1948 war. Set in motion and by mutual agreement between Jordanian and Israeli officials, we were given permission to cross from East to West Jerusalem in January of 1949.

Two small flatbed trucks, one driven by Naim Halaby, and the other by a United Nations official, a kind and gentle American citizen in his twenties (perhaps older), left Jericho and wound their way west just past the well known Inn of the Good Samaritan, where, according to tradition, the Good Samaritan took the bloodied victim to an inn, thus earning a name for himself for eternity. The twenty-mile ascent to the Mandelbaum Gate, the only official conduit between East and West Jerusalem, seemed like an eternity.

In 2010, Pulitzer Prize-winner Kai Bird published his book *Crossing Mandelbaum Gate: Coming of Age Between the Arabs and Israelis, 1956-1978* (Fig. 7). As the son of an American Consular Officer who lived in East Jerusalem, Kai and his family had the privilege of crossing the border as frequently as they wished. And when Kai later attended the Anglican International School in West Jerusalem, the crossings became almost a daily routine. As soon as I looked at the cover of Kai's book I saw a photograph of Mandelbaum Gate's one-car narrow strip of road and the lateral massive concrete barriers and concertina barbed wire. I recognized the spot, and I immediately recalled my family's January 1949 harrowing experience of our *Awda* (return). On what must have been the coldest day in snow-covered 1949 Jerusalem, we arrived at the Jordanian side of the crossing by 9:30 a.m. and were processed rather quickly. My uncle, mother, and two older brothers rode in the cab of one truck, and my sister, my twin brother, and I rode in the cab of the other truck, driven by the American United Nations official. As we proceeded to the Israeli checkpoint, barely 200 feet away, we were stopped for what would have appeared to be a routine document and vehicle inspection. What should have taken less than an hour dragged into a seven-hour ordeal under the watchful eyes of machine-gun-toting Israeli guards who would emerge from their warm barrack-like structure to walk around the trucks, kick the snow while smoking cigarettes, and then standing just a few feet away from the truck doors, spit their phlegm at us. We were stuck in the snowy no man's land where the "The evening was blue, bitter," and "The snow gave [this small piece of land] a drawn, bleak look."[16]

Fearing that the petrol would run out, the driver turned the engines on only intermittently to provide just enough heat to keep us warm until the next brief run. Stranded in no-man's land, almost at the same spot depicted on the cover of Kai Bird's book cover, we were suspended in a Kafkaesque dark forest, a world circumscribed by monstrous cyclopean concrete barricades and an ugly spiral of cold razor wire. When our teeth chattered, the kindly American gentleman would lead us in hand clapping, cheerful talk, and singing, much of which I didn't understand. And to this day I remember him opening his heavy winter coat and placing my twin brother and me on either side of him and wrapping us for extended periods of time to ward off the brutal cold. And for days my sister suffered from serious frostbite. Finally, in the late evening hours, and only after Mr. Simon was reached, were we allowed to

Figure 7. Kai Bird's book cover showing the Mandelbaum Gate.

drive the few miles to our stone home in Upper Baka'a. Had it not been for al Tal, Bassan, and Simon, our lives would have undoubtedly taken a different course.

And somewhere out there, if he is still alive, is an American Schindler, a man whose memory still warms my heart, and a man to whom I will forever owe a deep debt of gratitude. Beamed through this retelling and hoping to soon hear from him or his family, I am sending this message out to:

"Dear American Good Samaritan, if you are still alive and or if someone out there, friend or family member, knows of your whereabouts, please let me know. Sixty-six years later I would love to personally honor you and to express a deep gratitude on my family's behalf for the magnanimous deed you rendered to a desperate family aching to go home." In the words of ET, the child in me will always say, " Halaby go home."

Raouf J. Halaby is a Professor of English and Art. He is a peace activist, a sculptor, a photographer, a gardener, and a former beekeeper.

The Mandelbaum Gate
Raouf Halaby relates some of his experiences[17] living near the Mandelbaum gate.

In the aftermath of the 1948 Arab-Israeli war the armistice line divided the city of Jerusalem into two sectors. East Jerusalem fell to Jordan, and West Jerusalem fell to Israel. The only point of access between Jordan and Israel was through what was then known as the Mandelbaum gate. The Mandelbaum gate was merely a former family residence that was located on the armistice line. The back of the house was the official checkpoint for the Israeli side; what used to be the front yard was a paved no man's land area that led to the Jordanian checkpoint some 40 yards away.

In his narrative, Stranded in No Man's Land, Raouf Halaby related his first memory of the Mandelbaum gate in the winter of 1949. However, since that time, the gate has become a symbol of oppression and apartheid. As Halaby continues:

"Once a year, however, the small number of Christian Palestinian families throughout Israel were allowed to cross through Mandelbaum gate to spend either 24 or 36 hours (depending on the military governor's whim) with their relatives in East Jerusalem.

"Because of the humiliating and demeaning experiences at the checkpoints, I remember these brief Christmas pilgrimages with more horror than joy. Very early on the 24th day of December we would line up at Mandelbaum gate. Israeli soldiers with Uzi machine guns at my eye level would walk by and hurl profanities or indignities. Aged men and women talked humbly to 20-year-old soldiers.

"Once the gate was opened, the long process of producing documents, answering numerous questions and being subjected to body searches began – often there were humiliating strip searches and cavity checks. One moved ever so slowly through an endless maze of barbed wire, rooms, partitions, desks, counters, soldiers, customs and numerous officials. Once processed, we were moved in groups to another maze of barbed wire in the no man's land area whereupon Jordanian soldiers took over and carried on in the same manner. On the average it took some five hours to walk the short distance.

"The letdown and the physical and emotional stress made the return trip equally horrifying. Only this time one had to make sure that gifts and other purchased items were not confiscated. I distinctly remember the following incident. A small battery-operated red plastic Morris-Minor car I had received as a Christmas present was taken by an Israeli customs agent to some back room 'to have it checked for explosives.' I never saw that car again.

"In 1988 my native American-born wife and I traveled to Jordan, Israel, the West Bank and the Gaza Strip. Upon entering Israel [at the infamous Allenby Bridge crossing], my wife, another American-born citizen of Palestinian background, and I were pulled out of the group for a 3 1/2-hour interrogation-search session. Not only was I strip-searched, but an Israeli soldier attempted to confiscate, 'for security reasons,' my wife's hair drier and curling iron. Remembering my plastic red car, I snatched the items out of the soldier's hands and defied him. Yes, I could do that; I am an American citizen now."

In 1967 Israel invaded and occupied the remaining sections of Jerusalem, which were controlled by the Jordanians. They dismantled the Mandelbaum gate. Halaby further states, "While the Mandelbaum gate and the ugly symbol for which it stood have disappeared, an infinitely more sinister and vile symbol of oppression has sprouted across Palestine in the form of an abominably loathsome 25 ft. high concrete 'Wall of Separation'."

It Was Like a Huge Tsunami
Laura Baramki Khoury

April 1948 is a date I shall never forget. It is the month and year when the Nakba was at its height. My parents and I were terrorized and ordered to leave our home in Jerusalem, Palestine. Woefully our experiences do not differ from those of other Palestinians who were forced to leave their homes and country, fleeing for their lives and the lives of their children.

My story begins on an evening in January 1948 when my grandmother and I were alone at home in Talbieh in Jerusalem. I was studying for my exams at the Teachers Training College and wishing I would finish studying, so that I could visit my friend who was living nearby. All of a sudden we heard a menacing voice emanating from a monstrous tank that was completely closed except for two slits, ordering all Arabs in the Talbieh quarter to leave now, now! We panicked, especially because my parents were not at home and we did not know what to do. Eventually my parents came home. The armored tank was relentless and insistent! It continually drove around and the shouting voice emanating from it succeeded in terrorizing us to leave our house and go to my uncle's house in lower Baka'a in Jerusalem. That was the second time that we had moved house while still in Jerusalem.

I had lived all my life until that fateful year in a house that my father had built near what became known after 1948 as the Mandlebaum gate. My father, Andoni Baramki, was an architect, and he owned two houses, which he had built. We were living in one of these two houses until we had to take refuge in the Talbieh quarter because the area became very dangerous, due to the Hagana Jewish underground terrorizing the area and shooting indiscriminately at any passerby. The other house, almost across the street from where we were living, was always rented out and became a museum with changing names from time to time. And to add insult to injury, the Israeli curators of the museum never acknowledged the fact that the building belonged to my father. They only mentioned that the home, with its special architectural beauty, was constructed by Mr. A. Barmaki and omitted that it was built and owned by A. Baramki.

After hearing the order that we had to leave, once again we moved to a rented house in lower Baka'a, because the area was more secure and housed mostly Palestinians. However, the situation was getting worse, and random shootings were becoming an everyday happening. I almost got killed one evening as I was going home after I was returning from the College, when a stray bullet grazed my hair. At first I thought it was a bird flying over until a man passing by told me how lucky I was barely missing the bullet.

In April of the year 1948, when everybody was leaving in the wake of the Dayr Yasin massacre and no place seemed safe enough, we left our home in Jerusalem, taking nothing with us except some of our clothes, thinking that it was a temporary period. That is why we took refuge in Birzeit (in the West Bank) so that we would be close by to return when all would be well again. But it was never well again. My family and I never again saw the Jerusalem in which we had lived.

When we eventually returned to Jerusalem after living in Gaza and then Beirut for a few years, we found a destroyed city; a city with its soul gone. Our families and friends were no more there. Our homes were full of bullet holes - all run down and neglected.

I mourned for my lost youth in Jerusalem. Oh how I have yearned to be a young adult in Jerusalem after finishing boarding school in 1947. I longed to live all year round in my city, wondering what my life would have been like. I was just about to be on the threshold of a new teen-age life full of expectations, of romance if you like, or just plain living.

Palestine was like a beautiful tapestry, with myriad brilliant colors all tightly woven together, with communities living together in harmony. Alas, we came back to a ravished tapestry, all torn, its threads scattered all over the country – indeed countries.

My plight, as I mentioned at the beginning of my narrative, is from my point of view, describing what my family and I went through, but this is nothing compared to the rest of Palestine, to all the villages that were destroyed, their lands taken, their men, women, and children shot at and driven out of their homes at gun point, never to return again and thus to become refugees in camps till this day.

What about the indelible trauma that all the families of my parents' generation that had to leave their homes, their work, and all their achievements, and their dreams for their children? It was like a huge tsunami that happened and obliterated everything that ever was, except that that tsunami was man-made by evil people with the collaboration of other countries, not least the British, who thought our country was theirs to give away and partition. But of course the British did this everywhere they occupied and ruled.

We will never forget; our stories will continue to be passed on from one generation to the next, and someday justice will prevail.

Laura Baramki Khoury lives in Jerusalem and is the wife of the late Dr. Abdallah Khoury. Laura writes commentary articles that are circulated through the Internet.

Loss After the Nakba and Life under Occupation
Gaby Baramki

What follows are some of Dr. Gaby Baramki's personal and family experiences after the Nakba in 1948 and the Israeli invasion and takeover of the West Bank in 1967.

"According to the United Nations plan, my home city, Jerusalem, was meant to be shared by both sides under United Nations trusteeship, but as a result of the war our house, in West Jerusalem, was on the Israeli side and thus unreachable.

"My father was to pine all his life for this home he had created with so much care. Looking down on it from the East Jerusalem YMCA rooftop with me, he assured me that we would get it back some day. What we got, eventually, was a chance to stand outside its front door. After the Six-Day War in 1967, Israel occupied all of Jerusalem, and my father was able to visit his house at last. When he arrived there, he found that the house had been badly damaged by shelling in 1948. Worse, it now had an Israeli army reservist as a squatter and was under the auspices of the Israeli 'Custodian of Absentee Property'. When my father presented himself at this government department, he was told that he could not reclaim the property as he was an 'absentee'. My father, a tall, well-built man, failed to see how anyone could consider him 'absent' given his indisputable presence.

"He went on to file a claim for the house, but was informed that we would only get it back when there was peace between Palestinians and Israelis. When he asked if could at least rent it, he was fobbed off with ever-changing excuses. One official claimed that it was unfit for habitation. My father replied that, as an architect, he was undoubtedly able to restore it. Nevertheless, he was not allowed to set foot in the house again to his dying day.

"My parents, who had been staying with relatives in Birzeit during the 1948 hostilities, found that they had lost not just their home but every asset acquired during my father's working life."

Next Dr. Baramki narrates some of his experience in 1967 of the Israeli invasion and takeover of the West Bank:

"My parents, my sister, and her children, as well as Haifa carrying our unborn child, our son, Hani, were all cooped up in the house with me. Then a few soldiers walked up to our house. They were carrying guns. . . . When I opened the door, one of the soldiers pointed his gun at me. I am sure I looked deadly pale. . . . The soldier addressed me in Arabic '*La tkhaf* (do not be afraid), we're not going to shoot'. 'What is it that you want?' I asked. 'Is there anyone else in the house with you?' he said. 'Yes' I said. 'My wife, my parents, my sister and her four little children.' He ordered them all out, onto the veranda, and the soldiers went into the house. They searched it for a while and then came out again.

"The soldiers had been quite polite and so my mother said to them 'Can I make you some tea?' They replied, 'No we've got beer.' When they had gone we went inside and discovered that they had helped themselves to the beer from our fridge. Unfortunately, we later found out that they had also taken my mother's jewelry, a golden pen that belonged to Haifa, a pair of binoculars and some gold coins my father had kept. Having one's home looted, which was to become a standard feature of the occupation, was only one of several unpleasant new experiences.

"Living under Israeli rule was unlike anything we had ever known. For a start, we were now under a military government. The local military governor, an Israeli brigadier, was our chief, but any soldier carrying a gun was a Palestinian's superior. Military orders poured forth, setting out what we could and could not do. To repair our house, raise chickens or plant a tree now required an Israeli permit."

With the permission of Haifa Baramki, the wife of the late Dr. Gaby Baramki, and the Publisher, Pluto Press, the material of this narrative has been excerpted from Dr. Gaby Baramki's book, Peaceful Resistance, Building a Palestinian University under Occupation, Pluto Press, 2010.

My Multicultural Family

Samia Halileh

As a young child, I did not know I was Palestinian. As I grew older I learned that I was and what it entailed. My grandparents were evicted from their homes in Yafa [Jaffa – on the coast of Palestine and now on the Southern outskirts of Tel Aviv] and Yazur [village near Jaffa] during the Nakba in 1948 to Nablus in the West Bank, which became part of Jordan. Shortly after the Nakba and the creation of Israel in our homeland, both sides of my family went to Kuwait, where the oil industry provided jobs to thousands of Palestinian refugees. My father and mother met there and were married. In 1959, after I was born as their third child, they came back to Jericho, in the West Bank, which had become part of Jordan in 1948. That's when, like everyone else, I obtained a Jordanian passport.

My first memories are of growing up in Jericho, the oldest city on earth, with the Dead Sea close by, where you can float without learning how to swim. We lived on a farm, because I think my father had grown up on a farm in the village of Yazur in Palestine before being expelled. There were four children in my father's family: three went to school in Yafa, while the eldest girl, Zakiah, stayed home and helped her mother (my grandmother) around the house and in the fields. My mother grew up in Yafa in a large family of ten, three boys and seven girls. Her father was a policeman and all his children went to school.

After the 1967 war, Israel occupied the West Bank and took control of what had been under Jordanian control. During the military conquest we had to sleep under trees because Israeli planes targeted houses and Napalm burning bombs targeted those who had fled to prevent them from ever coming back. A few days later, we fled for safety, wishing to get away from the violence of the war and the bombs. I remember my mother crying fiercely, begging my dad not to flee; however he convinced her that it would be only for few days. We left in one car and my dad followed the next day in the other car, as bombing of civilians became more intense.

We went to Kuwait, where our extended family continues to live today, but my dad stayed in Jordan. After a short period of time, we came back to our home, kept our Jordanian passports and were given Israeli identity cards. Jericho and the West Bank became part of the occupied Palestinian territories. This kind of roaming and wandering from place to place became commonplace amongst Palestinians who became refugees in 1948 and then again in 1967. Being strangers in the land and living in exile is a story present in every family because those who left in 1948 have never been allowed to return to their homes and communities.

After my sixth-grade year, we went to live in Ramallah for better schooling and close access to the university where my sister enrolled. I attended the American

Society of Friends School, a Quaker school, in Ramallah. Our songs in the chapel were of peace and love. Sometimes, as we demonstrated against the Israeli occupation, our American teachers protected us from the Israeli soldiers.

In 1976, I went to study medicine in the United Kingdom, where hardly anyone had heard of Palestine except for foreign students and those who served in the British army during the British Mandate of Palestine (up to 1948). Others used to think I came from Pakistan.

When I registered at the college for my A-levels, I had to meet with an administrator to fill in my application. She asked me several questions, to which I knew very well how to respond, then she said, "What is your nationality?" For me, I had no doubt that I am a Palestinian, and I told her so; then as she was going to write it, I remarked that it does not exist anymore.

She said: "Where were you born?" I said, "Kuwait."
"You are a Kuwaiti?" I said "No!"
"What passport do you have?" I said, "Jordanian."
"You are Jordanian." I said, "No!"
"Where do you live?" I said, "The West Bank in Israel."
"You are Israeli." I said, "No!"
She banged the table angrily and said, "What are you then?"

I paused for a long while, as it slowly dawned on me that as a Palestinian, I didn't exist anymore! The other confusing question was when she asked my race; on the form only four racial categories were listed: "White," "Black," "Indian," and "Others." My confusion was because in my family, the colors range from blue eyes, blond hair, and white skin to black hair like mine, brown eyes, and brown skin, but this was not a category on her list, so I opted for "Others."

She asked about my religion. That was easy: I am a Muslim like my father. Many years ago his ancestors had come from Saudi Arabia. She did not ask about my mother, whose family was originally Jewish from Russia and who came to Palestine many years ago. And I did not tell her that in my extended family tree, two Jewish women married into the family. I only knew one of them, who had lived a good long life in Jericho. This very special area of Falastine [Palestine], the town of Jericho, attracted Christians, Jews, and Muslims from all over the world: blacks from Africa, Indians from India, and Europeans, many of whom came with the crusaders. Ironically, the crusaders, who came to claim the Holy Land for Christians, killed as many Arab Christians as Muslims.

This incredible mixture of peoples in all of Palestine has resulted in a mixed genotype that is specific to this part of the world. In certain areas, such as Gaza, Hebron and Nablus, many families have very fair and Western features, which is also true for Lebanon and Syria. In other parts, we are darker and more Eastern. What is also unique about this part of the world is that all the Abrahamic faiths have major shrines here - Christians, Jews, and Muslims all belong here. However, again uniquely, Isa [Jesus], born in Beitlahim [Bethlehem], is the only Palestinian among the prophets, as the prophet Mohammad came from the Arabian Peninsula and the prophet Musa [Moses] was from Egypt. Jesus is the only Palestinian prophet.

I will relate some of my personal convictions about religious affiliation in Palestine throughout its history. We know that the people of Palestine at one time were adherents of the Canaanite religion and that some of them converted to Judaism. During the Byzantine[18] Empire, most were Christians. With the advent of Islam into Palestine, many converted from Judaism and Christianity to Islam. So there are Christians, Jews, and Muslims with the same surname, Totah for example. There are many other such surnames along the Mediterranean coast of Palestine, Lebanon, and Syria testifying to the fact that religious affiliation is not necessarily indicative of the geographic origins of peoples.

In Palestine, intermarriage within religions, although small in number, exists especially among the Muslims. A woman can keep her religion if she marries a Muslim, but a man must become a Muslim to marry a Muslim woman. A male friend of mine with a surname of Khoury (priest in Arabic), married a Muslim woman after he converted to Islam. When his daughter was born, with a surname of Khoury, her religion was thought to be Christian and was so recorded on her birth certificate. Her parents never changed the entry on the birth certificate. So through intermarriage and conversion, I know of families who have members of both the Christian and Muslim faiths.

In this world where religion has so often been used to justify wars, I wonder by whom and why this has started, since ordinary people are tolerant of one another.

Professor Samia Halileh, M.D., Ph.D., is a practicing pediatrician and professor of epidemiology at Birzeit University, Palestine.

Al-Nakba of Haret al-Nammamreh
Jacob J. Nammar

I was born on May 16, 1941, in Madinat al-Quds, "the Holy City," known in the Western world as Jerusalem. We are a Palestinian family of ten who have lived and worshiped in this sacred place for generations. The City was accepted worldwide as having provided freedom and equality for a multi-religious pluralistic community. Jerusalem shaped our spirit, religion, heritage, identity, and earthly consciousness. In al-Quds, the Holy City, I always sensed the presence of God.

The Nammar extended family, also known as Nammari, was one of the leading families in al-Quds. We owned several tracts of valuable properties in the Old City and throughout Palestine. As the Old City became overcrowded, several wealthy families ventured outside the wall, including the Nammars. The relocation from the

Old City to the West of al-Quds created an exclusive community named Haret al-Nammareh, the Nammareh neighborhood, where they built palatial homes for the entire family.

From the time I was born, my life was privileged and shielded from the violent turmoil that was then brewing with great force. From the beginning, the Zionist strategy was one of Nikayon, Hebrew for "ethnic cleansing," to clear the land of Palestinian natives from their entire ancestral homeland to make way for the new nation of Israel. David Ben-Gurion, the Polish-born Zionist leader, knew very well that to create a Jewish majority he must illegally force the Palestinians out. He admitted as early as 1937, "We must expel the Arabs and take their land. . . . I support compulsory transfer. I do not see anything in it immoral".[19]

On one otherwise routine afternoon, the tranquility of my childhood was shattered when our bus was attacked on our way home from school. As we passed near the Montefiore Jewish Colony, machine gun fire broke out from the hilltop, forcing us to lie on top of each other on the floor of the bus while the driver sped ahead. Upon arrival at our neighborhood, with dread we discovered that two of my student friends had been killed and many had been wounded. I thanked God that, miraculously, my body had been spared, but I was shocked and spiritually wounded. This was the beginning of the end.

Later, the day before my seventh birthday, May 15, 1948, was one of the most horrible days of my childhood. That day, for me, marked the beginning of what became to be known as al-Nakba, the great catastrophe, the Palestinian exodus from our lands. Through terror the highly equipped Zionists spread panic in the Palestinian population, forcing about 80 percent to flee their homes to neighboring countries. Our relatives abroad pleaded with my parents that since the terrorists were approaching, our family, too, should leave, if only for the sake of the children. Yet, my father insisted that this was our home, and mother agreed that we must remain and exercise *sumud* - remain steadfast. We resolved to seek temporary refuge at the nearby German Colony[20] to protect ourselves from the violence.

My father, mother, and all of us children locked our lavish and wonderful home and left for safety. We walked close together, holding hands tightly. Suddenly, heavily armed Zionists stopped us at a street corner. "Where are you going?" they had asked. Father explained that we are going to the German Colony. After searching and questioning us for an hour, the Zionists allowed us to continue while detaining my father and older brother, Mihran. Before taking them away in a military truck, father pleaded to let Mihran go with the rest of the family, "He is only seventeen years old and a minor, please let him go!" But the soldiers took him anyway.

At the Colony the nuns welcomed us with open arms. After about a week, we reluctantly decided it was time to go back home. Two nuns insisted they accompany us for our protection. It was our first glimpse of the damage and destruction of buildings and homes. On arrival we could not believe our eyes. Our home had been broken into and vandalized. Anticipating the war, my father had stocked large amounts of food in the house. It was heartbreaking to find all our food stolen. Our family was in despair. We saw trucks full of furniture, valuable Persian carpets, appliances, and mattresses being hauled away. In addition, homes were looted of jewelry, books and valuables, and worse, Palestinian women were violently raped.

A few weeks later several groups of armed Zionist militias came to our home demanding we relocate to another neighborhood. They said it was for our own protection, that it would be "only for a few days" and that we would return "soon." Our spirit sank. All we took this time were a few personal belongings. We were escorted to a vacant, dilapidated apartment building still under construction next to the railway tracks. We discovered that we had been forced under military administration law into a fenced security "Zone A", confined with other Palestinian families. The military zone was a ghetto and a large open prison camp, surrounded by eight foot high barbed wire, with armed guards preventing anyone from leaving or entering under strict curfew.

Two-and-a-half years after the state of Israel was established, this prison zone was dismantled. We were issued a Teu'dad Zehut. This was an identity card, issued by Israel's Ministry of Interior to differentiate Jews from Palestinians. With this new policy, and by coming under the control of the new country of Israel, our civil rights were now undermined.

After receiving these new papers, my family's first instinct was to move back to our own home in Haret al-Nammareh neighborhood where we belonged. But when we arrived there, we were astonished to discover that our home was already occupied by two new Jewish families from Eastern Europe who spoke only Yiddish. They considered us strangers and would not allow us inside. After many agonizing hours, we were informed by a Jewish soldier, who was stationed outside our house to protect them, that, "These Jews believe that God promised them this land, so they came from Poland to claim it."

We promptly protested to the authority, but they advised us that under the newly promulgated 1950 property law we were now classified as and considered "Present Absentees," the same status as "Absentee Land Owners" and "Internal Refugees." Their new law stated that "land and homes left behind by Palestinians as of November 29, 1947, are deemed 'enemy' property and are liable for expropriation by Israel authorities." Desperate and demoralized, we were forced to return to the area of the dismantled prison zone to live in the same pitiful place.

To our surprise Mihran, my older brother, was released in 1951. My father, on the other hand, who was sick and weak, was deported to Jordan in a prisoner exchange. It took help from the United Nations and five years of pleading before our father was reunited with us.

The unconditional Western support of Israel's colonization is summarized best by the Israeli Nathan Chofshi:

> "We came and turned the native Arabs into tragic refugees. And still we have to slander and malign them, to besmirch their name. Instead of being deeply ashamed of what we did and trying to undo some of the evil we committed . . . we justify our terrible acts and even attempt to glorify them."[21]

Sadly, only a few years later my father, our rock, passed away from what I believe was a broken heart. His sudden death was painful to all of us, especially mother, who mourned him forever and never remarried. With discrimination and no future opportunities in sight, all my brothers and sisters began to emigrate one after the other. From no fault of our own, and against all our wishes, our nuclear family ended up scattered to faraway parts of the world.

My last experiences of Israel were sour. It was a state that didn't afford me a voice, let alone equality, independence, or even a future. It had torn apart my home, my family, my sense of a cohesive self, and had dispossessed not only my family but also my entire society. My own time in Jerusalem would last long. I was the last person from my family to leave my beloved Jerusalem and Palestine. I knew that I would always miss al-Quds (Jerusalem). Our family's tragic exodus brutally changed our lives forever. All we had was our attachment to our land and childhood memories, which we hold onto and treasure.

I am a man with a broken heart. I am from Jerusalem, my broken homeland, and Palestine makes me weep. Yet, I still have some memories to share and a story to tell. So I wish to add my own story to those of others who have lived through the ethnic cleansing of Palestine.

The symbol of Palestine is the olive tree, the tree of eternity, the tree of life, peace, hope, and survival. It endures for centuries, and then, even when it appears dead, life returns from its roots. This I pray for Palestine, that like the olive tree, it will be reborn from all of its deep roots. I pray for peace in Jerusalem and Palestine, that my prayer will offer *amal*—hope. I pray that my story will open doors. I lift my heart and hope for the City of God.

Jacob J. Nammar is a retired multi-lingual international business executive. He is an Arab Christan and the author of "Born in Jerusalem, Born Palestinian" A Memoir. Published in 2012 by Interlink Publishing, Inc.

I am a Palestinian woman. Here is My Story
Marlene Mourad

My story is not unique; like millions of other stories, mine is one of the trials, tribulations, survival, and hope of a people whose land was taken by those who pretended that Palestinians did not exist.[22] Their mantra was "a land without a people for a people without a land."[23]

I was born in Nablus in 1938. Nablus is an ancient city which was founded by the Roman emperor, Vespasian, in 72 CE. In 1099, the Crusaders took control of Nablus and held it for about a century, leaving its mixed Muslim, Christian, and Samaritan populations relatively undisturbed. In 1947, the proposed United Nations recommendation for the partition of Palestine designated Nablus to be part of the Arab State of Palestine. But in 1967, after the Six Day War, Nablus came under military occupation by Israel.

The day I was born, my mother took me in her arms and hid under the bed to avoid being hit by shrapnel during the 1936 to 1939 Palestinian uprising for self-rule against the British, who controlled Palestine. When I was one-and-a-half years old, my mother was depressed and could not nurse me any further, and there was no milk for me. I was starving, so my father and mother sent me to Jerusalem to live with my uncle and his wife, who was from Switzerland. My aunt suggested the Swedish powdered milk, Nestogen, which she was able to buy. This saved my life. Afterwards, I continued to stay with my uncle and Swiss aunt. Nestogen milk was a very new concept at that time. The irony is that Nestle, the producer of Nestogen, saved my life but is now supporting the Israeli occupation.

On March 29, 1948, on the Feast of St. Joseph, we, like St. Joseph and the Holy Family two thousand years ago, started our flight to Egypt – my Uncle, my Aunt, and I. I was ten years old then. Six weeks later, on May 15, 1948, the state of Israel was born. We were never able to return to live in our home in Jerusalem. Meanwhile, my Uncle and Aunt's properties, orchards, and assets were expropriated, some would say stolen, by the state of Israel.

Because my parents were living in Nablus (which is in the central West Bank and was not occupied by Israel at that time), and I was with my Uncle and Aunt in Jerusalem (which was occupied by Israel), I became separated from my parents. After my Uncle's home and property were confiscated by the Israelis, much of their furniture was either taken or thrown out on the street. My mother, writing to me later after they had occasion to visit Jerusalem, sent me a letter in which she told me, "We found your doll in the street – crushed in the mud, with one leg lost!

Having lost everything, we settled into what seemed like a depleted life in Cairo and watched as more and more Europeans arrived in our homeland to claim it as theirs. With not much to our names but the proceeds from the sale of the car that brought us to Cairo, my uncle opened a restaurant called Tomy's Bar. I began attending school in Cairo, and life seemed to settle down and have some stability for a while, until four years later, in 1952, everything collapsed around us yet again. "Black Saturday," sometimes referred to as the "Cairo Fire," occurred in January 26, 1952, when Egyptians rioted against their British occupiers. Many European business establishments, along with retail shops, cafes, cinemas, hotels, restaurants, theaters, nightclubs, and the country's Opera House in downtown Cairo were burned down. Our restaurant was burned to the ground. For the second time, we lost everything. We had hoped our new home in Egypt would be stable and safe, but it was not to be. The Egyptian government provided some compensation for those business owners who lost everything in the fires. My Uncle was able to begin anew with a small restaurant.

I continued in school, and during the summer vacations, I travelled with my Aunt to Switzerland, where I had the opportunity to continue to improve my French. Shortly after completing my school, I met my future husband, Samir Mourad. We were married in 1958 and had three children, Joseph, Mona, and Noha, all born in Egypt.

Because we keenly felt discrimination against Christians in Egypt, we decided to leave the country. My husband and I along with our three children emigrated to the United States in 1968; five years later we became U.S. citizens, and for the first time, we lived without concerns for security and more upheaval. Though we assimilated quickly into life in the United States, we have never forgotten from where we came and our struggles for survival.

In 2004 my husband and I co-founded the "Interfaith Council for Peace in the Middle East," which is a faith-based organization located in Northeast Ohio. We, along with a group of dedicated Christians, Muslims, and Jews, utilize education, peaceful activism, and dialogue as the means for raising awareness about the situation in Palestine, Israel, and the Middle East. The group is dedicated to working for a peaceful resolution to the various conflicts in the Middle East. We aim to put a human face on the suffering and hardships of its people and to help bring to life their aspirations for peace, justice, dignity, and freedom. Today, with hope against hope, I continue to work and advocate for peace and justice for the land that God gave to ALL who live in the Land we call 'Holy'.

Questions for Reflection

1. What role did the massacre at Dayr Yasin play in the flight of Palestinians?

2. What are the reasons most Palestinians from the Jerusalem District fled from their homes?

3. Do you see similar threads in the narratives from the Jerusalem District? If so, what are these common threads?

4. What became of the homes of Palestinian Jerusalemites in the well-to-do suburbs of Jerusalem such Talbieh and Lower and Upper Baka'a?

5. The Mandelbaum gate was a checkpoint between and East and West Jerusalem before the Israeli occupation of East Jerusalem and the West Bank in June 1967. The Mandelbaum gate is now replaced by the wall, which as Raouf Halaby relates, is a "sinister and vile symbol of oppression." The wall divides people from their schools, places of business, and hospitals. How would you feel if you were living in a situation similar to that in which Palestinians in the West Bank and East Jerusalem find themselves?

6. There are checkpoints between the West Bank, East Jerusalem, and Israel and hundreds more within the West Bank. Delays and humiliations are commonplace at these checkpoints. They impede movement of Palestinians as they go about their daily lives. Going to work, school, places of worship, and hospitals become a major undertaking and sometimes impossible when the Israeli military declares a curfew. How would you feel if you had to face checkpoints daily, similar to those, which Palestinians in the West Bank and East Jerusalem have to face?

Jaffa District

Jaffa District lies on the central coast of Palestine. Twenty-three villages in the Jaffa district were destroyed and/or depopulated by the Zionist forces before the end of the British Mandate in May 1948.[24]

Jaffa, before its surrender on May 13, 1948, was sometimes called the Bride of Palestine. It was a major cultural center with 12 newspapers and many business and commercial interests. At this time, Jaffa was the largest city in Palestine, with a population of 77,000, and the second most important next to Jerusalem. Jaffa's seaport was believed to be one of the oldest continually used seaports in the world. It was also famous for its oranges and was at times called the "City of Oranges".[25]

In Jaffa as in other districts, "the decisive factor in the forced depopulation of its people was the violent intimidation by Zionist forces."[26] Jaffa was strategically vulnerable. In the United Nations recommendation for the partition of Palestine, the city of Jaffa was to be part of the Palestinian state and was to be completely surrounded by the Israeli state.[27] Moreover, prior to the creation of Israel, Zionist settlements encircled Jaffa: Tel-Aviv to the North, Hatikva to the Northeast, Mikvet Israel to the East, Holon to the Southeast, and Bat Yam to the South.[28] As the mandate was coming to a close and the British were leaving, the inhabitants of Jaffa became concerned about the power vacuum.

Arab League members also grew fearful that a power vacuum was developing, which the Zionists could exploit as the British evacuate. The [Arab] League's political committee saw this as a consequence of British assistance to the Jews "both before and after the war [World War II], which contributed to the formation of their Hagana force [the precursor of the Israeli Defense Force], another terrorist army. Azzam Pasha [the Arab League secretary general] protested that the British had extended 'no assistance of any kind' to the Palestinian Arabs 'to help them defend their towns and villages from an armed force or to undertake such defense.' He complained that the British had 'completely disarmed them during the 1936-39 period', thereby exposing the 'defenseless Arabs to the wiles and horrors of the Jewish terrorists'."[29]

In other words, the Palestinians were largely defenseless, and this was particularly so in the outlying villages in the Jaffa District. Abd al-'Azis Khayr from the village of Kafr 'Ana, in his interview with Esber, recalled that Kafr 'Ana was hit with mortars while women were winnowing wheat, and explosions beheaded some of them. He went on further to say:

> "Some shots hit children. [The Jews] did not spare any house from their shooting. They did this all day long from sunset until dawn for two months before they attacked the village, until the night when they expelled us. Before that they did not have enough force to enter the village, but when they got it, they fired on the village with mortars. . . . What could we do?

We had no one outside to help us. We begged for bullets. We used to buy each [bullet] for a quarter lira to defend ourselves. We all defended our village, but we did not have enough weapons. What could we do against their might?"[30]

On April 26, Jaffa's inhabitants were subjected to widespread terror. IZL [Irgun Zva'i Leumi, a Jewish terrorist group] mortars began to shell Jaffa at 8:00 a.m., destroying numerous civilian Arab homes.[31] Esber, in her book, *Under the Cover of War: The Zionist Expulsion of the Palestinians*, continues to relate:

"General Horatius Murray reported that Jewish units started 'systematically to mortar Jaffa,' continuing for 48 hours. Rows and blocks of houses were blown up.[32] 'Abd Al-Ghani Nasir, who worked for the British military in Jaffa, recalls that the attack on Jaffa consisted of artillery shells aimed at crowds in places like the central market. Bombing would start and then cease until civilians ran to the site frantically looking for friends and family; then bombing would recommence more intensely with the aim, Nair said, 'to inflict the maximum killing that they could.'[33] The Zionist record corroborates the indiscriminate slaughter of civilians that the Palestinians recall, as well as the intent to remove the Arab population. One of the objectives of the mortar barrage, according to the instructions of the IZL commanding officer, Amihai Paglin, was 'to cause chaos among the civilian population in order to create mass flight'."[34]

According to the British military, "refugees [were] fired on by Jewish snipers as [the refugees] moved off."[35] Esber further states, "Zionist snipers had also shot at fleeing Arabs and ambulances during Haifa's evacuation, further heightening the Arab's terror." An unknown number of Palestinian Arabs also drowned during the exodus by sea;[36] most went to Gaza and some to Beirut, Lebanon.

Intimidation targeted the entire civilian population. Shukri Salameh, a Palestinian attorney, reported a Zionist clandestine radio station broadcasting constantly in Arabic, "urging the population of Jaffa to escape with their families before their houses were blown up over their heads." The radio broadcaster reminded the Arabs ominously of the Dayr Yasin slaughter.[37]

Various British military observers and Israeli sources corroborate that the Palestinians of Jaffa left due to heavy, indiscriminate shelling of civilian areas.

Figure 8 is an artist's view of how many of the Jaffa residents were expelled. The artist "Tamam Al Akhal was twelve years old when she left Yafa [Jaffa], Palestine, with her family in 1948. Their sudden escape from Zionist terror was in a dangerously small boat. They used to live within the walls of the ancient city of Yafa. At dawn of April 28, 1948, Zionist soldiers went from door to door, getting people out of their homes at gunpoint and pushing them towards the harbor. Those escaping Yafa

Figure 8. Tamam Al Akhal. *Uprooting, 1998.* Oil on canvas, 65 x 79 in, 165 x 200 cm.

that day were forced onto boats and pursued by armed Zionist soldiers throwing explosives. It was a day of many deaths, most by drowning."[38]

On May 14, Jaffa capitulated to the Israelis. In a three-page document[39] (Figs. 9, 10, and 11) circulated to the civilian leaders of Jaffa, amongst them, Asaad S. Halaby, and reproduced below, the Israeli Hagana (the Israeli armed forces, which were to become the modern Israeli military, the so called Israeli Defense Forces) made promises, which they did not intend to keep. One such promise was, "It is understood the Hagana does respect and will always respect the Geneva Convention and all International Laws and uses of war (Fig. 9)." Despite this promise, the Israeli Hagana's occupation of Jaffa was brutal.

As reported by Pappe, Red Cross representative's reports depict a "collective abuse of basic rights."[40] "The occupying Israeli troops intimidated, screened, beat, tortured, and concentrated the remaining inhabitants, about 4,100, in one or more areas encircled by barbed wire. Private property was looted, vandalized, robbed, and destroyed. Some prisoners were used as forced labor. Atrocities continued after the occupation under the military governorship of Yitzhak Chizik. Fifteen Arab men

AGREEMENT

Between   The Commander of the HAGANA, Tel-Aviv District
             (which includes Bat-Yam, Holon, and Mikve Israel);
and   The Arab population of the area enclosed by Tel-Aviv,Mikve-
On   13th May 1948
at   Headquarters, Hagana, Tel-Aviv District

Whereas the undersigned,

               AHMAD EFFENDI ABU LABAN
               SALAH EFFENDI EL NAZER
               AMIN EFFENDI ANDRAUS
               AHMAD EFFENDI ABDUL RAHIM
are the Emergency Committee of Jaffa ;

And WHEREAS they are in Jaffa in order to direct the
affairs of the Arab in the area above defined, following their declaration that Jaffa is an underfended area;

AND IN ORDER TO preserve and maintain the peace and welfare
of the Arabs in the area above defined;

THEY THEREFORE HEREBY solemnly declare and affirm that all
Arabs in the area above defined are represented by them;

AND THAT they will carry out all instructions given and to
be given by the Commander of the Hagana, Tel-Aviv District, and/or by
any Officer designed and/or authorized by him, to day and at any
further date;

And they further solemnly declare and affirm that they have
read the instructions given today by the Commander of the Hagana, Tel-
Aviv District, to the Arab in the area above defined, and have coun-
tersigned these orders as a token that they have fully understood them
and that they undertake full responsibility that the instructions will
be properly carried out by the Arabs.

IT IS UNDERSTOOD that the Hagana always does respect and
will respect the Geneva Convention and all International Laws and Usa-
ges of war.

IN WITNESS WHEREOF they affix their signatures this thirteenth day of May 1948, whilst at the Headquarters of the Hagana, Tel-
Aviv District.

Ahmad Effendi Abu Laban

Salah Effendi El Nazer   The Commander of the Hagana,

                              Tel-Aviv District
Amin Effendi Andraus

Ahmad Effendi Abdul Rahim

We hereby testify and solemnly affirm the signatures of the
above Ahmad Effendi Abu Laban, Salah Effendi El Nazer, Amin Effendi
Andraus and Ahmad Effendi Abdul Rahim.

Figure 9.

INSTRUCTIONS TO THE ARAB POPULATION

by the

COMMANDER of the Hagana,

Tel-Aviv District

Given on

13th May 1948.

WHEREAS your representatives signed an Agreement today, I hereby direct as follows :

1.   Any shot fired at a Jewish area or at a Jew or at any member of the Hagana, or any resistance to them, will be sufficient reason for the Hagana to open fire at the Offender.

2.   All arms, ammunition and military equipment of any kind will be stacked at a place and time which will be notified later, and handed over to my representative. Any person found in possession of any article of military equipment after that time will be severely punished.

3.   Any person having any knowledge or information of the location of mines or booby traps or any similar devices, will at once submit such information to the nearest member of representative of the Hagana. Any person also obeying this order will be severely punished.

4.   (a) All males in the area defined in the Agreement will concen-
                trate in the area between Feisal Street, Al Mukhtar Street,
                Al Hulwa Street and the Sea until everybody has identified
                himself under arrangements, the particulars of which will
                be notified later.

            (b) During this time, any male found outside this area will be
                severely punished, unless in possession of a special permit.

5.   After the termination of the identification, all persons with the exception of those defined in Paragraph 6 will be issued with a special identity-card and will be free to return to their former homes unless they live in an area which will be declared as a military enclosure.

6.   All persons who may be dangerous to the peace and security of the area will be interrogated and, if necessary, be interned. The Representatives of the Arab population may attend in an advisory capacity during these proceedings.

        The Commander of the Hagana declares that it is not his intention to detain and/ or to intern the male population of the area defined, even if they or any of them did take part in the hostilities in the past. Only criminals or persons suspected of being a danger to the peace are liable to internment.

Figure 10.

- 2 -

7.   The number and the size of the military enclosures, i.e. areas out of bounds to civilians, will be limited and directed by military necessities only. Outside those enclosures, normal life for all peaceful Arabs may continue in the whole area.

8.   Any male wishing to leave may apply to my representative for a permit to do so; likewise any male Arab who left Jaffa and who wishes to return to Jaffa may apply for a permit to do so. Permits will be granted after their bonda-fides have been proved, provided that the Commander of the Haganais convinced that applicants will not, at any time, constitute a threat to peace and security. This will be done with the cooperation of the representatives of the Arab population, who will funtion in an advisory capacity.

9.   All public Offices, Municipal and Government, must be kept intact and all documents and registers therein must be kept safely in good condition so that any claims of residents may be checked.

10.   The removal or transfer of any property within the area defined must be previously authorised by my representative.

11.   The ensure that these and any further instructions will be carried out, I shall nominate a representative who will help restore law and order in Jaffa.

12.   Public Health and other Public Utility Services of the Municipality of Tel-Aviv will endeavour to assist you until normal life is established in Jaffa.

Figure 11.

were found shot dead on May 25 in the al-Jabaliyya neighborhood. A 12-year-old girl was raped by Israeli soldiers on May 14 or 15 and numerous other attempted rapes occurred."[41]

Item 9 in a document of instructions also distributed by the Hagana to inhabitants of Jaffa on May 13, (Fig. 10), promises that "All public Offices, Municipal and Government, must be kept intact and all documents and registers therein must be kept safely in good condition so that any claim of residents may be checked." In fact, once they took Jaffa, they proceeded to loot and destroy.

Yafa, My Home
Nahida H. Gordon

I was born in Al-Quds (Jerusalem) to a Presbyterian (Church of Scotland) Palestinian family in 1939, the year that marked the end of the Great Palestinian Uprising (1936-1939) and the beginning of the Second World War. These two events served as bookends to the year of my birth and defined my life in ways I could not appreciate until much later.

When I was two years old, our family moved from Jerusalem to Jaffa, known to me in Arabic as 'Yafa'. Yafa's history, as well as most of Palestine's, has been one of occupation by invaders and empires. The most recent invaders were the British and the Irgun Zva'i Leumi and Hagana forces of the Yishuv (the Jewish community in Palestine).

Some of my most vivid memories are connected with our home, which I visit whenever I am in Palestine - my latest visit was in November 2015. For me, it is emotionally difficult and distressing to think of my lost home in Yafa. The distress comes not from the loss of bricks and mortar as some people think, but the loss of my Palestinian life and the loss of a sense of belonging in my own community. To Palestinians, connectedness within family, community, and land is vital and extends over generations.

We lived in the land of the Bible, and even in the 1940s, so much of our traditions and surroundings were connected to the time of Jesus. This made the Bible come alive as though the events told there happened only yesterday. Yafa is the city where Simon the tanner (Acts 9) lived. His home is thought to be close to the shore and was a short walking distance from our house. The church of St. Simon is built on what is believed to be the site where Simon the tanner's shop stood. The apostle Peter was staying with Simon when he had a vision, which he interpreted as God telling him to carry the message of Jesus Christ to the gentiles. It is a message of inclusiveness of people of differing ethnicities. In Acts 9:36-40, we read the story of Tabeetha, who was brought back from death by Peter. My school, the Tabeetha School for Girls (Fig. 12), was named after Tabeetha of Acts and was established in

1863 by the Church of Scotland. My school was a short two blocks from our home, and my memories of school, as of everything else in my life in Yafa, are a mixture of the happy and the sad. In November, 1947, not too long after the beginning of the school year, the United Nations General Assembly, with strong lobbying by the world Zionist groups and the support of the United States' Truman Administration, chose to recommend the partition of Palestine against the wish of the majority of its people. This was an egregious violation of my human rights and the human rights of all Palestinians, who were the majority population. In addition to being against international law, the partition plan privileged the Jewish minority population at the expense of the Christian and Muslim majority population. Yafa was to be part of the Palestinian state surrounded completely by the new Israeli state, thus making Yafa a target of acquisition by the Israeli State. As the battle for Yafa began, it had its effects on every part of our lives.

A few of my childhood memories will draw a picture of the atmosphere then - an atmosphere filled with the tension among the adults in our lives and among the visitors to our home. Our house was adjacent to the old city and near the waterfront, a few hundred yards from the Yafa lighthouse (Fig. 13) . Its sweeping light would shine through the door transoms from the veranda and I could watch it at night as I was falling asleep. It was a constant comfort. It made me feel safe from the chaos outside. In the spring of 1948, we fell asleep at night to the sound of bombs aimed at Yafa. In my childish imagination, the bombs sounded like large pipes being thrown around by giants. The memory is strong and vivid to this day. It was frightening and going to sleep was difficult. The lighthouse became a friend as I watched its hypnotic recurring sweep of light through the transom of my bedroom door, and this friend lulled me to sleep every night. To this day, a lighthouse elicits feelings of safety, warmth, and wellbeing.

Figure 12. Tabeetha School.

Figure 13. The Yafa lighthouse.

Snatches of sound and sights from this period persist vividly in my mind to this day. As a historical background to one of my most frightening memories is a description I read in Adam LeBor's City of Oranges.[42] "On January 4, 1948, a truck, piled high with oranges, was parked in an alley off Clock Tower Square, alongside the New Seray [the new municipal building], which housed Yafa's municipal offices, welfare workers and a kitchen for needy children." My father's office was in the Clock Tower Square. "Soon after the truck driver and his companion left, a thunderous explosion shook the city. Broken glass and shattered masonry blew out across Clock Tower Square. The New Seray collapsed in a pile of rubble. Windows shattered for yards around, and a thick choking cloud of dust billowed out. After a moment of silence, the screams and moans began. Twenty-six were killed, and hundreds injured. Most were civilians, including many children who had been eating at the charity kitchen."[43]

That day Mother was nervous. It was cold outside with a persistent drizzling rain with thunder mixed in with the sound of explosions. She was worried because Father was late arriving home. We heard a car drive up the street. She asked me to run out to the veranda to see if it was Father. He had come into the side gate and garaged his car. When I arrived at the veranda and looked over the parapet, I saw him walking below me. He had his over coat on with the collar turned up high. He had what looked like a dirty handkerchief around his forehead and his hair was smoky white. I ran in to tell Mother that it was indeed Father and that he was dirty and had pebbles in his hair. My next memory is looking into the bathroom. Father was standing over the washstand and Mother was trying to clean him up. His necktie and shirt were soaked in blood and he had grit and dirt all over his face and hair. The handkerchief was one lent to him by a fellow victim and was also soaked in blood. My father, the anchor and keeper of our lives, had just survived a Zionist terror bombing. Father was wounded, but he had remained behind to help move some of the wounded to the hospital. That evening as we sat by the fireplace, I told my father that I was cold. His reply to me was "you are not cold – you are frightened!"

During this time, the students in my class were thinning out. It came to a point when I remember that class consisted of three students and no teacher. We played school and took turns playing the role of teacher. Our favorite pastime was drawing the flag of Palestine. Soon after that, the bombing in our neighborhood increased. . One day, as my sister recalled, there was a fight outside our house between the Hagana and the defenders of Yafa. Father was not at home and Mother was terrified. She locked up all the windows and doors and we hunkered down. Later, my brothers collected empty bullet shells and the spent bullets that landed on the veranda from the previous night's fighting. As Israeli historian Ilan Pappe relates in his book, ethnic cleansing "operations were also Yigael Yadin's brainchild. They began on 13 February 1948 and focused on several areas. In Jaffa, houses were randomly selected and then dynamited with people still in them."[44] I remember these operations by the sound of the bombs and the blasts! Later, Yadin became acting chief of staff of the Israeli armed forces.

No wonder we were never allowed out on the street! I have no memories of the streets of Yafa because as a child growing up in Palestine, I did not have the experience of walking alone to school. We were always escorted by an adult or taken by car. It was not an uncommon occurrence for the soldiers of the Yishuv (the precursor of the Israeli leadership) to pepper our street with live fire. So carefree playing outside our home was not a possibility. My parents, however, provided us with opportunities to have carefree and wonderful times by spending our summers either in Ramallah or in resort areas in Lebanon. This allowed us to escape the heat of the coast and give us children the space and freedom to run outdoors in safety for the whole summer. When I visited our old neighborhood as an adult and was astounded to discover that school was a short two blocks away from home.

My parents throughout this time tried to make our lives as normal as possible. I have many happy memories of friends, school, and cousins. At least once a month, my parents took us to Jerusalem to visit with my maternal grandmother, her children and grandchildren. My grandmother would have the most wonderful meals with all of us arranged around a large table. We formed close ties with all the cousins, which lasted in spite of exile and in spite of thousands of miles of separation.

Our house had two large verandas overlooking the beautiful Mediterranean Sea. One was adjacent to my parents' bedroom and the second much larger veranda was our playground from which we could see and interact with the children living in the Old City. Interacting with other children was always a matter of setting a play date – to use the modern language of my grandchildren. Mothers and their children would come to visit. Mothers would visit with each other and we children would play together. We were never allowed out on the street and never went anywhere without an escort.

An event in April of 1948 lives very clearly in my memory. On the night of April 9, 1948, the Irgun Zva'i Leumi (Menachem Begin's terrorist group), surrounded the Palestinian village of Dayr Yassin, located on the outskirts of Jerusalem, and attacked the village of more than 600 people, killing and wounding men, women, and children. I remember clearly the terror I felt when hearing about it in the loudspeaker broadcasts in the streets. Vans of the newly arrived European colonists were traveling through our streets blasting the message: if you do not want the same thing to happen to you as what happened in Dayr Yassin then you should flee. I agonized as a child about what I would do if they were to come to my house to kill my family as they did in Dayr Yassin.

One day, I heard a noise out on the street. I ran to the balcony outside my brothers' bedroom, which faced the street. I saw a coffin cover carried vertically by a man who was walking down the street towards me. The cover had a cross down its entire length. Following the coffin cover was the coffin itself being carried by six pallbearers. The noise I heard was the shuffle of their feet on the pavement. As the coffin arrived just below me, I saw its occupant – a very young smooth-faced man. He was incredibly beautiful and peaceful. He was dressed in charcoal gray pants with pin stripes and a black jacket. He looked as though he was dressed for his wedding, which was never to be. Then I noticed a woman walking behind – she was my mother's friend, a frequent visitor to our house. She was dressed in black and had a veil down across her face. She was weeping inconsolably, and was supported on each side by two other women whom I did not recognize. The funeral cortège continued to move below me and then went into the yard of St. Simon Church, which was further down the street towards the waterfront. Later I found out that the man was the younger brother of my mother's friend and that the Zionist forces killed him.

Nothing seemed safe anymore. Days later during the night, the bombs fell across the street and hit St. Simon Church where the funeral of that young man was held. A few feet farther northeast and they would have hit our house! By now it was April, and my father, having had enough of violence, decided to take our family to safety away from Yafa. It was our custom to leave every summer to the mountains of Lebanon or to Ramallah to escape the summer heat of the seacoast. So my father decided that we would leave early for our summer stay and return at the end of the summer in time for school. Alas, we were not allowed to exercise our right to return!

On April 22, we hurriedly packed a few suitcases and drove out of Yafa. On the way, I remember seeing houses burning. My father and mother worried about whether the Jewish soldiers would let us leave. Again we did not realize that they would be more than glad to have us leave. All was left behind – our dog and our cat, all our family pictures and mementos of a life – all gone! As soon as we were safely settled in Lebanon, my Father returned to Yafa and remained for a few weeks, but then shortly after May 14, when Israel declared its statehood, he rejoined us in Lebanon.

And what would we have experienced had we stayed in Yafa? Going back to LeBor's City of Oranges, "By April 26, 1948, using the tons of shells that the Irgun had taken from the British munitions train, the battle for Yafa began in the early hours of Sunday 25 April. Irgun gunners directed a steady rain of mortar fire onto the city. In theory, the gunners were not supposed to target hospitals, religious sites, or consulates. In practice, the shells fell indiscriminately across Clock Tower Square, smashing into the markets and south into the heart of Ajami (near where our house is located), killing and wounding large numbers of civilians. Panic and hysteria swept through the city."[45] How could we have known that we would miss this tragedy by just three days?

My father was a prominent and prosperous businessman who imported appliances and automobile tires from the United States and automobiles from England. He had places of business in Jaffa and Haifa. Because the inhabitants of Yafa had few arms and equipment, my father contributed to the defense of Yafa by installing armor plates on trucks used in the city's defense. Going through my father's papers after his death, I discovered a three-page document (Figs. 9, 10, and

11 above) issued by the Hagana. The document is dated May 13, 1948, just two days before Israel declared itself a state and the United States recklessly recognized it within hours. Esber discusses this document in some detail.[46] In this document, signed by the Hagana and four leaders of the Yafa community, the Hagana admonishes the citizens of Yafa to obey all statements in the agreement and pledged to the Palestinians of Yafa that "IT IS UNDERSTOOD that the Hagana always does respect and will respect the Geneva Convention and all International Laws and Uses of war." This is just another deception in a long line of deceptions presented to the Palestinian people and to the International community, deceptions that continue to the present day, first by the Hagana and later by the Israeli government, about honoring the rights of the indigenous people of Palestine.

The fourth article of the instructions (Fig. 10) proclaims: "(a) All males in the area defined in the Agreement will concentrate in the area between Feisal Street, Al Muktar Street, Al Hulwa Street, and the Sea until everybody has identified himself under arrangements, the particulars of which will be notified later, and (b) During this, any male found outside this area will be severely punished, unless in a possession of a special permit." I had two teenage brothers at this time. We knew what this meant – had we stayed my father and brothers would probably, at best, be transported elsewhere leaving my mother, sister, and me alone and defenseless. In the eighth article, it assured residents of Yafa that if they left, they could return. Article nine claimed: "All public Offices, Municipal and Government, must be kept intact and all documents and registers therein must be kept safely in good condition so that any claim of residents may be checked." Articles eight and nine together reassured residents that leaving would be all right since a return was assured. In reality, shortly after Yafa fell, the Hagana destroyed documents in municipal and government offices as well as schools, wiping out history and possible future claims. Here is another deception from the Hagana and the new Israeli government. They never intended to let us return! School records from Tabeetha School where my sister and I were students were destroyed. The registrar of the Tabeetha School, who is a Palestinian, managed to save a few registers. When I visited her in Yafa in 2006, she showed me the register, where I could see my name.

One frequently hears that Palestinians wanted to drive the Israelis out to sea, when in fact in Yafa and Haifa, it was the Israelis who put many of its Palestinian inhabitants into small boats and pushed them out to sea, where many drowned. Further, as these frantic Palestinians went to the boats, Israeli snipers shot at them. I often wonder; had we stayed in Yafa after May 15, would we have been forced onto one of these boats? Another claim by the Israeli government is that the Arab leaders told the Palestinians to flee. Reality was quite the contrary. We were terrorized by the Israeli forces and fled for our lives.

On occasion I think about one of my childhood friends, Leticia, from Palestine. Her mother, I was told, was Jewish and her father was Christian. She would come with her mother; our mothers visited and we played. My musings are that here we were in Palestine, probably in 1944-46; Mother had a Jewish friend and I had a Jewish/Christian friend. And we were both Palestinian. Oh – what could have been and should have been!

I have visited our house several times since April 22, 1948. Our property consisted of my father's place of business below and our home above. We think the property was formerly a consulate building for a South American country. My father bought it and remodeled it to suit our family. The first time I went back to Yafa to visit our home, I found it had been made into a restaurant, and the lower floor of the property was made into a small shopping mall. They had removed the small verandas outside the doors of the two bedrooms facing the street. One had been my brothers' bedroom and the second was a guest bedroom. They also had covered the veranda next to my parents' bedroom and made it part of the restaurant. Wanting to see the back end of the property, my sister, husband, and I walked through an alley east of the house and then climbed a set of stairs leading to a second-story apartment in the Old City complex. When we reached the top of the steps, we were able to take photographs of the restaurant, which was vacant and abandoned at that time. We also encountered the occupant of the apartment whose steps we climbed. She was a young woman, sitting on her doorstep and smoking a cigarette. When asked whether she felt guilty about living in someone else's home; she replied: 'No. I have had a hard life and deserve this apartment. I was born on a kibbutz and life was hard there.' In other words, her past suffering entitled her to take other people's property. Why don't these settler colonists understand that it is not we Palestinians who caused their suffering? They are benefiting from their Government's theft of Palestinian property.

My second visit to the family home was in 2003, at which time the property was undergoing a major renovation. The façade was the same and this time they had replaced the missing two small verandas adjacent to the street-facing bedrooms. When my driver told one of the workmen that I used to live in the house, his reaction was "She better leave if she knows what is good for her." At a later visit in 2006, the house was further transformed with apartments below and some above. Our large playground veranda now contained apartments with views of the Mediterranean Sea. Surprisingly, the door leading to the steps to our house was still there. However, the two steps leading to the door were removed. These two steps contained a little treasure. My father said that when he remodeled the property, he built a chamber within the steps into which he placed several bottles of wine that he planned to serve the guests at my older brother's wedding. That wedding did not take place in Yafa but in exile. Someone else had the pleasure of drinking that wine!

On October 20, 2010, I had the opportunity to visit Yafa once more, and of course I included a side trip to view our old house (Fig. 14). My traveling companions were my husband, my older brother, the pastor of Westminster Presbyterian Church

Figure 14. Southwest view of the Halaby property in Yafa.

in Wooster, Ohio, and two friends from the church. The entire trip was a memorable experience. I had two encounters with Israelis that afternoon. They were as totally different as two encounters can be. The first was a man of about 40 who was coming out of a small shop on the first floor of the property and facing West. His shop was called The Israeli Experience, and as he was walking to his motorcycle, I asked him why he does not also talk about the "Palestinian Experience?" He became irritated and started talking rapidly, telling me that he knew nothing of these things. I told him softly that I had the deed to the property. The volume of his talk increased markedly and he started yelling at me, telling me that I was attacking him with unsubstantiated claims.

My second encounter that day was very different. Thanks to my brother, who pressed every one of the buzzers of the 15 apartments carved out of our family home, one of the occupants, an Israeli design artist, answered the buzzer and consented to invite us into the apartment she occupied. She generously welcomed us to her living room and gave us water to drink. I will preface my remarks by saying that she was a brave and thoughtful person. She allowed us into her home even though she knew who we were. We sat and reminisced about the house as though it was a common acquaintance, which it was! We told her about her apartment – that it used to be part of the veranda next to our parents' bedroom. I asked her if the lighthouse still operates, and sadly, she said: "No." I told her how I used to go to sleep watching its light move across the walls of the hallway leading out to the veranda. Sitting with the previous, dispossessed owners, she listened with respect, acknowledging my sorrow and loss. This colonist told us that she rents the apartment and thought that the Catholic Church, which had a large property on the high point of the old city overlooking our house, owned it. She now had in front of her the previous, and dispossessed, owners.

We then began talking about present-day politics in Israel. She told us that even though she owns a house in Jerusalem, she prefers to live in Yafa. She was concerned about the rising fascism in Israel. I asked her if she thought Lieberman could or would become Prime Minister. She shrugged her shoulders and said that she hoped that he would not. She was progressive in her thinking, and I found much with which to agree. In a different place and time, I think we could have been friends. With gentle questioning, she told us about her life and her parents' lives. They came to Palestine in the 1920s from Pinsk in Eastern Russia. The family wanted to escape discrimination and the pogroms. She ended her recounting of her family's experiences by saying that she just wants to live a normal life. This is yet another tragedy – I wondered how she can live a normal life when she is living in stolen property and a stolen country. I felt her suffering and was deeply touched. We both struggled with our emotions. I hugged her when we left and she returned the hug. We shared a bond of suffering inflicted by a senseless and unfeeling world.

I began this account by asking myself why it is so painful and distressing to visit my home in Yafa. I think the answer may be in seeing the present-day reality, I see the death of warm and wonderful childhood memories. It may be less painful to forget the present and just hold onto old memories. This is particularly so when I see what has been done to my grandmother's house in Jerusalem.

I always envied those Palestinians who were able to remain. During one of my visits to Yafa, I met with three of our friends from childhood days. During dinner, one of them asked me: "Nahida, who do you think is better off - you who left Yafa or me who stayed?" Her question was asked with a combination of bitterness and sadness. I then realized that even though she is still living in her childhood home, she also lost her community. Palestinians were torn apart and had to regroup in refugee camps or other Arab towns. She is living among Israelis who surround her in her original home, and she was just as separated from our Palestinian community as I was!

To continue my family's story, we emigrated from Lebanon to the United States in 1951. I arrived in the United States barely a teenager. It was in the United States that my sister and I received our high school and university educations and my brothers their university educations. I am now a grandmother, happily married to my husband of 55 years. We are immensely proud of and grateful for our three children and four grandchildren. I am a professor emerita of biostatistics at a prestigious American university. My husband's ancestors were earlier immigrants; they came from Scotland, England, and Germany to America, some decades before this country was founded, to escape political persecution.

I am active in my local Presbyterian Church, and in the denomination at the national level, on behalf of Palestinians. But, I sometimes wonder whether my Church here in the U.S.A. has room in it for Palestinians. When Presbyterians continue to affirm Israel's "right to exist," even though they qualify it by saying "within established borders," as a Palestinian, I feel hurt, rejection, and sadness.

Naturally, I hear those words differently than others. To me, these words mean that Israel had and has a right to dispossess me, my family, and other Palestinians, and to continue to kill, terrorize, and repress Palestinians to the present day!

In my experience, the Church, as well as much of Western Christianity, is complicit in not only the theft of my home but also the loss of a life lived within my Palestinian community. I was robbed of living as a Palestinian among other Palestinians near my extended family in my ancestral homeland. The Bible, the basis of my faith, has been used to dispossess me of the land where I was born and of the people to which I belonged.

But I acknowledge that I am still among the fortunate of the dispossessed, for I had the privilege of having a father with the means to protect his family and I have lived a productive life, albeit as an unintended immigrant in a land not of my birth. But what of the Palestinians who were not so fortunate, who lost their homes, land, villages, and communities, and who were killed or dispossessed as the Zionist colonists from Europe drove them from their land? What of those Palestinians who fled to live elsewhere, many in refugee camps in Palestine or adjacent countries? What of the dispossessed Palestinians who live in Gaza, many of whom came from Yafa and its surrounding villages and who now live and suffer with an unremitting Israeli blockade, who are demonized as terrorists, and who only wish to return to their land and homes? Now near the end of my life, I know that some losses can never be compensated – not for me or for all other Palestinians in exile for decades.

The year 1939, my birth year, marks a period in history of profound tragedy for humankind with the outbreak of World War II. Persecution, pogroms, and discrimination experienced by Europe's Jews for many centuries in Europe, as well as the killings during World War II, brought some of them to Palestine in search of a safe homeland. The leaders of these Europeans Jews proceeded to compound their tragedy by inflicting upon Palestinians a modern form of pogroms, persecution, discrimination, and killings.

But this has not always been the history of the Land of Palestine. For centuries Christians, Jews, and Muslims lived together peacefully in Palestine. This Palestinian and many others only wish for the two peoples to live together in this land which both call their own. It should be one land, where we all enjoy equal rights with equal access to political, legal, economic, cultural, religious, and educational rights. I echo the wish of the Israeli woman who is currently living in one of the apartments of my former home: a wish that we both can live a normal life united as human beings in the common suffering of our humanity.

Nahida Halaby Gordon, Ph.D., professor emerita of biostatistics, is active in seeking peace and justice for the people of Palestine. A life-long Presbyterian, she is an elder and serves in several committees of the General Assembly of the Presbyterian Church (U.S.A.).

Dear Teta: A Letter from My Granddaughter

Dear Teta,

When I was traveling with my fellow students from Berkeley to Palestine, I took the time to find and visit the house where your Teta [grandmother] lived. I am sending you a jar. Inside the jar are rocks, earth, and other things that I picked up when I went to visit your Teta's house in Jerusalem. The ground was torn up from construction, but I knew this earth was the earth your grandmother and your family lived on. It is your land, so I wanted you to keep a piece of it with you (Fig. 15). I love you!

Madison

Dear Madison,

I am moved beyond words knowing that you understand and care about my feelings for my lost homeland. I am getting old now and will probably never live long enough to see my dream of returning to my home in Palestine. The Nakba tore our lives up so that we lost not only our homes but we also lost something much more valuable – our communities and the freedom to live our lives as Palestinians in our own land. With passing time, it is now difficult to see how we can live our dreams of return, but we can hold onto wonderful memories of home and family. These rocks and this earth will help me remember.

Most of all, dear granddaughter, I treasure that you understand our loss and hold our memories of our old lives to be dear. I am proud of your intelligence and your sensitivity. I am confident that you will live a life dedicated to justice for those who are dispossessed. Keep Palestine and Palestinians close to your heart and pray as I do for a free Palestine.

Love,

Teta

Figure 15. Rocks and earth from Madison's great-grandmother's house located in lower Baka'a, Jerusalem.

Questions for Reflection

1. The Hagana, the precursor of the Israeli Defense forces, promised to abide by the Fourth Geneva accords. Based on what you know about the present occupation, do you think they have lived up to their promise?

2. Who was pushed out to sea as Jaffa fell to the Israeli forces? And is this contrary to what you have been led to believe?

3. Under the fourth Geneva Convention, refugees have the right under international law to return to their homes. Why has Israel created insurmountable obstacles for the refugees to return to their homes? Specifically, what do you see are the impediments Palestinians face in trying to return to their homes and communities?

4. As the older Palestinian generation is dying, do you see that the younger generation feels as strongly about the expulsion of their parents and grandparents from their homeland?

5. The Zionist founders of Israel often remarked: "Palestine was a land without a people for a people without a land." Further, they stated the people inhabiting the land at the time of the founding of Zionism were "Arabs from the desert." How would you respond to these assertions based on what you now know about Jaffa?

Al-Ramla District

The Al-Ramla district is south of the Jaffa district and west of the Jerusalem and Ramallah districts. In addition to the towns of Al-Lydd and Al-Ramla, 58 towns of the Al-Ramla district are documented as being totally destroyed and or depopulated.[47]

The expulsion of approximately 60,000 Palestinians from the towns of Al-Lydd and Al-Ramla in July 1948 is just one example of outright forced expulsions. Masalha writes:

"Ben-Gurion and three senior army officers were directly involved: Yigal Allon, Yitzhak Rabin, and Moshe Dayan. Shortly before the capture of the towns, Ben-Gurion met with his army chiefs. Allon, commander of the Palmach, the Hagana's elite military force, asked Ben-Gurion: 'What shall we do with the Arabs?' Ben-Gurion answered (or according to one version, gestured with his hand): 'Expel them.' This was immediately communicated to the army headquarters and the expulsion implemented."[48]

Benny Morris, one of the first Israeli historians to write about the Nakba, writes:

"At 13:30 hours on 12 July 1948 . . . Lieutenant-Colonel Yitzhak Rabin, Operation Dani head of operations, issued the following order: 'The inhabitants of Al-Lydd must be expelled quickly without attention to age . . . Implement Immediately.' A similar order was issued at the same time to the Kiryati Brigade concerning the inhabitants of the neighbouring town of Al-Ramla, occupied by Kiryati troops that morning. . . . On 12 and 13 July, the Yiftah and Kiryati brigades carried out their orders, expelling the 50-60,000 remaining inhabitants of Al-Lydd and Al-Ramla and refugees camped in and around the two. . . . About noon on 13 July . . . Al-Lydd's inhabitants were forced to walk eastwards to the Arab Legion lines; many of Al-Ramla's inhabitants were ferried in trucks or buses. Clogging the roads . . . the tens of thousands of refugees marched, gradually shedding their worldly goods along the way. It was a hot summer day. Arab chroniclers, such as Sheikh Muhammad Nimr al Khatib, claimed that hundreds of children died in the march, from dehydration and disease. One Israeli witness described the spoor: the refugee column 'to begin with [jettisoned] utensils and furniture and, in the end, bodies of men, women and children.'"[49]

"Ismail Shammout was born in al Lydd [Al-Lydd] in 1931 and was seventeen when on July 13, 1948, he was evicted from his home along with the majority of the population of Al Lydd. They were ordered at gunpoint to leave their homes, surrounded by armed Zionist soldiers and overseen by sharpshooters on roofs. They were herded into the town squares and thence forced eastwards into the wilderness. On the way, Zionist soldiers molested them and at gunpoint stole their valuables and confiscated the little provisions they had. The painful march took three to five days to complete. Many died. With his family, Ismail ended up in the refugee camp of Khan Younis, where he painted the suffering of women and children and the agonies

Figure 16. Ismail Shammout. *A Sip of Water*, 1953. Oil on board, 18 x 24 in, 45 x 60 cm.

of long lines for food and water."[50] The painting, *A Sip of Water* (Fig. 16) depicts Ismail Shammout's experience on the death march from Al Lydd. He is pictured as the boy giving his mother a sip of water. At first he found a can and some water to give to his mother, but an Israeli soldier shot it out of his hands. He tried again and the second time he succeeded, but found his little sister dead of thirst.[51]

Death March

Rev. Audeh Rantisi

I cannot forget three horror-filled days in July of 1948. The pain sears my memory, and I cannot rid myself of it no matter how hard I try.

First, Israeli soldiers forced thousands of Palestinians from their homes near the Mediterranean coast, even though some families had lived in the same houses for centuries. (My family had been in the town of Al-Lydd in Palestine at least 1,600 years). Then, without water, we stumbled into the hills and continued for three deadly days. The Jewish soldiers followed, occasionally shooting over our heads to scare us and keep us moving.

Terror filled my eleven-year-old mind as I wondered what would happen. I remembered overhearing my father and his friends express alarm about recent massacres by Jewish terrorists. Would they kill us, too?

We did not know what to do, except to follow orders and stumble blindly up the rocky hills. I walked hand in hand with my grandfather, who carried our only remaining possessions – a small tin of sugar and some milk for my aunt's two-year-old son, sick with typhoid.

The horror began when Zionist soldiers deceived us into leaving our homes, and then would not let us go back, driving us through a small gate just outside Al-Lydd. I remember the scene well: thousands of frightened people being herded like cattle through the narrow opening by armed soldiers firing overhead.

In front of me a cart wobbled toward the gate. Alongside, a lady struggled, carrying her baby, pressed by the crowd. Suddenly, in the jostling of the throngs, the child fell. The mother shrieked in agony as the cart's metal-rimmed wheel ran over her baby's neck. That infant's death was the most awful sight I had ever seen.

Outside the gate the soldiers stopped us and ordered everyone to throw all valuables onto a blanket. One young man and his wife of six weeks, friends of our family, stood near me. He refused to give up his money. Almost casually, the soldier pulled up his rifle and shot the man. He fell, bleeding and dying while his bride screamed and cried. I felt nauseated and sick, my whole body numbed by shock waves. That night I cried, too, as I tried to sleep alongside thousands on the ground. Would I ever see my home again? Would the soldiers kill my loved ones, too?

Early the next morning we heard more shots and sprang up. A bullet just missed me and killed a donkey nearby. Everybody started running as a stampede. I was terror-stricken when I lost sight of my family, and I frantically searched all day as the crowd moved along.

That second night, after the soldiers let us stop, I wandered among the masses of people, desperately searching and calling. Suddenly in the darkness I heard my father's voice. I shouted out to him. What joy was in me! I had thought I would never see him again. As he and my mother held me close, I knew I could face whatever was necessary.

The next day brought more dreadful experiences. Still branded on my memory is a small child beside the road, sucking the breast of its dead mother. Along the way I saw many stagger and fall. Others lay dead or dying in the scorching midsummer heat. Scores of pregnant women miscarried, and their babies died along the wayside.

The wife of my father's cousin became very thirsty. After a long while she said she could not continue. Soon she slumped down and was dead. Since we could not carry her we wrapped her in cloth, and after praying, just left her beside a tree. I don't know what happened to her body.

We eventually found a well, but had no way to get water. Some of the men tied a rope around my father's cousin and lowered him down, then pulled him out, and gave us water squeezed from his clothing. The few drops helped, but thirst still tormented me as I marched along in the shadeless, one-hundred-plus-degree heat.

We trudged nearly twenty miles up rocky hills, then down into deep valleys, then up again, gradually higher and higher. Finally we found a main road, where some Arabs met us. They took some of us in trucks to Ramallah, ten miles north of Jerusalem. I lived in a refugee tent camp for the next three-and-one-half years. We later learned that two Jewish families had taken over our family home in Al-Lydd.

Those wretched days and nights in mid-July of 1948 continue as a lifelong nightmare because Zionists took away our home of many centuries. For me and a million other Palestinian Arabs, tragedy had marred our lives forever. Throughout his life my father remembered and suffered. For thirty-one years before his death in 1979, he kept the large metal key to our house in Al-Lydd.

After more than four decades I still bear the emotional scars of the Zionist invasion. Yet, as an adult, I see what I did not fully understand then: that the Jews are also human beings, themselves driven by fear, victims of history's worst outrages, rabidly, sometimes almost mindlessly searching for security. Lamentably, they have victimized my people.

Four years after our flight from Al-Lydd I dedicated my life to the service of Jesus Christ. Like me and my fellow refugees, Jesus had lived in adverse circumstances, often with only a stone for a pillow. As with his fellow Jews two thousand years ago and the Palestinians today, an outside power controlled his homeland – my homeland. They tortured and killed him in Jerusalem, only ten miles from Ramallah and my new home. He was the victim of terrible indignities. Nevertheless, Jesus prayed on behalf of those who engineered his death, "Father, forgive them..." Can I do less?

Father Rantisi was born in Al-Lydd in 1937. He was 11 years old when he and his family were expelled from Al-Lydd and onto the death march that ended in Ramallah. From 1955 to 1958, he attended the Bible College of Wales. In 1963, with the help of First Presbyterian Church in Aurora, Illinois, he continued his studies. Following his stay in Illinois, Rev. Rantisi served as a mission worker for 18 months in the Sudan with the United Presbyterian Church. In 1965, he married Patricia Greening, the daughter of a British Anglican clergyman, and they settled in Ramallah. In the same year, Rev. Rantisi opened the Evangelical Home for Boys in Ramallah. In 1967, they experienced the horrors of the Naksa (setback) of the West Bank by the Israelis). In 1976, Rev. Rantisi was elected as Ramallah's deputy mayor.

The narrative provided here is from a book by Rev. Audeh G. Rantisi and Professor Ralph K. Beebe titled "Blessed are the Peacemakers: A Palestinian Christian in the Occupied West Bank."[52] Rev. Rantisi's autobiography is a life filled with hardships but is a triumphant testimony to the spirit of Palestinians and their will to flourish. Rev. Rantisi had a full life and died in 2001 at the age 64 years.

The Haunting Memory of Refugees from Al-Ramla and Al-Lydd

Samia Khouri

When the Palestinians left their homes in 1948, either out of fear for their lives or at gunpoint of the Jewish terrorists, we were living in Upper Baka'a in Jerusalem. But my brother and I were already at boarding school in Birzeit, and my sister was at the College in Beirut. So I did not experience the trauma of running for my life as others did. However Birzeit, the hometown of my father's family, and where my aunt Nabiha was running a boarding school, became the receiving end for many Palestinian families. My parents had arrived earlier than other members of the family while it was still easy to travel. My father had sensed the mounting tension, and because he was helping my aunt at the school, he did not want to be far away during those days.

Later on we were told by my aunts and uncles, who eventually found refuge in Birzeit, that after the Dayr Yasin massacre in April 1948 by the Jewish terrorist gangs, those same gangs started terrorizing Jerusalem's residents by circling around in trucks carrying some of the victims of Dayr Yasin so that the sight would scare them enough to flee. The gangs certainly succeeded in scaring everybody, which eventually led to the exodus of most of Jerusalem's people. My husband, whom I did not meet until the late fifties, had a similar story, as he was living in lower Baka'a in Jerusalem at the time.

But then with all the teen-age cousins around, we thought of that summer in Birzeit as a vacation. I remember uncle Labib, who had come from the YMCA of Jerusalem with his wife and a baby, calling that exodus a "Shatha," a picnic, because everybody carried the bare minimum of their belongings, thinking that in a short while they would go back. But that never happened. And eventually the family dispersed, each trying to get settled in a different part of the world. However, uncle Labib stayed in the country and eventually established the YMCA of East Jerusalem.

But what really kept haunting me, for years, was the memory of that July afternoon when the first stream of refugees from Al-Ramla and Al-Lydd started arriving into town. Old and young, babies being carried and little children dragged along that tedious walk. They had been forced by the Jewish terrorist gangs to leave at gunpoint and had been walking for miles. En route they lost dear ones, and as they were searched on their way out they were robbed of a lot of their money and jewelry. According to eyewitnesses, earlobes had to go with the earrings, fingers with the rings, and hands and even arms with their bracelets. Birzeit and Ramallah were the first two towns where most of those people found refuge. I can still remember how we went out to the street to invite them in for a meal after that horrific experience and their tedious journey on foot. Aunt Nabiha ordered the kitchen staff to bring out whatever food supplies were available in the storeroom to prepare a meal for those refugees. Some were in a complete daze; others were so relieved and grateful to find some food and water. I specifically remember one woman who went on and on talking incoherently. It seemed as if she had sunstroke and was delirious. The images of those people lying around in the school hall, in the churches, and under the olive trees are still vivid after sixty-five years. The Red Cross came to their rescue by putting up some tents under the olive trees, and they had a Swiss nurse who was staying at the school, so we used to help her in the evenings preparing bandages and cutting cotton and gauze, and would go out with her to the tents to check up on the families where some of the children were absolutely dehydrated.

From the early months of 1948 Birzeit became the headquarters of Al-Jihad el Muqaddas (hallowed struggle), led by Abdel Qader Husseini.[53] I remember how much we, the female students at the school, took pride in knitting sweaters for those young men to protect them from the cold evenings of Birzeit. So it was a day of mourning in Birzeit when Husseini was killed at the Qastal battle in April 1948, and for the 1948 class it was a special loss, as he was supposed to officiate at their graduation ceremony at the end of April.

Samia Khoury serves on the boards of Sabeel Ecumenical Liberation Theology Center in East Jerusalem and on the board of trustees of Birzeit University in Birzeit, Palestine. Samia writes about justice, truth, and peace for the Palestinian people, the relationships between people and the land, the context of Christian-Jewish-Muslim relationships in the Holy Land, concerns for children in conflict, and gender issues.

We Remained
Farah Munayyer

We stayed in our home the first day when the Israeli soldiers came into Al-Lydd. The next day I observed hundreds of Palestinians being expelled from their homes and told to walk to Jordan. I saw this through the shutters of our windows while we were still in the house.

The next day, some Israeli troops came by and wanted to search the house for arms. They found none, but they stole money from my uncle, who was living with us. The next day another group of soldiers came and gave us ten minutes to leave the house, and told us that they would shoot us if we did not leave. As we left the house, I noticed that the streets were littered with dead people, all civilians. Some of them were neighbors, some were relatives, and when I asked my father: "What are these people doing?" My father said, "They are sleeping." I was just seven years old, and he did not want to scare me.

It was late in the afternoon, so we stopped at the church in town to see if we could spend the night there and leave the next morning. Later we heard that many of the people who kept on walking towards Jordan died on the road. In church there were about 200 to 250 people from our hometown, both Christians and Muslims.

We stayed there for two nights. Eventually, the Israeli troops came by and dispersed those who had found refuge in the church to nearby homes that were vacant after the expulsion of their residents. We were given a room for all seven of us in my family. This is where we spent about a year – in one room. That included my grandmother, my uncle, my parents, my sister, and me.

The neighborhood where we were placed was referred to by the Israeli troops as the "ghetto." Living in a ghetto for a year wasn't easy. We were confined to that small location, and we had to manage, come what may. This ghetto was designed for those Palestinians who remained behind and was in the old part of Al-Lydd, next to the church and the mosque. The mosque was called the "Greater Mosque" because there was a smaller mosque in a different neighborhood. They gave us numbers, and every morning, the Israeli troops would call us into the main yard for a roll call and check on us to see what we were doing.

Some people wanted to know why Muslims took refuge in the church when the mosque was next door. We later learned that there was a massacre committed by the Israeli troops in the other mosque, known as Dahmash Mosque, where they machine-gunned scores of Palestinians in the mosque yard. As a child I saw, as did many others, the bloodstains that were on the ground of the mosque. This mosque was known as the little mosque, and it was closed for almost thirty-five years after the massacre.

We tried to go back to our home to pick up some pillows, blankets, and other necessities, but when we arrived at our house we found Israeli troops with their trucks in front of the house looting what they could. A year later our house was completely ravaged. After a year in the ghetto, my father got a job with the Red Cross and United Nations Relief and Work Agency (UNRWA) as a liaison officer for Al-Lydd, Jaffa, and Al-Ramla. He requested that the Red Cross give him an office and asked that we be returned to our home, where my father could have his office. The Red Cross intervened with the Israeli military governor in town, who eventually let us return to our home. The furniture, the library, the stockpiles of food, everything was gone. I was about 9 years old then, and I remember those days well.

When we moved back, the Israeli military governor was occupying a house about one hundred yards away from our house. His name was Matalon, and my father happened to know him from before the war. My father worked for the British Army in Sarafand, and Matalon had been a contractor who used to come to the British salvage depot to pick up merchandise. When my father went to visit with him in his office, he found Matalon was using our dining room table in that office. That was the only piece of the furniture that my parents ever located. Matalon, being a friend of my father, said, "Take the table back." We were the only family living in that neighborhood, except for one other family across the street. They were of Greek background, which is why they had been allowed to stay in their home. We knew them before we were forced out, so when we went back they were the only neighbors we had. The whole town was emptied of its population. Several weeks after our return, the first wave of Jewish immigrants started coming, and they were given the Palestinian homes that were sitting empty. It was uncomfortable for us to see these European immigrants occupy the homes of our Palestinian neighbors who lived there before the Nakba. And of course, these outsiders knew they were living in somebody else's home.

Within a few days, a new Israeli settler family from Bulgaria stopped by at our house. They occupied the house next door to us. Their son was about my age. We became friends – both the families and the children. We made other friends too, most of whom were from Bulgaria.

Growing up, I had only Israeli kids who arrived to Palestine from Europe as friends, and most of their talk at the time was about the Jewish holocaust and how they survived that horror. At first, I did not understand because it just didn't mean anything to me. As I grew older, as I learned about the Jewish holocaust, I remembered what the Israelis did to the Palestinians in my own hometown. I remembered with anguish the Israeli massacre at the Dahmash Mosque.

In 1956, I went to boarding school in Nazareth for five years. Traveling to school involved a trip to another town, which required permits and papers because I was Arab (which is how the Israelis like to refer to Palestinians). We were required to have a permit from the military government to move from one place to another. So, to go from Al-Lydd to Nazareth or to Tiberias, I needed a permit to travel in my own homeland. I remember well that my Israeli classmates would go to Tiberias, but I couldn't because I needed a permit. This also reminds me of my years at the Hebrew University; when my classmates were on a trip to the Syrian Golan Heights after it was occupied in 1967, I could not go because I was an Arab and I needed a permit to go. So from early on, the military rule that existed in Israel was specifically targeting Palestinians, who were called Israeli Arabs.

All Palestinian Arabs in what was called the state of Israel automatically became citizens of the state of Israel. We acquired passports and ID cards. Because we were Arabs, we were treated under different rules, and so every Arab who wanted to travel from one location to another needed a permit. All Arabs were assigned ID numbers beginning with "20" so it was always possible to distinguish between Arabs and other Israelis.

I will never give up my Israeli citizenship because I don't want to give the Israeli government the luxury of denying me the right to go back to my home. And this is my home, and it should be my choice whether I live there or not. I believe that my rights should not be at the discretion of someone who came from the Ukraine or Bulgaria or Romania.

When I go back "home," I usually go back for a family reunion. I go back to see my country. I enjoy very much going back to my parents' house and meeting the people that

I used to know when we were kids enjoying a watermelon sitting in front of the house. We still do that every time we return. It is my home.

I am a proud American and I am happy that America exists. It gives us the chance to enjoy democracy and freedom, which we lacked in Israel, being second-class citizens because we are not Jewish. As much as being a proud American, I also am a proud Palestinian living in diaspora.

Palestinians have a right to return to their homes and homeland; this is a right enshrined in the Declaration of Human Rights and is inalienable, meaning it cannot be taken away or given up by someone else on our behalf. In other words, we cannot give up our right of return in exchange for something. We, and our ancestors, have lived in Palestine for millennia. I believe all those who were forced out and became refugees must be repatriated and compensated. Others may come and live in Palestine, but they must abide by the laws of human rights. Specifically, I am talking about Jews that came from Europe. The Palestinians deserve to have their own country on their own land and not be forced out to somewhere in Africa or Asia.

I was born into a Christian Orthodox family, and I attended Catholic school for five years in Nazareth. My wife is a Muslim, and she was the driving force behind the move to go back to church, because she thought it best for the kids. Today, we are members of an Antiochian Orthodox Church.

The Israelis often repeated what became a mantra: "Palestine was a land without people for a people without a land." When the Jewish philosopher Martin Buber came to Palestine, he saw that Palestine was not without a people and called for a bi-national country. Alas, the Israeli leaders refused! Instead, it became clear that they wanted the land without its people. That is why they orchestrated the ethnic cleansing[54] of Palestinians from over 500 villages in 1947-48.

From my perspective, having lived through the birth of Israel and becoming part of the new nation, I believe that for the end of hostilities and for the sake of reconciliation between the Israelis and the Palestinians, the Israeli political leadership must have the courage to admit to their own people and to the world the crimes they committed against the indigenous Palestinian people. Such an admission, followed by apologies and restitution to the Palestinian people, is prerequisite to peace with justice and security for all.

I still yearn for the Palestinian people only what all other people also yearn: liberty, freedom, a flag, a national anthem, and self-determination for Palestinians in a country of their own.

Farah Munayyer is a pharmacist who lives in New Jersey with his wife Hanan Munayyer, who is the author of "Traditional Palestinian Costume: Origins and Evolution."

Questions for Reflection

1. Next to the massacre at Dayr Yasin, the death march from Al-Lydd has great and painful significance to Palestinians. If you were to put yourself in their place, what would you have done?

2. Was there any difference in the way the Israeli armed forces treated Palestinians according to their religious affiliation?

3. Farah Munayyer's family was able to remain in Al-Lydd. What was the reason they could stay?

4. Could the international community have done more to prevent the expulsion of the Palestinians from their ancestral lands?

Gaza District

The Gaza district is the southernmost coastal district of Palestine. Forty-five villages in the northern end of the district were depopulated and/or` destroyed by Israel during their 1947- 48 campaigns to expel Palestinians from their homeland. The village of Isdud (now Ashdod in Israel) had a population of 4,910 in 1945 and 763 building as of 1939.[55] Isdud was thought to be one of the five major towns of the Philistines dating back to the 17th century BC. The city came under Muslim rule in the seventh century CE and was inhabited predominantly by Muslims in 1948. There was fighting between the Egyptian and Israeli forces until October 1948, when the Egyptians withdrew south and most of the population of Isdud fled south towards Gaza. The other village of note is that of Najd, which had a population of 620 and 82 buildings in 1948.[56] The villagers fled towards Gaza. The advancing Jewish Palmach Negev Brigade forces depopulated the village on May 13, 1948. Two Israeli settlements were built on Najd land: Sderot and Or-ha-Ner.[57]

Rosemary Esber interviewed Abu Muhammad, a refugee from Najd who managed to flee to Jordan. The interview took place in the Hittin refugee camp in Jordan on August 11, 2001.[58] Abu Muhammad said that Najd was poorly armed. The village, along with Burayr and Simsim [two nearby depopulated villages], drew fire from Zionists who came from a nearby settlement. Abu Muhammad recalls how Najd's villagers were expelled on May 13, 1948:

> "[The Zionists] entered Najd with armored vehicles and they shot people. . . . They bombed Burayr badly. When we heard they entered Najd, we were frightened. We ran away from the village. They attacked Najd many times the same month, but we did not leave. But after what happened in Burayr [a massacre], all the people left Najd.

> "We walked from Najd to Dimra to Bayt Lahya [and] to many villages. We did not stay in any of them because of Jewish attacks. After days of walking, we arrived at Bayt Lahya because it was far away from war. People tried to sneak into Najd to bring some belongings and food – wheat and lentils. The people who were seen were killed or imprisoned by [the] Jews."[59]

What remained of the Gaza District the world now calls the Gaza Strip. Today, an estimated 1.8 million Palestinians, most of whom are refugees from districts as far north as Jaffa, live in the Strip. There are longstanding restrictions on the movement of people and goods to, from, and within the Gaza Strip, which undermine the living conditions of the people there. These restrictions were originally imposed in the early 1990's and continue in varying degrees until today.

In elections held on January 25, 2006, which were certified as fair by international observers including former U. S. President Jimmy Carter, Hamas won municipal seats throughout the West Bank and Gaza and 76 of 132 seats in the parliamentary election. With a majority of seats in the Palestinian parliament, Hamas could then form the government for the Palestinian Authority. Israel and its supporters, the United States and European Union, refused to recognize the new Hamas prime minister and instituted an economic blockade of the Gaza Strip and the West Bank in an effort to unseat the Hamas government. When the economic blockade failed, Israel, with the United States' cooperation, provided Fatah forces in Gaza with arms to battle Hamas. Violence erupted, with the end result that in 2007 Hamas controlled the Gaza Strip. According to the July, 2013, report of the United Nations Office for the Coordination of Humanitarian Affairs for occupied Palestinian territory (OCHA-opt), the blockade of the Gaza strip reduced access to livelihoods, essential services, and housing; disrupted family life; and undermined the people's hopes for a secure and prosperous future.[60]

OCHA-opt further states:

"The long-term restrictions have worsened preexisting gaps in key services such as health, education, electricity, water and sanitation. The situation has been compounded by rapid population growth and damage to infrastructure during recurrent hostilities. International organizations working to address these gaps continue to face impediments stemming from the restrictions on the import of construction materials and the related approval system.

" The restrictions on movement of people and goods between the Gaza Strip and the West Bank are part of a 'policy of separation' adopted by the Israeli authorities. As a result, people in Gaza are denied access to West Bank universities; cannot market their products or seek work in the West Bank; and cannot maintain normal family or cultural ties with Palestinians in the West Bank."

These conditions reported by OCHA-opt have only worsened after the 2008-2009 and the 2014 attacks against Gaza. During the latest bombardment and invasion of Gaza by Israel (July 7 to August 26, 2014), OCHA-opt published weekly Gaza crisis reports. Reporting the numbers of casualties can only begin to describe the pain and suffering endured by the victims of the blockade and siege of Gaza and their families. Deaths in Gaza documented by B'Tselem[61] from September 29, 2000, to March 31, 2015, are 7,057 Palestinians killed by Israeli military and 216 Israelis by Palestinians.

During the July 7, 2014, to August 26, 2014, bombardment and invasion of Gaza by Israel, a total of 2,168 persons were killed, of whom 297 were women and 521 were children.[62] The estimated number of wounded was 11,100, of whom 2,088 were women, 3,374 were children and 410 were elderly.[63] The United Nations estimates that 373,000 children require direct and specialized psychological support and that a thousand will suffer lifelong physical disabilities. During this same period, Palestinians killed 71 Israelis. Of these 71 casualties, 66 were soldiers.

The number of totally or partially destroyed housing units, schools, businesses, fishing industries, religious institutions including churches, hospitals, as well as the destruction of infrastructure such as the electrical grid and its resultant effects on municipal water supplies, conveys a picture of the horror visited upon the citizens of Gaza during the latest onslaught of the Israeli bombardment and invasion. According to the UN Conference on Trade and Development (UNCTAD), Gaza's economy was in a "state of total collapse" even prior to Israel's latest attack, warning on September 3, 2014, of "grave consequences" if Israel's siege and blockade are not lifted.[64]

This latest bombardment and invasion by Israel is the third in the last six years; the Israelis termed the first the Cast Lead invasion. However, one must not think that the killings and destruction occur only during such horrific invasions. According to B'Tselem,[65] Israelis killed a total of 4,859 Palestinians from September 29, 2000, to December 26, 2008, just prior to the Cast Lead invasion. Of these 4,859 deaths, 2,998 were in Gaza, 1,792 were in the West Bank, and 69 in Israel. During this same period, 492 Israelis were killed.

Dying Again: Memories of Freedom in Gaza
Ramzy Baroud

When you have no frame of reference for the concept of freedom, perhaps its absence is not so painful. My mother and father's generation lived in their own homes, on their own land. Their life was very simple, but it was still a life of dignity. I often ponder how the last six decades in refugee camps have been much more painful for the elderly than they have been for the young, who cannot fathom what it must be like to live outside the walls and barbed wire barricades of our open-air prison called Gaza.

Living under Israeli occupation means you live a life of uncertainty; you don't know when you wake up each morning if there will be electricity or if the Israelis have shut it off as a form of collective punishment. You don't know if the schools will be open or if the Israelis closed them all for a day, a month, or a year – as a form of collective punishment. You don't know if you can walk to the corner shop to buy food for your family, or if all the shops have been closed for a day, a week, or a month – as a form of collective punishment. You don't know if the Israelis will permit you to go across town to visit friends or family, or if they have imposed a curfew for a day, a week, a month, or more – as a form of collective punishment. You don't know if they will permit you to go to the hospital when you are ill. If you cannot be treated and you die, it is uncertain whether they will allow for your burial because the graveyards are closed – as a form of collective punishment. It is difficult to plan for the future because you don't know if they will permit you to live to see the future.

As children, my father shared with my siblings and me endless stories of life in his village of Beit Daras before the Israelis came and everything changed. I feel that it was his attempt to explain what life was like in the real world, how it should have been for all of us. As a young man, I had always aspired to be like my dad, to take a stand for my people and their freedom, and that day arrived when I was a young man. It was 1987, and the first Intifada (Palestinian Uprising) had broken out. It seems that the Palestinians had grown weary of sharing nostalgic stories of the days of freedom with their children, and that their children wanted a "hands-on experience" with freedom themselves.

Our decision came at a heavy price, and many people died. On this particular morning, Israeli soldiers killed a young man from my school. Our school was closed to mourn the falling of our classmate, but everyone arrived anyway, determined to hold our occupiers to account. Our numbers grew as the jeeps and tanks arrived. I was terrified as I picked up a stone, but stood still. Others ran away, but some ran towards the soldiers, with their rocks and flags. The soldiers drew nearer. They looked frightening and foreign. But when the kids ran in the direction of the soldiers and rocks began flying everywhere, I was no longer anxious. I belonged there. I ran into the inferno with my schoolbag in one hand and a stone in the other. "Allahu Akbar!" I cried, which means "God is Great," and I threw my stone. I hit no target, for the rock fell just a short distance ahead of me, but I felt liberated, no longer a negligible refugee standing in a long line before an United Nations Relief and Works Agency (UNRWA) feeding center for a bag of rice or powdered milk.

Engulfed by my own rebellious feelings, I picked up another stone, and a third. I moved forward, even as bullets flew, even as my friends began falling all around me. I could finally articulate who I was, and for the first time on my own terms. My name was Ramzy, and I was the son of Mohammed, a freedom fighter from Nuseirat refugee camp, who was driven out of his village of Beit Daras, and the grandson of a peasant who died with a broken heart and was buried beside the grave of my brother, a little boy who died because there was no medicine in the refugee camp's UN clinic. My mother was Zarefah, a refugee who couldn't spell her name, whose illiteracy was compensated by a heart overflowing with love for her children and her people, a woman who had the patience of a prophet. I was a free boy; in fact, I was a free man.

But the morning came when my father's ingenuity could no longer protect his family. A large boot pressing against my face awakened me. A swarm of soldiers were standing over me. My mother came running from the kitchen, to find an Israeli army unit handcuffing her children and dragging them out into the street. The event was customary. Soldiers often stormed into people's homes and broke the arms and legs of men and boys so as to send a stern message to the rest of the neighborhood that they would receive the same fate if they continued with their Intifada. Israeli Defense Minister Yitzhak Rabin called this mistreatment his "Break their Bones" policy.

Unable to speak a single sentence in Hebrew, my mother let out a howl, and cried out to one of them in Arabic, "I beg you soldier. My sons were sleeping. They have done nothing wrong. I kiss your hand; don't break their arms. I beg you, may Allah return you safe and sound to your family. How would your mother feel if someone came to break her children's arms? Oh Allah, come to my rescue. My children are the only things I have in this life. Oh Allah, I was raised poor and orphaned, and I don't deserve this."

At first, the soldiers paid no heed to my mothers' pleas and merely responded with "shut up and go inside," but her crying alerted the women in the neighborhood, who served as a first line of defense under such circumstances. Neighborhood women gathered outside their homes, screaming and shouting, as soldiers lined us against the wall and brought in their clubs. The custom was for the soldier to ask a person singled out for a beating, "Which hand do you write with?" before the club would break it, followed by the other arm, and then the legs. When the soldier asked one of my brothers the same ominous question, my mother's pleas turned into unintelligible cries as she dropped to the floor and held onto one of the soldier's legs with a death grip. The soldier tried to free himself, as two others came to his rescue, pounding the frail woman over and over again in the chest with the butts of their machine guns, and as my father forced his body between the angry solider and the desperate mother.

Made more courageous by the violent scene, especially as my mother seemed to be drowning in the gush of blood flowing from her mouth, neighborhood women drew closer, throwing rocks and sand at the soldiers. What was meant as an orderly beating of several boys turned into a chaotic scene where women braved guns and tear gas and verbal abuse by Israeli soldiers, who eventually retreated into their military vehicles and out of the area.

Thanks to my mother, our bones were left intact that day, but at a price. She was left bruised and bleeding. Her chest was battered and several ribs were broken. She was rushed to a local hospital and was incapacitated for days. Her health deteriorated, to the bewilderment of Ahli hospital doctors who hoped for an eventual recovery. Days later, doctors discovered that my mother had multiple myeloma. Apparently she had been sick for some time, but her illness was exacerbated by the violent encounter, which made her prognosis bleak.

Nuseirat was under a curfew, which meant that if you braved going outdoors, you risked being arrested or shot by occupation forces. The Israeli army agreed to allow her burial on the condition that only the immediate family was to be present under the monitoring of Israeli soldiers. We arrived at the graveyard, carrying the coffin, and were soon joined by grandmother, Mariam, who came running into the graveyard calling out her daughter's name. We began digging, but neighbors peeking through their windows quickly concluded that Zarefah had died and was being buried. My mother was a beloved neighbor. She was particularly adored among the older women of the camp, whom she treated with untold kindness. "Allahu Akbar," resonated a voice coming from one of the refugee homes. "Um Anwar has died," cried another. Within minutes, shouts of "God is Great" echoed throughout the camp. It is a call to prayer and also a call to action. People appeared from everywhere, carrying Palestinian flags; women, children, old men and women, and youth, all descending onto the graveyard. Refugees were outraged that the poor woman was to be buried based on military instructions and that she was followed, even to her grave, under the watchful eyes of the occupiers, their guns, tanks, and a hovering army helicopter. Youth began throwing stones, and soldiers responded with bullets and teargas. But the people were not to disperse easily this time. Thousands of them ensured that Zarefah would depart the earth and enter Paradise in the company of friends, treated as a martyr should be treated. As an ambulance hauled some of the wounded to the local clinic, Zarefah was lowered into the ground amidst chants and Quranic verses, recited en mass. Shouts of "Allahu Akbar" were intermingled with the whimpers and prayers of the crowd, with the sound of bombs, the teargas, and the hovering helicopter. Zarefah's burial represented everything pure about the Intifada - the unity of purpose, the courage, the sheer rage and resentment of the occupation, the sense of community, the resolve and the determination of the refugees. Zarefah, my mother, was 42 years old when she died.

Our subjugation continued. My neighbors still spent much of their days queuing up in charity lines where my mother once stood, lines for flour, rice, milk, or maybe used clothes from some European country. They must have pondered many things as they waited for so many hours in those lines. Perhaps they thought it strange that the same insignia from the United States imprinted on the two-liter can of cooking oil, or the 25-kilo bag of flour that was rationed to each family each month, was the same insignia on the random teargas grenade canisters littering the streets of Gaza. I often pondered the afterlife, and hoped that my mother could sense the gratitude I felt in retrospect for the boredom and embarrassment she endured for so many years in those charity lines in her children's stead.

But I did have one hopeful window to the outside world during those years after the death of my mother. The United Nations had started a pen-pal program with our school and a school in Stockholm. I was assigned to write to a young girl named Emily Svenson. When I received my first letter from her, it included a photograph of her and her family near a wooded lake in Sweden. More than taken by Emily's beauty, I became enamored with her surroundings. True, she had lovely fair hair and bright blue eyes, but more lovely was the place where they stood together smiling in the sunshine. There were no tanks, no checkpoints, no soldiers, no bullets – just trees and birds and smiles on everyone's faces. It was hard for me to imagine such a place of beauty and safety. Emily and I wrote to each other for years, and although our contradictory experiences were a source of sadness for each of us, it was an ever-renewing reminder of how God intended for us to live - in freedom.

The years passed, and I was strangely granted the opportunity to travel to the U.S. to study. I settled there and raised a family, and for past 20 years, it has been my home. I must say that I have had the most conflicting relationship with the United States; on one hand I am so grateful to finally get a taste of the freedoms that my people have always been denied. On the other, I realize that without the profuse financial and military aid provided to Israel by the United States, the Israelis couldn't possibly keep my people caged for all these generations. I have tried to return to Gaza to see my family, but the Israelis denied all attempts. And so, when my father fell ill, the only comfort I could provide was over the telephone.

He was incapacitated for a few weeks. There wasn't a hospital bed to be found in Gaza, for his illness coincided with a brutal Israeli military adventure in Gaza, and all hospitals were converted to function as massive emergency wards. His friends and family in Gaza took care of him and desperately tried to persuade the Israelis to grant him a permit to enter the West Bank for treatment, or at least to die in the company of his sons. Alas, it was determined that it was too great a risk for the security and the wellbeing of the state of Israel; he was sentenced to die at home with no treatment.

The night my father died, I had a dream. There we both were, sitting face to face, in the middle of one of our family's fields in Beit Daras. We were sitting in the glory of what once was ours. I was a young man; my father was wrinkled and withered. His battle scars were clear; his breathing labored. He looked to me and said, "I'm going to die again tonight."

A dream so vivid: it was springtime, a warm and peaceful afternoon. The trees were in bloom, the wind carried the perfume of the almond, lemon, and orange blossoms. Farmers were busy in their fields, children lying flat on their backs, basking in the afternoon sun, without shoes, without a care in the world. I felt a sense of belonging that I have never felt in my life, and I remember thinking to myself: "So this is what it feels like to be home." It was as if the dream was meant to give me just a short glimpse of the beauty and purity of those lovely years before the Israelis came. Until that moment, I don't think I was ever able to fully comprehend the overflowing love my father had for his homeland, for his freedom, and with that came an understanding of the incomprehensible sense of loss with the Nakba, our catastrophe. The sun poured its light on us. Then I shifted my attention from my father's tired eyes to the menacing band of soldiers on the horizon, from whence our nightmare started.

And once more, he caught my gaze and said, "I'm going to die again tonight."

Ramzy Baroud (www.ramzybaroud.net) is an internationally syndicated columnist and the editor of PalestineChronicle.com. His latest book is "My Father Was a Freedom Fighter: Gaza's Untold Story" (Pluto Press, London).

No Exit in Gaza: Broken Homes and Broken Lives[66]

Jen Marlowe[67]

Rubble. That's been the one constant for the Awajah family for as long as I've known them.

Four months ago (in the fall of 2014), their home was demolished by the Israeli military – and it wasn't the first time that Kamal, Wafaa, and their children had been through this. For the last six years, the family has found itself trapped in a cycle of destruction and reconstruction; their home either a tangle of shattered concrete and twisted rebar or about to become one.

I first met the Awajah family in August 2009, in the tent where they were living. I filmed them as they told me what had happened to them eight months earlier during the military invasion that Israel called Operation Cast Lead and said was a response to rocket fire from the Gaza Strip.

I had no intention of making a film when I went to Gaza, but after hearing the family's story, I knew I had to. I returned again in 2012 and have continued to stay in touch in the years since, realizing that the plight of the Awajahs opened a window onto what an entire society was facing, onto what it's like to live with an interminable war and constant fear. The Awajahs' story shines a spotlight on what Palestinians in Gaza have endured for years on end.

What stuck with me most, however, was the demand of the Awajah children regarding the reconstruction of their new home in 2012: they insisted that the house have two doors.

What The Awajahs Saw[68]

In separate interviews in 2009, Wafaa and Kamal Awajah told me the same story, each breaking down in tears as they offered me their memories of the traumatic events that had taken place eight months earlier – a night when they lost far more than a home. The next day, a still grief-stricken Wafaa walked me through her recollections of that night, pointing out the spot where each incident had taken place.

On January 4th, as Operation Cast Lead's ground campaign began, the Awajah family was at home. Wafaa's eldest daughter, 12-year-old Omsiyat, woke her up at around 2 a.m. "Mom," said Omsiyat, "soldiers are at the door." Wafaa jumped out of bed to look. "There are no soldiers at the door, honey," she reassured her daughter. When Omsiyat insisted, Wafaa looked again, and this time she spotted the soldiers and tanks. She lit candles in the window so that the Israeli troops would know that a family was inside.

Suddenly, the ceiling began to crumble. Wafaa, Kamal, and their six children fled, as an Israeli military bulldozer razed their home. No sooner had they made it outside than the roof collapsed. As tank after tank rolled by, the family huddled under an olive tree next to the house. Finally, when dawn broke, they could examine the ruins of their house.

Just as the Awajahs were trying to absorb their loss, Wafaa heard nine-year-old Ibrahim scream. He had been shot in the side. As more gunfire rang out, Kamal scooped up the injured boy and ran for cover with the rest of the family. Wafaa was hit in both hips, but she and five of the children managed to take shelter behind a mud-brick wall. From there, she saw Kamal, also wounded, lying in the middle of the road, Ibrahim still in his arms.

Israeli soldiers approached her husband and son on foot, while Wafaa watched, and – according to what she and Kamal both told me – without warning, one of them shot Ibrahim at close range, killing him. He may have assumed that Kamal was already dead. Despite Wafaa and Kamal's wounds, the family managed to get back to their wrecked home, where they hid under the collapsed roof for four days with no food or clean water, until a passing family with a donkey cart took them and Ibrahim's body to a hospital in Gaza city.

As far as I know, the Israeli military never investigated the incident. In fact, only a handful of possible war crimes during Operation Cast Lead were ever investigated by Israel. Instead of an official inquiry, the Awajahs were left with a dead son, grievous physical wounds that eventually healed, psychological ones that never will, and a home reduced to a pile of rubble.

Life Goes On

When I met them eight months later, the Awajahs were struggling to rebuild their lives. "What's hardest is how to offer safety and security for my children," Kamal told me. "Their behaviors are not the same as before."

Wafaa pointed to three-year-old Diyaa. "This boy is traumatized since the war," she said. "He sleeps with a loaf of bread in his arms. If you try to take it from him, he wakes up, hugs it, and says, 'It's mine.'"

"What you can't remove or change is the fear in the children's eyes," Kamal continued. "If Diyaa sees a bulldozer, he thinks it's coming to destroy a house. If he sees a soldier, whether an Israeli or Arab soldier, he thinks the soldier wants to kill him. I try to keep them away from violence, but what he experienced forces him to release his fear with violence. When he kisses you, you can feel violence in his kiss. He kisses you and then pushes you away. He might punch or slap you. I am against violence and war in any form. I support peaceful ways. That's how I live and raise my children. Of course, I try to keep my children from violence and help them forget what happened to them, but I can't erase it from their memory. The memories of fear are engraved in their blood."

I thought about Kamal's words as I filmed Diyaa and his five-year-old sister Hala scrambling onto the rubble of their destroyed home – their only playground – squealing with glee as they rolled bullet casings and shrapnel down the collapsed roof.

What moved me deeply was the determination of Kamal and Wafaa to create a future for their surviving children. "Yes, my home was destroyed, my life was destroyed, but this didn't destroy what's inside me," Kamal said. "It didn't kill me as Kamal. It didn't kill us as a family. We're living. After all, we must continue living. It's not the life we wanted, or had, but I try to provide for my children what I can."

The Fragility of Hope

In 2012, I returned to Gaza and to the tent in which the Awajah family was still living. It was evident that the trauma of their experience in 2009 – along with the daily deprivation and lack of security and freedom that characterize Gaza under siege – had taken a toll. "I had thought that those were the most difficult days of my life," Kamal said, "but I discovered afterwards that the days which followed were even more difficult."

In 2009, Kamal told me that the war hadn't fundamentally changed him. Now, he simply said, "I lost myself. The Kamal before the war does not exist today." He spoke of the screams of his children, waking regularly from nightmares. "The war is still chasing them in their dreams."

Most painful for Kamal was his inability to help his children heal. His despair and feelings of helplessness had grown to the point where he had become paralyzed with severe depression. "I tried and I still try to get us out of the situation we are in – the social situation, the educational situation for the children, and the mental situation for me and my family." But their situation, he added, kept getting worse.

My 2012 visit, however, came during a rare moment of hope. After nearly four years, the Awajah family was finally rebuilding their home. Trucks were delivering bags of cement; gravel-filled wheelbarrows were being pushed onto skids; wooden planks were being hammered down. In 2009, I had filmed Diyaa and Hala playing on the rubble of their destroyed house. In 2012, I filmed them climbing and jumping on the foundation of their new home.

"I am building a house. It is my right in life for my children to have a house," Kamal said. "I call it my dream house, because I dream that my children will go back to being themselves. It will be the first step to shelter me and my children, away from the sun, the heat, and the tents - our homelessness. The biggest hope and the biggest happiness I have is when I see my children smiling and comfortable...when they sleep without nightmares." Kamal added, "I can't sleep because of my fear over them."

For Wafaa, while the new home represented hope for their future, its construction also triggered flashbacks to that night of the bulldozer. As she told me, "Bulldozers and trucks bringing construction material came at night, and, at that moment, it was war again. When I saw the bulldozers and the trucks approaching with big lights, my heart fell between my feet. I was truly scared."

Planning for the new house also provided Wafaa and Kamal with a poignant reminder of the fragility of hope in Gaza. "The children say to make two doors to the house," Wafaa told me. "One [regular] door and the other door so when the Israelis demolish the house, we can use it to escape. We try to comfort them and tell them nothing like this will happen, but no, they insist on us making two doors. 'Two doors, Daddy, one here and one there, so that we can run away.'"

The Gaza War of 2014

After my 2012 visit, I periodically contacted the Awajah family. Construction was proceeding in fits and starts, Kamal told me, due to shortages of materials in Gaza and their lack of financial resources. Finally, however, in the middle of 2013 the home was completed and as the final step, glass for the windows was installed in February 2014.

Five months later, in July, the most recent Israeli assault on Gaza began. I called the Awajah family right away. "The children are frightened but okay," Wafaa told me.

The Israeli army had warned their neighborhood to evacuate, and they were now renting a small apartment in Gaza City. During a humanitarian ceasefire, Kamal was able to return to their house: it had been demolished along with the entire neighborhood (Fig. 17).

When I spoke to the Awajah family at the end of September, Kamal told me that rent money had run out. Seeking shelter at a United Nations Relief and Works Agency (UNRWA) school wasn't a viable option, he said, because there were already so many families packed into each room. The Awajahs were back in a tent next to the rubble of their twice-destroyed home.

Wafaa told me that she was cooking on an open fire, using scrap wood scavenged from the remnants of her house. For the first week, the children returned home from school every day and, surrounded by nothing but rubble, began to cry. Seventeen-year-old Omsiyat briefly took the phone. Her typically warm and open voice was completely flat, no affect whatsoever. Worse yet, Kamal still owes $3,700 for the construction of their previous house. Though the home no longer exists, the debt does. "We are drowning," Wafaa said.

The Awajah Family Today[69]: Drowning in Gaza

The Awajahs aren't the only ones in Gaza who are drowning. The true horror of their repeated trauma lies in the extent to which it is widespread and shared. Nine-year-old Ibrahim Awajah was one of 872 children in Gaza killed in the 2009, 2012, and

2014 wars combined, according to statistics gathered by the United Nations Office for the Coordination of Humanitarian Affairs and B'tselem, an Israeli human rights organization. (There was also one Israeli child killed by mortar fire in that period.)

The flat affect in Omsiyat's voice reflects the assessment of the United Nations Children's Fund that nearly half of the children in Gaza are in urgent need of psychological help. And Kamal's desire not to move into a communal shelter is understandable, given that 53,869 displaced people still remain crowded into 18 UNWRA schools. According to Shelter Cluster, an interagency committee that supports shelter needs for people affected by conflict and natural disaster, the Awajah family's house is one of 18,080 homes in Gaza that were completely demolished or severely damaged in the 2014 war alone. A further 5,800 houses suffered significant damage, with 38,000 more sustaining some damage.

Shelter Cluster estimates that it will take 20 years for Gaza to be rebuilt – assuming that it does not face yet another devastating military operation. As the last six years indicate, however, unless there is meaningful political progress (namely, the ending of the Israeli siege and ongoing occupation), further hostilities are inevitable. It is not enough that people in Gaza be able to rebuild their houses yet again. They need the opportunity to rebuild their lives with dignity. Kamal Awajah said as much. "I don't ask anyone to build me a home for the sake of charity. That's not the kind of help we want. We need the kind of help that raises our value as human beings. But how? That's the question."

There seem to be no serious efforts on the horizon to address Kamal's question, which has at its core an insistence on recognizing the equal value of Palestinian humanity. As long as that question remains unanswered and the fundamental rights of Palestinians continue to be denied, the devastating impact of repeated war will continue for every family in Gaza, and the terrifying threat of the next war will always loom. The Awajah children have every reason to insist that their future home be constructed with two doors.

Figure 17. Kamal and his children are sitting on the rubble of their twice destroyed home. Photo courtesy of Jen Marlowe.

Questions for Reflection

1. The blockade of the Gaza Strip is maintained primarily by Israel with the cooperation of Egypt. Do you see that this blockade would be maintained if the U. S. Government, that provides over 3 billion dollars of aid to Israel and to a lesser extent to Egypt, decided that it should stop?

2. According to Alison Weir of If Americans Knew,[70] "studies show that US news is extremely Israeli-centric. The main news bureaus for CNN, AP, New York Times, etc are located in Israel and are often staffed by Israelis. The son of the NY Times bureau chief is in the Israeli army; 'pundit' Jeffrey Goldberg served in the Israeli military; Wolf Blitzer worked for the Israel lobby, and numerous other journalists in the region have personal family ties to the Israeli military." Discuss how you think this affects the information available to the general American public. What should be done to address this problem?

3. In an the interim agreement signed by Israel and the Palestine Liberation Organization, Israel agreed to allow fishing boats from Gaza to fish up to some twenty nautical miles out to sea; however fishermen are not allowed to go farther than three nautical miles from shore and are frequently shot at by Israeli naval boats. Fishing provides a livelihood to many families and is an important source of food for residents of the Gaza strip. How does this draconian policy by Israel serve its security?

4. Considering the living conditions in the Gaza Strip due to the Israel blockade and siege, do you see how Palestinians may be justified in their belief that Israel is doing everything it can to make their life miserable so that they would leave or perish?

Ramallah District

Ramallah is in central Palestine, in what is now called the West Bank. Ramallah did not experience the 1948 *Nakba* directly, in that it was not conquered and occupied by Israel; however, Ramallah District experienced the effects of the Nakba. The population of Ramallah and the rest of the West Bank experienced the influx of huge numbers of refugees who were expelled from those areas of Palestine conquered and occupied by Israel. And later, during the 1967 *Naksa* (setback), Israel attacked and took the West Bank from Jordan; therefore the West Bank, including Ramallah, is now living under the repressive regime and practices of the Israeli military occupation.

Palestinians have been engaged in non-violent resistance against their occupiers for at least a hundred years, first against the British and then against the Israelis. One basic technique is *sumud*. Palestinians feel that if they persevere through life's hardships they will inherit the land. In Mathew 5:5, we are told, "Blessed are the meek, for they will inherit the earth." Some Palestinians, when asked what they think of all of the land confiscation and building by Israel, simply say, "Let them. They will eventually leave, and we will still be here." There is a sign (Fig. 18) painted on the huge cement wall (separation barrier) inside Bethlehem that simply says, "To exist is to resist." Many share this sentiment. Since the Zionist agenda is to force as many Palestinians off their land and into exile elsewhere, just to continue existing in one's home is a form of resistance.

Another example of peaceful resistance is that of the villagers in the Galilee, who were the first to use the Israeli legal system to resist expulsion from their villages.[71] Qumsiyeh, in his book *Popular Resistance in Palestine: A History of Hope and Empowerment*, cites two examples.

Figure 18. Graffiti on the separation wall encircling Bethlehem.

The first example was the "all-Catholic Palestinian village of Iqrith [that] was occupied on October 31, 1948, without any resistance, and five days later the residents were told to vacate it temporarily for two weeks. When the two weeks turned into months the villagers petitioned the Israeli High Court of Justice, which surprisingly ordered on July 31, 1951, that they be allowed to return. . . . Yet the military authorities ordered full evacuation on September 10, 1951, and the village was completely destroyed on Christmas Day 1951."[72]

The second example is the village of Kufr Bar'am, whose story is narrated in the documentary, *The Stones Cry Out,* by Yasmin Perni. The residents of Kufr Bar'am were also "ordered to evacuate so they too decided to go to the High Court, which ordered in early September 1953 that they be allowed to return. Instead, the Israeli army attacked the village by air and land; the bombardments completely destroyed it."[73]

Another simple form of resistance, one that carried the risk of death, was the attempt of many Palestinians to return to their villages after having been forced out during the Nakba of 1947- 49. Under international law, refugees have a right to return to their homes after war. Many attempted to return to their homes and farms, but most were shot on sight. It is estimated that "between 1949 and 1956, between 3,000 and 5,000 returnees were killed, the vast majority unarmed."[74]

So where are the Palestinian Gandhis? Here are three! It is only the conspiracy of silence by the United States media that keeps such persons hidden! Here in this section are three more examples of peaceful resistance to the violent Israeli occupation.

We Refuse to Die in Silence
Iyad Burnat

Iyad Burnat: "We want our people to have their freedom like everybody in the world. We do not like to be in jail or to be killed. We demonstrate because we refuse to die in silence."

Iyad Burnat (Fig. 19), leader of the Bil'in Popular Committee, which is responsible for the non-violent popular resistance against the wall, narrates stories of Bil'in and life under the Israeli Occupation of the West Bank. Bil'in is a village of approximately 1,800[75] inhabitants located 12 kilometers (approximately 7.5 miles) west of the city of Ramallah in the central West Bank. Since 2005, Bil'in citizens have been joined by Israeli and international peace activists as they demonstrate each week against the Separation Wall that has taken 60 percent of Bil'in's land for illegal settlements. They have maintained a commitment to non-violent resistance in spite of armed, military opposition by Israel that has resulted in injuries and deaths of Bil'in residents. Bil'in's popular resistance is documented in the award-winning film *5 Broken Cameras,* which was made by Iyad's brother Emad Burnat and Israeli director Guy Davidi.

Here is Iyad's narrative.

"My name is Iyad Burnat, I am not Mahatma Gandhi, or Martin Luther King, or Nelson Mandela, but I like these people. I love their way because they give us more hope to continue and more hope to win. Resistance against foreign occupation in Palestine began in 1936. I was 15 years old when I joined the 1987 intifada [uprising]. I joined with friends from school. In Bil'in village there were no checkpoints or soldiers, so we demonstrated in the streets in support of our friends in Gaza. When I was 17 years old, a group of soldiers raided my home at nighttime and arrested me because I participated in a non-violent demonstration at school.

"They said to my father that they would keep me for 4 or 5 minutes. They took me to Tahriyeh jail in the Hebron area. I remember there was snow in Palestine then. It was February, and it was very cold. So I went to jail, and I saw two soldiers who seemed very big to me because I was a child. They put me outside in the snow and the cold for a day and afterwards they took me to a small room, which had barely enough room to stand. They did this every day and every night. For one or two hours a day they interrogated me, beat me, and asked me to sign a paper written in Hebrew. They did this to all the prisoners. So I signed it after 21 days. They took me to court where I discovered that in the paper I signed, which was in Hebrew and which I could not read or understand, stated that I was throwing stones at the soldiers. So they sentenced me to two years' incarceration. I stayed for two years in the desert in Israel – in the Neqeb jail. [It is illegal under international law to incarcerate individuals under occupation in areas outside the occupied territories.] When I entered the Neqeb jail, I found 20,000 prisoners in this jail, and many of them were children. So this is how I started my life. I lost my years in school, and when I came out of prison, I decided to continue my resistance and my struggle in a non-violent way.

Figure 19. Iyad Burnat. Iyad Burnat is the leader of the Bil'in Popular Committee, which is responsible for the non-violent popular resistance against the wall.

"In 2003, the Israelis started to build the apartheid wall [separation barrier] in the north. At this time, the international media were looking at what was happening in the Palestinian cities, which were being attacked by the Israeli Army of Occupation. In December of 2004, they started to build the apartheid wall in Bil'in village. Before the demonstrations in Bil'in, I participated in demonstrations to support our friends in Budros and Khardatba[76] and their villages. When it started in Bil'in, I was ready to lead the people in non-violent demonstrations. In the beginning in December 2004, demonstrations were held every day. The people were demonstrating against bulldozers, which were destroying the olive trees. The olive tree is the lifeblood of the Palestinians, and it provides food for families. In 2003, they began building the Modi'in Ilit settlement, which now has 46,000 people. Now in the West Bank there are about half a million settlers. The apartheid wall snakes deep into West Bank territory, cutting Palestinians from their farmland as it does in Bil'in.

"The wall also cuts off Palestinians' access to water. Before the wall was built, Palestinians had enough water for every day. Now, the Israelis control the Palestinian aquifers and give us water one day a week. These actions give us, and all villages in the area, the right to resist the occupation and to resist the wall and settlements.

"Later we decided to have our demonstrations every Friday, and we have done so for the past eight years. We have internationals and Israeli activists participating with us. We adhere strictly to non-violent means in our demonstrations. We put ourselves in barrels and in cylinders. We tie ourselves to the olive trees. Every week we have a new idea. The wall is not a security wall, as Israelis say. Our message to all the people in the world is that Palestinians want peace, and they can live in peace with Israelis. We are not against the Jews of the world. We are against the occupation. So this is our message. We want our people to have their freedom like everybody in the world. We do not like to be in jail or to be killed. We demonstrate because we refuse to die in silence.

"The Israeli occupation uses a lot of violence against us. Every week, we have people who are injured. We are 1,800 people who demonstrate. They use many kinds of weapons against us, and most of these weapons are made in the United States, in spite of the fact that it is illegal under United States law to use these weapons against civilians. For example, a black rocket that killed our friend Bassam Abu Rahman was made in the U.S. by a company in Pennsylvania. In Bil'in they fire this weapon close to the targeted people, from a distance of only 15 to 20 meters. They also fire tear-gas canisters directly at people, which frequently injure and sometimes kill them. Rubber bullets [steel bullets covered with rubber] are also used to maim or kill. Since the beginning of these demonstrations, forty people have been killed by these weapons in non-violent demonstrations. Just a few weeks ago, we lost one of our friends in Nabi Saleh. He was shot to death by a rubber bullet.

"The Israeli military also tries to break our spirit by using all kinds of weapons. They arrest and kill us because they do not like our demonstrations, which send our message to the world. They have also attacked the village at nighttime, sometimes every night for a long period of time. They scare the children, scare the people, and break into houses. They attack the village from the fields.

"I have four kids at home, and it happened that when they were sleeping in the middle of the night big soldiers with dogs came into the house. The kids covered their faces so that they would not have to look at the soldiers. When I look in the eyes of my little daughter, who is eight years old and has grown up with the wall, I see the pain and fright. The first time she smelled tear gas, she was one month old. She has grown with the fear of the soldiers at night. So she can't sleep alone. So many times she wakes up at night crying and shouting. The same is happening to many of the children in the village.

Many people ask: "Do the women participate in the demonstrations?" Yes, in Bil'in, in Nil'in, and in Budros everybody participates in the demonstrations. Women, children, men, and even internationals participate. Anyone can participate. So we use many kinds of ideas in our demonstrations. We change our strategy every time.

Figure 20. In December 2009, due to the non-violent demonstrations, the Israeli Supreme Court made the decision to move the wall back 500 meters. This was the first time the Israel Court decided to demolish part of the wall. It was the first victory for the Bil'in people. The villages got 1,000 donums (1 donum equals approximately one quarter of an acre) back for their farmers. Map by courtesy of Al-Haq.

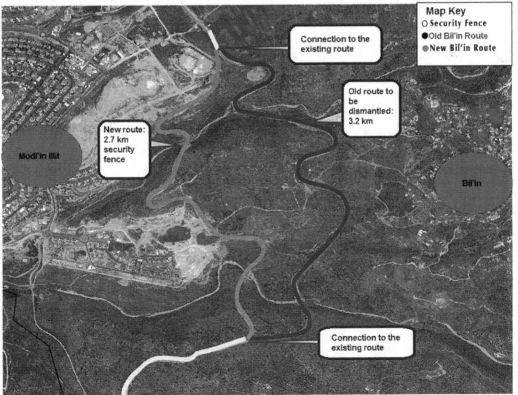

"I have been arrested many times – like many of my friends. They [the Israelis] wanted to put pressure on this struggle. So they have arrested us many times and put us in jail. They shoot us and attack our houses. They do not want us to lead the people in a non-violent struggle.

"Many famous people have visited Bil'in and participated in these non-violent demonstrations: Jimmy Carter, Desmond Tutu, and even members of the European parliament, Nobel Peace Prize winners, and groups from everywhere."

Peaceful Resistance, Building a Palestinian University under Occupation
Gabi Baramki

Dr. Gabi Baramki (1929 – 2012) was the vice president of Birzeit University and as acting president, assumed the responsibility of the administration of the university from 1974 to 1993, the time during which its president, Hanna Nasir, was deported from the West Bank. Dr. Nasir was exiled by the occupying Israeli military during a period of the occupation when the Israelis were actively suppressing education in the West Bank. Through peaceful means and a dedication to the education of Palestine's young people, Dr. Baramki persisted against extreme odds for the human rights of Palestinian people to education, self-determination, freedom, and justice. This narrative has been excerpted from Dr. Gabi Baramki's book,[77] *Peaceful Resistance, Building a Palestinian University under Occupation*, Pluto Press, 2010, with the permission of his widow, Haifa Baramki, and the publisher, Pluto Press.

In Dr. Baramki's words:

"Birzeit University in the Israeli-occupied Palestinian West Bank has been perceived by Israel as a threat. I happen to agree with this analysis but for reasons diametrically opposed to those offered by the Israelis. Birzeit is not a threat because there are 'guns instead of books on shelves' as Israeli tales would have it, but rather because, as an academic institution and testing ground for ideas, it has become a place that has produced many Palestinian leaders at both international and community levels.

"I could not have envisioned the reality of running a university under Israeli occupation. The storming of its campus by armed soldiers, the regular imprisonment of students, and the killing of so many of our students haunt me to this day. Still, we have never given in. Palestinians have the same right to education as young people anywhere, and they need that education to build the free, successful society they deserve.

"Each year on 15 May, Palestinians commemorate the Nakba, the events of 1948 that led to the loss of their homeland. It is a day of mourning for us, a reminder of the mass expulsions and destruction of villages wrought by Zionist troops. Birzeit students, like other Palestinians, usually demonstrate on that occasion. This often leads to clashes with Israel's army of occupation.

"In 1979, Israel's 'Independence Day', whose date moves each year due to Israel's lunar calendar, fell on 3 May. All day, settlers had been driving past the university in their cars, shouting, waving flags and celebrating Israel's 'independence' in a provocative manner. Some students reacted to this by throwing stones at them. In response, the armed settlers started shooting at the students.

"The Israeli army rolled up to support the settlers and there was a confrontation. I was called to the Post Office in Birzeit, which the Israeli army had turned into an operations centre. Colonel Feldman, the same military governor who had deported Hanna Nasir, took me to task about the students' behaviour. I told him that if settlers really wanted to avoid such clashes, they should keep away from the students. It would be best, I suggested, if the army advised the settlers to avoid driving through Birzeit, especially on such an emotive day. Instead, Feldman's soldiers went off and made all the students stand outside in the yard for hours, some of them in handcuffs. Following this incident, the army ordered the university closed for an 'indefinite period of time'.

"We protested against the closure with a massive letter campaign directed to the media in the United States and Europe. In addition, we called on our contacts in the United States to encourage at least some congressmen to try to put pressure on Israel, so it would rescind the closure order. Almost two months after the closure, George Assousa, an Arab American who had contacts with the State Department, asked me if I was prepared to meet with the Israeli Minister of Defence, Ezer Weizman. I could then ask him to solve the closure problem. I agreed, and within a couple of days, Assousa made the arrangements for the meeting.

"Weizman was polite and was joined in his office by the military commander of the West Bank, Binyamin Ben Elizer ('Fuad'). Weizman skirted around the subject for a bit. Instead of mentioning the closure, he talked about Karim Khala, the mayor of Ramallah, and Bassam Shak'a, the mayor of Nablus, in a friendly way. The two men were proud Palestinians, and their cars had been booby-trapped some time ago by Israeli settlers. Bassam had lost both legs in the attack and Karim part of his left foot. Weizman referred to the former as a 'hard nut to crack,' [Here Dr. Baramki relates that Weizman was merely expressing the opinion that Bassam was a tough man and losing both legs would not stop him.]

"There was, of course, a connection with Birzeit. The year before, Israel and Egypt had signed the Camp David accords. This had been a great disappointment to us, as the accords failed even to mention Palestinian national aspirations. By signing the accords, Israel had gained recognition from the largest Arab state without offering freedom to the Palestinians. The West Bank was rocked by public protests, and Birzeit's students had invited the mayors to speak at the university about their political views.

Figure 21. Press conference at the American Colony Hotel after closure of the university by the Israeli military authority in 1979. Dr. Baramki is speaking at the microphone.

"I told Weizman frankly about our students' feeling and made it clear that they needed to resume their studies. The university was a centre for serious learning, I explained. In fact its quality of education was so important to us that we picked applicants purely on the basis of their academic performance.

"After I had expanded on this for a while, Weizman turned to the commander who was sitting on his right and said, 'Fuad, my boy, let's open the university.'

"The next day, I was asked to meet with Fuad. He started our conversation by laying down conditions for re-opening of the university. If we really wanted him to revoke the closure order, we would have to promise that there would be no more violent student protests.

"I pointed out that I could not possibly make any such promises on behalf of the students. As a university, our role was to do our best to keep the place in order and to run the education process in a proper fashion. Fuad clearly did not like hearing this, and the prospect of returning to our classrooms started to recede again. However, I remained optimistic, and sure enough, two days after the university was allowed to open again.

"No head of any other Israeli university ever enquired about the difficulties we might be facing as a university under occupation, or showed any interest in visiting us. All remained aloof, even when Birzeit was closed down. There was no sympathy whatsoever for our plight. You might have thought our university was on a different planet from theirs, yet the Hebrew University was no more than 16 miles away; most others were within an hour's drive. It was as if, in the view of Israel's academic leaders, Palestinians' attempts at organizing higher education were beneath contempt. Preoccupied with their own grim past, Israeli academics seemed indifferent to the sufferings of others.

"Over time, we managed to build links with a handful of sympathizers, the 'Solidarity Committee with Birzeit University,' which was active in the 1970s and 1980s. But it was three decades before a group of the country's higher education professionals issued its first joint protest in 2008 against restriction of academic freedom in Palestine. Even then, no university rector signed [the protest].

"Birzeit's closure lasted for a full two months in the end. It also set a new precedent by depriving Palestinians of education for a significant length of time.

"We realized that these orders were not just a new way of punishing our students for demanding their national rights. Used often enough, they would eventually turn us into an ignorant, disorganized, fragmented, and easy-to-control subject population, or so the Israelis clearly hoped. We could not allow this to happen, but the problems facing us were formidable. Students whose parents had scrimped and saved to send them to Birzeit, and who had themselves worked hard to achieve their academic aims, had suddenly been deprived of access to education. Fourth-year students needed to prepare for graduation and take their final exams. Many students could not afford to hang around and wait for the university to reopen. They needed to complete their studies and start earning their keep. With the possibility of a graduate job receding into the distance, some girls were encouraged by their families to marry instead.

"Faced with those prospects, we racked our brains for ways to keep the education process going. We needed to find other places in which to teach and ways for the students to make up for lost time. By the third Israeli closure, we had formulated a back-up plan.

"As soon as a closure order was issued, effectively turfing us out of the university, secretaries would grab their files and teachers their books. News would then be circulated about locations in which secret classes would be held. Science students, whose practicals would be shifted elsewhere, would be smuggled into the campus at night to do their lab work. A student who needed specific books would indirectly contact our librarian, who would climb into the closed library through a back window, find the volumes in question, and pass them to the student outside. None of us was ready to give up, but the challenges this form of alternative education would throw up for us proved far greater than expected.

"The first of these derived from the fact that many of our students lived some distance from the Birzeit-Ramallah area. Closures were invariably accompanied by an increase in military checkpoints. Youngsters carrying book-bags could expect to be stopped, searched, and sent back. Anyone objecting to this, or even casting a defiant look, risked a severe beating plus a couple of weeks in jail. Students took to staying over at friends' houses near the campus or found ingenious ways to bypass the checkpoints, which often involved a long trek across hills.

"We held classes in private homes, fields, company offices, mosques, and churches. The whole community pulled together to lend premises and support our continuing efforts to keep the university functioning. During weekends, junior schools would sometimes let us use their classrooms (the Roman Catholic school nearby was very cooperative). Students and lecturers would make their way cautiously to a location whispered to them, then try to get on with academic work. In return for this local help, the university provided services to the community. Our students started to teach in neighbourhoods whose schools had also been shut down. This was important, as the military governor did not allow any school, once closed, to extend its school year. He considered the year to be completed even if pupils had been taught for a mere 50 days of it. We also set up support groups for the unemployed and for families who had lost their breadwinner. Both staff and students would collect food and clothing and distribute it to needy families.

"Meanwhile, soldiers would scour the town for such classes. What this often meant was that they would look inside buildings for young people with books sitting around a table. Having identified them as students engaged in the illegal act of furthering their education (to be gambling instead would presumably have been legal), the soldiers would storm in and try to arrest all those present. Our university's financial manager, Harbi Daraghmeh, who was an undergraduate during several periods of closure, still remembers how students tried to escape by jumping through windows or running across roofs.

"The Israeli army would frequently announce: 'We have uncovered cells of illegal education. We believe there are more of them and will remain in pursuit.' The term 'cells of illegal education' was eagerly adopted by Israeli politicians, who seemed unaware just how absurd it was.

"Nevertheless, both academic staff and students caught in the education raids were often sent to jail. Even Israel's statute books do not list a crime called 'running a cell of illegal education,' so military judges would convict them of public-order offences instead.

"To bypass the army, we also experimented with holding classes in Jerusalem. Having been annexed by Israel against international law, the city was not technically under military occupation, so West Bank rules did not apply there. Birzeit maintained friendly relations with St George's, a highly reputable Church of England school. Many of its pupils came on to study with us, and so it agreed to help. Teaching space and facilities were put at our disposal. As we were still allowed to enter the city in those days, teaching at least some of our students on its premises seemed to offer a solution.

"However, the army quickly found out about these arrangements and started to threaten the school. The headmaster was told that the Israeli authorities would take action against him if he helped university students to meet on his premises. This put us into a very difficult position: although it seemed unlikely that the Israelis would carry out their threat, we did not wish to bring harm to this excellent school.

"While the headmaster was still considering his decision, Israeli soldiers (who were plentiful in the city despite its civilian status) swooped on a group of our students who had gathered outside the school. It was no longer a safe environment. This was an unhappy outcome, not just for us but also for the school. After some discussion among our staff, we decided to abandon the arrangement, canceling the classes that we had arranged there.

"Jerusalem's YWCA and YMCA, institutions which have long offered facilities to Jerusalem's Arab community irrespective of religious affiliation, were also sympathetic but had little space to offer us. Still, we decided to teach some of our students there, those who were already living in the city. But we could send out lecturers in only a few subjects.

"Continuing to study under such circumstances required tremendous commitment, even on a good day. We had to make do without phones, photocopiers, or a cafeteria. Our first-year engineering students were taught calculus in a rented room in al-Bireh [city adjacent to Ramallah], physics in Birzeit's student hostel, and chemistry in Jerusalem. Each journey meant that the student had to cross at least one checkpoint and so carried an inherent risk of arrest. Not only did this mean that students regularly missed classes, but their degree courses became discouragingly long. As detention periods increased, some first-years had to restart their courses two or three times.

"Eventually, our Israeli lawyer, Lea Tsemel, raised the issue of closures for an 'indefinite period of time' in the High Court, and we obtained a ruling saying that a closure should be for a 'reasonable' period of time. This ruling was observed, especially during the subsequent closures of 1981 and 1982 – but that period was never less than two months. During that academic year alone, we were closed three times: twice for two months and once for three months. This cut a total of seven months from one academic year.

"The third closure of the university in 1982 was especially galling, as it was caused by the Israeli invasion of Lebanon. Having marched into a sovereign neighbouring country, carpet-bombed its capital, and then helped its local allies to slaughter thousands of Palestinian refugees, Israel nevertheless insisted it was a highly vulnerable state. As such, it could not allow strong, dangerous institutions such as Birzeit University to operate.

"Over the years, the closures became an increasingly distressing feature of our lives. One of their main effects was to prolong the time a student needed to complete his or her degree. To understand how this worked, it helps to look at the experience of two individual students.

"Tahsin Alyan from Jalazon [refugee camp seven kilometers north of Ramallah] was planning to study English literature, and he arrived at Birzeit when the university was shut. All we could offer him were informal lessons, which were frequently interrupted by army raids. Soldiers would throw teargas grenades into the room to force all the students out, then split up so one group could arrest those who fled while the other would destroy science equipment or photocopiers and, later on, computers.

"Tahsin could not always attend even those unsafe classes, because he was often turned back at one of the checkpoints between his home in the refugee camp of Jalazon and the university. On one occasion a soldier manning the checkpoint arrested Tahsin because he refused to sing an Arabic pop song when ordered to. Another time, soldiers came to Tahsin's home at night to take him to prison. Before delivering him up, one of them told him not to kid himself that he would be treated well because he was a student. 'Things are different here from how they are abroad,' the soldier explained.

"They were indeed. Tahsin was held for two weeks in a tiny, boxlike cell and not allowed to see anyone. Moreover, as he had been arrested during his exams, he missed out on the credits. In the end, it took him five years to complete his degree. He was 26 years old when he could finally set out to find a job, a crucial step as he has a large, disadvantaged family.

"Emad Ghaiadah had to wait eight years before he could graduate in his field, political science. This was partly because the university was closed down so often and partly because he spent time in jail.

"Students who were in their first year when a closure occurred were most deprived, sometimes having to restart their course two or three times. What we tried to ensure was that finalists, at least, were prepared for their exams during a closure and had somewhere they could sit them. This, of course, assumed that they were free to do so.

"Not surprisingly (to us, at least), the closures did nothing to lower the tension or change the anti-occupation mood in the West Bank. Angry, frustrated young people with nothing to do and nowhere to go to will find ways of expressing their feelings. This prompted what the military would describe as security-threatening 'flag incidents.'

"Whenever someone raised the Palestinian flag, which was often, the military would instantly intervene. To the soldiers, the black, red, white, and green flag was like a red rag to a bull. The fact that it originated at the time of the Arab Revolt [of 1916-1918], when Arab forces helped the British expel the Turks from Palestine during the First World War, was of no interest to them. They saw it purely as a reminder that the Arabs of Palestine, the original inhabitants, refused to go away and leave the land to the Jews. The students knew this, and regarded it as a challenge to hoist the flag wherever and whenever they could. Raising the Palestinian flag was a symbolic action, a sign of our struggle against the occupation, and the students' way of asserting themselves as Palestinians. The flag fluttering in the air affirmed our presence.

"So flags were quickly and illegally hoisted from roofs, treetops, and electricity poles. At one time, the students managed to attach one to the top of the minaret in Birzeit village, at another time they flew it from the bell tower of the local Catholic

Church. The soldiers would rush to get it down, but often could not work out how. Reaching high places like these clearly required a long ladder, and they could not imagine how on earth the students had managed to do so without one. Neither, frankly, could I.

"'Flag incidents' that involved a minaret or a church would often bring down collective punishment on a town. Shops or schools might be shut for a time, or local people would be made to stand outside the building for several hours. Soldiers would also randomly pick up young men and at gunpoint make them climb up to bring down the flag.

"The university would not be blamed directly if a 'flag incident' happened outside campus. One day, though, during one of the short stretches in which the university was actually open, our students managed to attach a flag to the roof of the student cafeteria in the Old Campus. This resulted in an almost instant call from the military governor. He did not just complain about the incident but ordered me to have it taken down immediately.

"My reply was that the university was not a military garrison. I did not have the kind of authority enjoyed by the military governor, and the students were not soldiers. Therefore, I explained, he needed to give me time. This did not go down well. The governor threatened to close down the university and send his soldiers in unless I obeyed.

"We couldn't always avoid following military orders, but there seemed to be no need to rush. It was noon, and we left the flag to flutter in the breeze for a bit. The military governor called again after half an hour, then again every half hour after that. At around four in the afternoon, I gathered the students and suggested that we salute the flag, sing the Palestinian national anthem, Biladi ('Our country'), and lower it ourselves. The students duly lined up, we saluted the flag and then slowly lowered it.

"Our response prevented a confrontation and the storming of the university by the army. However, it did not increase my popularity with the military governor. The next day, he rang me up and insisted that this kind of incident must never happen again. I could hardly guarantee this.

"Indeed, one bright, sunny morning on my way to campus, I noticed a huge flag, at least two meters long, hanging between the second-floor windows of our administration building. No one could possibly miss it. I went into my office, secretly thrilled at the sight, and decided not to do anything about it.

"As expected, I soon got a call from the military governor. 'There is a flag,' he barked. 'Oh?' I said. 'I am not sure what you are talking about.' He described where it was and ordered us to take it down immediately. You cannot, of course, just say 'no' to a man commanding several hundred armed soldiers, so I replied that I would see about this. We took our time, as usual, and then pulled down the flag. We dispensed with the ceremony this time. I really did not know who had put it up, or how and when. Still, it was nice to set eyes on it once in a while.

"On another occasion, Birzeit was holding a book fair in the yard of the old campus. As I walked up to give the opening speech, I saw two students carrying a giant Palestinian flag. Once I had taken up my position on the improvised outdoor speaker's platform, they stretched out the forbidden item right behind me. The event was widely reported in the press. The next day the governor called, asking me questions about it and wanting to know whether I had really stood in front of the flag. I brushed this aside, telling him that he ought not to over-react to such normal student activities.

"Most of the time, though, we were playing cat and mouse with the military, trying to keep our students' education going outside when they closed the university. During the first intifada (1987-92), the YMCA premises in Ramallah became one of our key locations, where we would display announcements about students' classes. Although we had built up a good messenger system, it was not very fast, and this was the quickest way of notifying students of changes in their schedules. We could not actually teach in the YMCA, but used it for administrative tasks and as a staff common room.

"The army was always milling around outside, and one-day soldiers tried to break in. YMCA staff held them off at first, but then asked me to come in. I arrived together with Albert Aghazarian. Walking up to the Israeli officer at the door, we explained to him that there were no classes taking place in that building. He refused to believe us and sent in his men. There was no way of stopping them. Once inside the building, though, the soldiers had a surprise. There were indeed no classes. However, there were notice boards displaying the names of students who were graduating on such and such a date, as well as instructions telling students about to receive their degrees where and when to meet. These announcements showed that we had an ongoing education programme.

"The soldiers, although disappointed by their failure to catch anyone in the criminal act of learning or teaching, photographed all they found. I later went to the office of the military governor to protest about the raid. He couldn't have cared less. Raids like this were almost routine.

"What was striking about Israel's persecution of Birzeit was the weakness of the Israeli arguments when it came to justifying it. When talking to the local military governor once, I asked him to spell out his reasons for closing us down. His reply was that having over a thousand people together in one place constituted a 'security problem.' I resisted the temptation to point out that most of the world does not see a university in those terms and asked him to elaborate instead. He refused. The magic word 'security' was all that was required to shut us down.

"Still hoping to persuade him, I went on: 'Look at it this way – if all these one or two thousand people are gathered in one place, at least you know where they are.

You can control them. Now, though, they have spread out to 30 or 49, maybe 100 different villages. And if you regard the students as agitators, keep in mind that they can now agitate in all of these places.'

"We ended up repeating this conversation, almost unchanged, every few months, and the governor never offered us a deal. We had hoped that he might list some conditions, which, if met by us, would lead to the university being reopened, but the Israelis clearly just wanted Birzeit shut.

"When the closures began to be reported abroad, the Israelis did not like this and so gradually eased the pressure on our so-called 'underground education activities.' These had never been a security matter, of course. Faced with growing public resistance to their rule, the army had merely sought to assert its control over the streets.

"So we kept going and even expanded our activities. As the standard of high-school matriculations declined, we devised our own university entrance exams. When the First Gulf War broke out in 1991 and Israel imposed a 40-day curfew that made travel impossible, we revised our graduation procedures. Students were allowed to sit their finals in Bethlehem or Gaza, as well as Ramallah. Most of them had been unable to work with us beforehand through the entire year's syllabus, so we sent out teaching notes and set up regional offices in which students could consult academic staff from various departments, as in an open university. The pressure that such restrictions and procedures put on our academic staff is hard to imagine. Still we held out, admitting students whether the university was officially open or not.

"Closure orders normally came from the military governor. When the orders continued beyond the first and the second year, even the military governor was apologetic when giving us the news. The source of the orders, we knew, was the then Defense Minister, Yitzhak Rabin. It was he who had launched the infamous Israeli 'iron fist' policy against the uprising, so we were not keen to meet with him and glad that the other Palestinian universities had adopted the same policy. We were also aware that Rabin's government was beginning to come under some outside pressure about the closures. I felt Rabin had not grasped the unpopularity of the occupation among all sectors of the population and had no real intention of re-opening the universities. "

"Eventually, Bethlehem University was to be the first to be reopened, in 1991. As usual, the Israeli propaganda machine started to spin right away. Two weeks after Bethlehem's reopening, a delegation from Europe's Lutheran churches was visiting Jerusalem. As its members were concerned about the welfare of the Palestinians, they met with people on both sides, including the new Minister of Defense, Moshe Arens. During that meeting they were told that Palestinian schools and universities were open and that everything was normal.

"That very evening, the Lutheran church in Jerusalem had arranged a reception for this delegation. I was there, and when they congratulated me on the fact that the university was now open, I had to point out that this was totally untrue. Only one university out of the six had been allowed to open. The rest remained very much closed. 'But the Minister of Defense told us a different story,' they countered. I explained that it was untrue.

"The next day I went to the military governor and told him: 'You'd better open the universities; otherwise you turn your defense minister into a liar.' While this argument did not work, the authorities gradually rescinded the closures, one every six months. Birzeit was eventually to reopen after almost five lost academic years.

"We held a huge, especially festive, graduation ceremony for six different intakes, whom I described as the 'wave of steadfastness and challenge' in my speech. We recalled those who had given their lives for freedom with deep sadness and the hard-won academic achievements of the students present with great pride. For the first time, we also formally hoisted the Palestinian flag."

Community and Public Health: Institution Building as an Act of Resistance
Rita Giacaman

I was born in Bethlehem and immigrated with my family to the United States as a result of the 1967 Israeli invasion and takeover of the West Bank. When I returned to Palestine in September 1978 to join the Biology Department faculty at Birzeit University, I found that the faculty, staff, and students were involved in community development and outreach activities. Community service was and is an integral part of Birzeit University's mission. This was one of the features of nonviolent resistance to Israeli military occupation in the form of community service and the building of Palestinian institutions independent of the Israeli military.

One of my students and I began to develop a community and public health program from a garage/storage "office." Because Birzeit University was small, faculty and students had close, informal, and cooperative relationships, which facilitated the development of multidisciplinary teams of researchers/activists. This proved to be crucial for our approach to public health, which combines biomedical knowledge with an understanding of societal phenomena and the context in which people live.

Early on, we set out to generate the data needed for the planning and implementation of health services. At the time, most Palestinian health-service planning was based on assumptions regarding people's health needs rather than the actual knowledge of what those health needs were. Our first study was completed in Zbeidat, a small farming community in the Jordan Valley. We assessed the social impact of the introduction of drip irrigation techniques and we observed health conditions in Zbeidat. The study demonstrated that housing, water, sanitation, and nutrition are key elements in producing health or disease; and that clinics and hospitals addressed disease only after it set in rather than addressing preventive care. We concluded that work was needed both with existing health services and with communities in order to prevent disease and to promote and protect health.

The results of this study were used to set up a clinic in Zbeidat and to train a village health worker from Zbeidat at Bethlehem University (which was at the time training male village health workers) in order to work on issues such as sanitation, health education, and nutrition. Unfortunately, the clinic did not survive long, because we did not provide the necessary follow up and support to the isolated village health worker. The experience taught us that conducting research was not enough; we had to maintain ongoing involvement through training and supervising workers and monitoring and evaluating health projects that we helped initiate. Indeed, this has been the work cycle and cardinal rule we implemented at Birzeit University's Institute of Community and Public Health (ICPH).

Our knowledge and understanding of health was gained first in practice. We then generated theory for effective primary care using the evidence that we generated from lived experience and from research. This reliance on data drawn from both research and practice continues to characterize the approach of ICPH.

We also learned from the mistakes of others. When we began our second health survey in 1981 in three villages near Birzeit, we knew from the Bethlehem University experience that we should train female and not male health workers, because only women are able to enter homes and gather information on the home environment and family nutrition. Such information is essential in planning effective primary health care.

The Birzeit village study turned into one of the most important ICPH programs because it succeeded by building on previously gained knowledge. This study taught us to continually assess before moving forward and helped us appreciate the importance of collaboration with other local institutions. This program was conducted jointly with Birzeit Women's Charitable Society, which was already operating a clinic in Birzeit village. This clinic had an attending physician who spent a few hours a week monitoring the growth and development of the children of Birzeit village and surrounding villages. Immunization services for children were also offered.

As can be seen by this example, we built on what existed. We set up a clinical laboratory, needed for quality diagnoses, and we increased the number of hours the physician attended the clinic. We developed curricula and trained women village health workers from seven villages near Birzeit, and we employed a midwife for clinic work and home visiting. We supervised and supported village health workers and focused on home visits, health education, and community mobilization for the solution of selected problems, such as sanitation and housing problems. We worked closely with all relevant parties to operate a comprehensive primary health care program, including working with the villagers to install tube/potable water supplies to improve sanitation and to bring the University's Literacy and Adult Education Program into the villages in our area. We also combined the village health program with student health care. That was the beginning of student health services at the university.

The successful Birzeit clinic program became a model for other primary health care programs in the West Bank that are still running today. The Palestinian Ministry of Education and Higher Education, which was established in 1994 after the formation of the Palestinian National Authority, accredited the community health-worker training as a post-high school middle diploma in the late 1990s. Given that

Figure 22. Rita Giacaman.

community health workers are at the core of primary health care principles, and that such an accreditation is unique to Palestine and exists in no other Arab country, the establishment of a diploma program is a testimony to how collective action and the struggle for liberation could bring about fundamental advancement in the nature and practice of public health. And that is the paradoxical nature of our situation under continued Israeli military occupation: it can bring about major changes in structures that otherwise would have been difficult to change.

During the 1980s, we sought to obtain scholarships for our students to get their master's degrees abroad, because local universities did not offer such degrees. Institution building as a mode of resistance to occupation entailed first and foremost increasing the number of health care professionals with specialties in research and health care practices relevant to local health needs. The first parasitologist, nutritionist, health educator, and sanitation specialist in the country were biology students I taught. Teaching at the Biology Department provided the opportunity to influence students and help them realize the importance of these public health specialties.

The middle 1990s required a major shift in ICPH's operations. In line with our commitment to define our activities in terms of societal needs, it became necessary to help train Palestinians to take charge of health services. We thus conducted a survey of all clinics in the West Bank and Gaza Strip in 1994, in preparation for setting up programs that would offer a post-graduate Diploma in Primary Health Care and a Master's degree in Public Health (MPH). The results were used to develop curricula, which were endorsed by local and international public health experts and practitioners, including those from the World Health Organization. As of June 2009, there were 235 graduates with a Masters of Public Health degree, half of whom are women, and about a third of whom have been promoted to key positions in the various sub-sectors of health. We continue to solicit doctoral-level scholarships for our research assistants and students, after mentoring them for a period at ICPH.

Our teaching follows principles similar to those of our research orientation: we bring in results from field research to students, and discussions with them help to clarify our understanding of the findings. We also visit students and alumni regularly in their workplaces through our ongoing field-visits program. Our exchanges during these visits help them deal with some of the constraints of practical work; they help us learn about changes that are occurring in the healthcare environment. Through these interactions with our students and alumni who are practicing in their communities, we are able to learn and incorporate new information into our research and teaching. This approach is necessary for the continued relevance of our teaching programs to the healthcare needs of the population.

Throughout the 1980s, we combined research, capacity building, planning, and model building with emergency work, such as providing first aid to students who were shot or attacked by the Israeli military. Later, during the first intifada, we launched initiatives such as testing the cistern water of Ramallah/al-Bireh twin cities for bacterial contamination and chlorinating them, just in case the Israeli military government retaliated by withholding tubed water supplies from the area. When the Israeli army closed our schools, we taught in our homes, in defiance of the closure orders, and our kitchens turned into labs, with microscopes and other equipment transported from the university.

During the second intifada, we followed the combined development/emergency imperatives. We did emergency first-aid work and offered online and telephone support to those who needed help – patients waiting for ambulances during curfews, families with a woman in labor who had to wait out a curfew to go to the hospital, and ambulance drivers and health care providers who had to get medications and other essential items such as baby food to isolated and needy villages with whom we were in touch.

During unrest, we continued to teach our students, even when we had to operate out of a garage, as we had when we started out (only this time the garage was in Ramallah). However, unlike our situation during the first intifada, we were supported in reaching students by the excellent Birzeit University web portal RITAJ, the Internet, and mobile phones. We also sought to document people's experiences with Israeli army violations such as pilfering, destruction of property, and the seizure of homes to use as resting or observation stations after having locked up the families in one of the rooms. We documented the consequences of the Israeli army's wanton destruction of the infrastructure and institutions, and the death, injury, disability and other health problems facing people living under severe political violence since 2000. In fact, some of our most cited articles focused on the consequences of the invasions of West Bank towns on population health in 2002, and, more recently, on the health status and health services of Palestinians under Israeli military occupation, published in 2009 in The Lancet.[78]

As of April 2010, we had completed a study on the consequences of Israel's December 2008 –January 2009 onslaught on the Gaza Strip and presented the initial findings in the second Lancet Palestinian Health Alliance conference, which convened in early March 2010 at ICPH. We continue to document the social suffering the war inflicts on the Palestinian population. We provide evidence of what it means to live under such difficult and unjust conditions, and elaborate on the consequences of war on health. We do this for policy and planning purposes, to assist health services in accommodating people's needs.

But there is another purpose for our research: the world must know.

Dr. Rita Giacaman is professor of public health at the Institute of Public and Community Health, Birzeit University, Birzeit, Palestine. She earned a doctorate in Clinical Pharmacy from the University of California, San Francisco Medical Center, San Francisco, California, U.S.A., in 1977 and a Master of Philosophy degree in Sociology/Social Policy with a focus on health and women from the University of Essex, Colchester, England, in 1985. Professor Rita Giacaman is a founding member of the Institute of Community and Public Health at Birzeit University, located in Birzeit, Palestine. Professor Giacaman served for many years as the chair of the Institute and was instrumental in its success.

Questions for Reflection

1. Nonviolent resistance can take many forms: peaceful marches and demonstrations, civil disobedience, economic pressure such as boycotts and divestments, political pressure such as sanctions by governments. Based upon your reading thus far, can you name and discuss the different ways that Palestinians are engaged in nonviolent resistance to the Israeli occupation?

2. The text of the Palestinian civil society call for boycott, divestment, and sanctions (BDS):

   "We, representatives of Palestinian civil society, call upon international civil society organizations and people of conscience all over the world to impose broad boycotts and implement divestment initiatives against Israel similar to those applied to South Africa in the apartheid era. We appeal to you to pressure your respective states to impose embargoes and sanctions against Israel. We also invite conscientious Israelis to support this Call, for the sake of justice and genuine peace."

   These non-violent punitive measures should be maintained until Israel meets its obligation to recognize the Palestinian people's inalienable right to self-determination and fully complies with the precepts of international law by:

   • Ending its occupation and colonization of all Arab lands and dismantling the Wall

   • Recognizing the fundamental rights of the Arab-Palestinian citizens of Israel to full equality; and

   • Respecting, protecting and promoting the rights of Palestinian refugees to return to their homes and properties as stipulated in UN resolution 194.

   Are you aware of boycott and divestment campaigns in the United States and Europe, which are a response to the Palestinian call for BDS?

3. Palestinians are exercising civil disobedience much as Mahatma Gandhi did in India. Do you see any similarities or differences between the situation in Palestine/Israel and India?

Nablus District

Nablus district, located in the central highlands of Palestine, has been under Israeli occupation since 1967. The seat of the governorate of Nablus is the city of Nablus, which has a population in excess of 150,000 according to the 2007 Palestine Bureau of Statistics.

To understand the milieu of the narrative by Majeda Akram Fidda, an elected member of the Nablus municipal council at the time of her imprisonment, a brief history of the 2006 elections in the West Bank will be presented here.

The West Bank and the Gaza Strip are divided into 16 governorates, of which Nablus is one; 11 are in the West Bank, including East Jerusalem; and five in the Gaza Strip. Municipal and village councils, of which there are 557, have administrative responsibility for water, electricity, waste disposal, schools, planning and building control, road construction and maintenance, and control of public markets; however the Israeli authorities limited their powers and took control over policies and budgets. The Arab Jerusalem Municipality Council was completely dissolved. Of the total number of municipal and village council members, 13.4 percent were women, mostly in the West Bank.[79]

The Palestinian Authority held elections on January 25, 2006, for the Palestine Legislative Council. These elections were monitored by international observers,

Figure 23. Abd Abdi, *Prisoners*, 1981.
Woodcut on paper, 28 x 20 in, 70 x 50 cm.

including former U. S. President Jimmy Carter, and were certified as fair and democratic. On September 26, 2005, during the campaigns for the elected seats in the Palestine Legislative Council (PLC), Israeli Occupation Forces arrested 450 members of the Hamas party, most of whom were actively campaigning for the municipal elections or the PLC. The majority of those detained were kept in administrative detention for "varying periods of time".[80] This demonstrates Israel's practice of imprisoning elected municipal officials.

Ms. Fidda ran and won election to the Nablus municipal government under the Change and Reform Party in 2005 at which time this party was not declared to be "illegal" by Israel. However, Israel did declare this party to be illegal in 2007 and used this declaration as a pretext to arrest Ms. Fidda.[81] Israel describes itself as "the only democracy in the Middle East", yet its policies and practices in the West Bank are designed to thwart democratic practices.

The work of the Addameer (Arabic for conscience) Prisoner Support and Human Rights Association (www.addameer.org) is a valuable source of information on Palestinian adults and children in Israeli prisons and on Israeli policies and practices involving their imprisonment. The group monitors legal procedures and solidarity campaigns to end torture and other violations of prisoners' human rights.[82]

According to Addameer, "approximately 700 Palestinian children under the age of 18 from the occupied West Bank are prosecuted every year through Israeli military courts after being arrested, interrogated, and detained by the Israeli army. The most common charge levied against children is throwing stones, a crime that is punishable under military law by up to 20 years in prison. Since 2000, more than 8,000 Palestinian children have been detained."[83]

In practice, there are no special interrogation procedures for children detained by the Israeli military, nor are there provisions for an attorney or even a family member to be present when a child is questioned. The majority of children report being subjected to ill treatment and having forced confessions extracted from them during interrogations.[84]

United Nations International Children's Emergency Fund (UNICEF), Defense for Children International – Palestine (DCI-Palestine), the Special Rapporteur on the situation of human rights in the Palestinian territories, and the U. S. Department of State Reports on Human Rights Practices have "repeatedly condemned Israel" for its widespread and systematic ill treatment of Palestinian children under Israel's military detention system.[85] "During 2013, 76.5 percent of Palestinian children detained by the Israeli military in the occupied West Bank endured some form of physical violence during arrest, transfer or interrogation, a slight increase from 2012."[86] The tabulation, below, indicates some but not all common violations collected by DCI-Palestine during 2013.

Common complaints and areas of concern between January 1 to December 31, 2013	West Bank	
	Number of cases	Percentage
Hand ties	98	100.0%
No lawyer present during interrogation	94	95.9%
Not informed of right to silence	91	92.9%
Blindfolds	92	93.9%
Not informed of reason for arrest	96	98.0%
Physical violence	75	76.5%
Verbal abuse, humiliation and intimidation	73	74.5%
Strip searched	78	79.6%
Denial of adequate food and water	76	77.6%
Threats or inducement	39	39.8%
Denial of access to toilet	68	69.4%
Night arrest	55	56.1%
Position abuse	32	32.7%
Transfer on vehicle floor	49	50.0%
Shown or signed paper in Hebrew	21	21.4%
Solitary confinement for more than two days	21	21.4%

The Israeli military uses a procedure called "administrative detention" to imprison Palestinians indefinitely on secret information without charging them or allowing them to stand trial. Administrative detention was used both by the British during their mandate of Palestine and later by the Israelis beginning after the 1967 occupation of the West Bank. The rate of administrative detention has steadily risen after the second intifada in 2000. Immediately before the start of second intifada, Israel held 12 Palestinians in administrative detention; however, "between 2005 and 2007, the average monthly number of Palestinian administrative detainees held by the Israel remained stable at approximately 765."[87]

An Administrative Detainee

Majeda Akram Fidda

Majeda Akram Fidda, a member of Nablus municipality council, was arrested by Israeli soldiers on August 6, 2008. She was acquitted of all charges against her on December 31, 2008, but instead of being released, she was placed in administrative detention for over a year. She was finally released on January 25, 2010. In this video [www.addameer.org/evideo.php?id=109], she talks about her experience as an administrative detainee and as a female political prisoner in an Israeli prison.

The following narrative is a transcript of that interview, courtesy of Addameer, the Palestinian Prisoner Support and Human Rights organization.

"I was a prisoner twice; the first time was in 2005 and the second in 2008. The total time I spent in jail was two full years. I am a pharmacist. I graduated from the former Soviet Union. But I was more committed to social work, so I spent most of my time in social work.

"Currently I am an elected member of the Nablus Municipality Council."

Detention

"I never thought that a person who is engaged in social work or even an elected municipality member would be subjected to detention. In the middle of the night of August 6, 2008, they [the Israeli military] came to my house at around 2 a.m. They came to my house and invaded it. They took my neighbor as a hostage and used her as a human shield. They invaded the whole building; they even invaded and searched uninhabited flats whose owners lived abroad. The small shops underneath the building were also invaded. Later on, they came back to my house and arrested me."

The Court

"I was transferred to the [military] court in Salem. I was surprised that the accusation against me was that I ran for office and was elected. What kind of arrest is based on ones' electoral victory from a list they do not approve of? [She is referring to the Change and Reform Party list.] I was detained for five months and was found innocent at the end of the legal procedures. The judge issued a decision to release me because there was no evidence, proof, or accusation, and the judge considered that five months was enough for my case. Instead, I was surprised that they transferred me to administrative detention. This was the biggest shock for me. The judge issued a decision stating that this administrative detention was illegal, and if there was no investigation on other issues, then the administrative detention was illegal. I should be released. But instead the administrative detention was extended by six months, and then by three months more, and yet again by another four months, and so on.

"They extended my administrative detention five times based on a non-existent accusation. It was a very harmful situation for me. My lawyer was from the West Bank; he did not have a permit to enter the 1948 territories [this refers to Palestinian territories taken by Israel in 1948, i.e., what is now called Israel], so I was never able to see him except during court sessions. Even then, when I was waiting in a cell before the court, I would ask the guards to call my lawyer, but they never did. It was only when I came across other prisoners going to court before me that I could tell them to call my lawyer.

"For the Israeli occupier, administrative detention is based on a secret file – a security file. It is as though our presence on Palestinian land has become a danger to the security of Israel. Administrative detention is a very unjust detention. There are a lot of people who lost their jobs, lost their families while they were in jail going through one extension of administrative detention after the other with no end to it."

Female prisoners in Israeli jails

"The female prisoners who had life sentences would pity us, because at least they knew that they were to remain in prison. With administrative detention, we felt it was a life sentence on hold, not knowing when we would be released or if we would be released. The prisoner always tried to ask the people around her: do you think I will be released? Do you think there is no more information about me they could bring? Do you feel optimistic? Pessimistic?

"What dreams did you have recently? Dreams used to have a great effect on us inside prisons. What did you dream? Prisoners would ask if the dream was before or after dusk in order to see how recent it was and predict the possibility of it coming true and when. We shared many human feelings together, dreams, optimism, pessimism, asking each other if we were going to be released or not.

"What hurt me most was my concern for my parents. My parents are not young, and they don't have any children in Palestine. All their children except me are abroad. I was worried for them. I worried about their reactions more than I was worried about myself. I later found out through my sisters (who happened to be here from abroad) that once, when they already knew about my latest extension, they came home and saw my mother preparing my favorite food and delicious sweets. When they saw all the food, they asked for who it was. My mother replied, 'It is for Majeda because she is coming out [of prison] today or tomorrow!' They didn't know how to react, how to tell her that her daughter had received another extension when she had prepared all this. They told me they used to avoid these situations. My sisters would take turns informing my mother because they could not bear to see her reaction. My father would get tired and collapse. And I was afraid that I would come out and not find him alive.

"The hardest extension for me was the fourth one. I learned from the prosecution that the last piece of information they gathered on me was in July. And so after two extensions, I thought it should be over and I would be released. So I prepared myself. They informed me in the evening that I would be released the next day. I gave all my clothes and personal items to the other female prisoners. Everyone was congratulating me. We were singing and cheering and we had a party. We agreed to celebrate again in the morning. They prepared sweets, and I was dressed to leave, holding a bag of presents for my parents – handicrafts that I made. The head of the prison came, looked at me, and asked the prisoners' spokesperson, 'What is Majeda waiting for?' She replied: 'She was informed that she will be released, and she is waiting for the bus to pick her up.' He spoke to her in Hebrew. I could get a few words and understood that there would be no release. He said that I was given another extension. This was at 8:30 a.m., half an hour before my intended release! I can't deny that I was completely shocked. It was hard for me to recover at that moment. Of course I thanked God, but I went to my cell and couldn't sleep. Later, I read on the BBC news that the Israeli administration accepted to release 20 prisoners to obtain in return a one-minute video of Shalit. I was again surprised that my name was not amongst the 20 mentioned in the deal. It was extremely hard for me; it was an all-day emotional roller coaster. However, I controlled myself again because I was happy for the three female prisoners about to be released. They were mothers: Zahra Hamdan, Fatima Saad, and Rawda Saad."

Green Nablus

"When I won the election in the municipality, I was fortunate to become responsible for the best two departments: the cultural and the garden departments. All those in the cultural organizations I was overseeing hoped for big projects – for instance, establishing a theater in Nablus city with a theater troupe. Since I am an artist, I would draw a garden, how and where it should be. And I would sit with the agricultural engineer to plan for more than one place. When you are in a state of depression in prison, to overcome the psychological pressures, you think of the sun, the air, the seashore, the water, the rain, the sound of birds, things you are denied, so you can relive all this; otherwise you will die inside the jail. You would be killing yourself if you don't think of these things."

Questions for Reflection

1. One of the most frequently repeated Israeli talking points is that "it is the only democracy in the Middle East." Do you think that a democracy would imprison a democratically elected public official, as they did in the case of Majeda Akram Fida? What legal irregularities do you see in the imprisonment of Ms. Fida?

2. The International Covenant on Civil and Political Rights,[88] article 2, part 1, states that "Each State party to the present Covenant undertakes to respect and to ensure to all individuals within its territory and subject to its jurisdiction the rights recognized in the present Covenant, without distinction of any kind, such as race, color, sex, language, religion, political or other opinion, national or social origin, property, birth or other status." Do you think Israel is violating this International Law?

3. Palestinians living in the West Bank live under Israeli military law, while Israeli colonist settlers living in the West Bank live under Israeli civil law. The treatment of Ms. Fidda directly violated elements of the International Convention on the Suppression and Punishment of the Crime of Apartheid,[89] article II parts

    (a) (iii): Denial of a member or members of a racial group[90] or groups of the right to life and liberty of person by arbitrary arrest and illegal imprisonment of the members of a racial group or groups; and

    (b): Any legislative measures and other measures calculated to prevent a racial group or groups from participation in the political, social, economic and cultural life of the country and the deliberate creation of conditions preventing the full development of such a group or groups.

    The United Nations defines "racial discrimination," as "any distinction, exclusion, restriction, or preference based on race, color, descent, or national or ethnic origin that has the purpose or effect of nullifying or impairing the recognition, enjoyment or exercise, on an equal footing, of human rights and fundamental freedoms in the political, economic, social, cultural or any other field of public life."

    Do you think the treatment of Ms. Fidda and others like her constitutes a crime of apartheid?

Tulkarm District

The Tulkarm District lies on the coast of Palestine north of the Jaffa district and extends inland to the central highlands. Half of the villages of Tulkarm were either depopulated or destroyed before the end of the British Mandate. According to Esber,[91] Christians and Muslims owned 77.9 percent of the district, while Jewish inhabitants owned 17.3 percent. There were 34 Arab villages in 1948: "17 were forcibly depopulated and a total of 16 villages were demolished." Esber[92] interviewed individuals from several villages. The pattern of dispossession and expulsion was similar to other Zionist campaigns and was composed of intimidation and violence.

The campaign of violence and massacres continued long after the 1947- 48 campaign of expulsion. An example is the massacre of Kafr Qasem in 1956. Kafr Qasem was a village just inside the 1949 armistice line between Israel and the West Bank. Samia Halaby began her work with the Kafr Qasem villagers in 1999. She made numerous trips to Kafr Qasem to interview the villagers. The narratives below are part of her work, which is due to be published in 2016. Several of her artworks depicting the massacre are in private collections.

A Massacre Is Like a Hammer Blow: The Kafr Qasem Massacre of 1956
Samia A.Halaby

King Husein of Jordan ceded the village of Kafr Qasem to Israel in 1949 as part of the Rhodes Armistice Agreement. Thus the residents of Kafr Qasem found themselves transformed from citizens of an Arab village in an Arab country, Jordan, free to live and move, into captives of a brutal Israeli military rule which limited their movements and their ability to work and subjected them to massive theft of their farmlands.

On October 29, 1956, the day that Israel, England, and France conducted a surprise attack on Egypt's Suez Canal, the Israelis created an artifact. They announced less than 30 minutes in advance that there would be a strict curfew on all the Arabs of Kafr Qasem and other neighboring villages. Then they lay in wait for innocents returning home; the villagers had absolutely no way of knowing of the curfew and were mercilessly shot to death. Forty-eight villagers and one unborn child died that evening, and many were wounded.

A massacre is like a hammer blow that shatters a hard mass to smithereens. At first the pieces do not all see the hammer and do not know whom to blame. Painful energy flies in all directions. The town receiving the blow is shattered, broken to pieces, and as the pieces settle there is blame, anger, pain, loss, recrimination, shock, disbelief, desperation, and in the case of the Kafr Qasem massacre all this is added to the poverty and depression resulting from a brutal military occupation. What does the father tell his wife when he returns home alive, that their eight-year-old child who she sent to fetch him dies in the massacre? Why is a small girl unable to tell her mother that her father lies wounded in the street except to say that dinner need not be prepared for him? Why do men and women, unable to believe their own experience, return to the scenes of the massacre to confirm its reality with those who shared it only to find death instead of fellowship? Why was the only survivor of one of the events of the massacre asked why she was the only one to survive? Why does a wounded man, who had escaped, return on seeing Israeli soldiers executing fourteen women, only to be shot dead himself?

There is a level of vicarious curiosity even in honest, sympathetic reporting. The townspeople of Kafr Qasem exhibited great hesitancy in dealing with journalists and historians, or with artists like myself, in spite of the fact that they really wanted their story told. Thirteen years into this project, and after repeated visits to Kafr Qasem, trust developed between us. In October 2012, on the occasion of the annual memorial march, I received lengthy interviews and was treated like an old friend. I did not receive such welcome on my first visits there in 1999 and 2000. If I were to live in Kafr Qasem for at least one year, I might begin to unravel all it means to a community to experience a massacre like the one that took place there in 1956.

The narrative of Abdal Tamam (born 1944), who lives in Kafr Qasem, is one of the narratives recorded in Arabic and translated by me.

In Abdal Tamam's words:

> "I was 12 years old when the Kafr Qasem massacre took place in our village in October of 1956, and it politicized me. At age 14, I began drawing about the massacre, and three or four times the Israeli police entered my home and took my drawings. I was put in prison from 1967 to 1970 and placed under administrative detention; that meant I had no legal recourse and might remain there forever.

> "In prison I did a lot of drawings, but the Israeli jailers did not give me permission to send them out. They took them all, promising to give them back when they let me out, but then they refused to give them back to me. In prison I did not draw about the massacre or about Palestinian politics because they would have made life impossible for me. So I drew about Viet Nam.

> "On the day of the massacre they let us out of school earlier than normal, a good while before sunset. We were happy running along the roads, which were not paved then. In our whole lives we had only seen two or three cars. Suddenly a military jeep came past us. The soldiers had their weapons ready on their laps and they were staring at us. We were amused by the novelty

of it. On our way home we met a crowd of adults in the village center. They were saying that there is a curfew and that the workers in the fields were not informed. One man rode a bicycle to call his daughter and the women who worked in the fields where my mother was working.

"Two boys that I knew, Jamal Saleem Taha, who was 11 years old, and Riyad Raja, who was eight years old, said that they were going to bring back their family members who were out working and wanted me to go with them to get my mother. I thought the man on the bicycle would get her sooner. I was lucky, as the soldiers killed both of them. The square emptied and I heard shooting and got scared and went home.

"They had told us that the curfew was at five, but we had no watches'. [Kafr Qasem in 1956 had no electricity and no running water.] Not enough time had passed for it to be five; it was still light. One could still see. I started looking through the cracks between the wooden boards of the door. I saw an old woman, a neighbor, whom I used to call 'aunty'. Her son tried to get her into his house, but she wanted to get sugar and a teapot for the long hours of curfew. She ran into a soldier who shot at her, but she got away. There were maybe two meters between the soldier and me. I heard him curse the old woman in Hebrew, and this curse I had never heard before; there is no need to repeat it. [I said repeat it, and Abdal Tamam continued.] He said 'kus umek eylef shaneen' or in English, 'fuck your mother for a thousand years.'

"I was still near the door and saw him move westwards into an alley and heard him shoot again, when suddenly my mother came running out of it. She entered saying she saw the flashing of fire, and she was asking where is Abed, where is Abed. In her panic she was asking for me. My oldest brother was still missing; there was curfew and no communications, and no one knew where the other was. The firing got really heavy, and my mother began saying Jum'ah Sarsour is gone, Mousa is gone, Abdallah is gone. I was just listening. She knew who was still on their way.

"On the day after, old men came to us with the military asking for hoes, pick-axes, and other tools for digging. The adults of course realized that there had been killing and there would be burial.

"We were cooped up and knew nothing of what happened. On the third day they let people out for a short period. This is the sight that I remember. Men and women stood about not knowing the fate of their missing family members, whether they got killed or had stayed at their work place. They were wondering who died and asked each other about who was still missing.

"We the children heard people saying there was killing and burial, and we wanted to see. As we went one boy yelled: "This is my father's bicycle" and took it. It was covered with blood. I saw the truck that had the 13 women who were killed. I had never seen such a sight. The earth, the dirt; the place was like black oil and blood all mixed together and bullets and bullet casings. Oh God! The place was full of brass casings, piles of them. It was like a battlefield! Oh so much shooting! The truck had no area greater than 12 centimeters that was clear of bullet holes, even the wheels. In the cactus fence there were bits of their flesh and splattered blood, clothes, shirts, scarves. A terrible, terrible sight!

"Now among the old people who came asking for tools for digging was Thiab Abed Hammad, God rest his soul, a respected man in the village who had two sons still missing. The military took him with them when they wanted to bury the dead so he would identify the bodies. As they brought the first body down [from the truck] in order to bury it he saw that it was his son, and he fainted.

"They brought 50 workers from Jaljoulia [the neighboring village] and told them to dig 50 graves. They feared that they were digging their own graves. They did not dig deep, maybe only 20 centimeters. I lived nearby and saw the wrappings of the dead. They were visible – poking up from the dirt. If you pulled on the wrapping you would pull out the body. It was one month later that the villagers were finally permitted to bury their loved ones. I was there and something happened in front of my eyes. A woman whose husband was old and who normally wore an *umbaz* [traditional dress] was being helped to bury her husband. When they dug they found a young man wearing pants. She said this is not my husband. As this situation was repeated several times, it was generally agreed that it is better not to go searching among the other bodies and abuse the survivors. So they buried the body properly and marked the grave as though it was the husband. I knew the young man whose body they dug up, but I will not reveal his name, and I too will let everyone pray peacefully at the graves marked with their loved one's names."

There were eleven waves of killings during the Kafr Qasem massacre. What follows are three examples from these waves of killing.

In the northern fields of the village, three shepherd boys were out watering the family's flock of sheep, not knowing that Israel had launched a surprise attack on Egypt just hours before; nor did they know of the curfew imposed on their village. The oldest boy, Abdallhah Easa, was 16, and the youngest, Abed Easa, was nine years old. Ibraheem Easa, 35, had learned of the curfew and left the safety of his home to bring them back. They returned immediately, with Ibraheem leading. Abed and Abdallah were just behind him while the third boy, Sami Mustafa, was watching the rear of the herd. They were met by Israeli soldiers of the Border Guard, who immediately shot and killed Ibraheem, Abed, and Abdallah. Sami saw them being shot. He fell to the ground playing dead, and survived (Fig. 24).

Figure 24. Samia A. Halaby. *The Kafr Qasem Massacre of 1956: Killing in the Northern Fields, 2012*. Conté crayon on paper, 40 x 44 ½ in, 102 x 113 cm. Killed: Abdallah Ahmad Easa. 16; Abed Mahmoud Easa, 9; Ibraheem Abdal-Hadi Easa, 35. Escaped: Sami Mustafa.

In the second example, five minutes before the curfew, and unaware of it, four quarry workers were returning home to Kafr Qasem on bicycles (Fig. 25). When confronted by Israeli soldiers with whose harassment the men were familiar, they reached for their identity cards. Instead, an order to 'harvest them' was given. Two, Ahmad Freij, 35, and Ali Taha, 30, died. Both were fathers of young children. Two others, Mahmoud Freij and Abdallah Bdier, managed to escape. Mahmoud was wounded in the thigh and managed to crawl to an olive tree and hide until morning.

The third example is from the ninth wave of killing. Night had fallen when the truck arrived at the location of the massacre. Among the victims of the ninth wave were two men in the cab of the truck and 14 women with two boys in the back. The driver, seeing the scattered dead, tried to escape at high speed. This alerted the singing women, who unwittingly began to scream, thus alerting the recumbent soldiers, who ran after the truck, shot its tires and gas tank, and stopped it. Safa Sarsour, having just seen her 16-year-old son, Jum'a, dead on the side of the road, now witnessed her second son, 14-year-old Abdallah, being killed with the men. The women, some pregnant, elders, and girls, pleaded for their lives. The only survivor was Hana' Amer, 15 years of age, who reported that the women clung to each other for protection (Fig. 26). Even the two girls who had managed to escape returned to the circle. As they were being shot they turned in a big group, and one by one they fell. The soldiers continued shooting

113

Figure 25. Samia A. Halaby. *The Kafr Qasem Massacre of 1956: First Wave of Killing at the Western Entrance to the Village,* 2012. Color pencil on paper, 22 x 30 in, 56 x 76 cm. Killed: Ahmad Muhammad Freij, 35; and Ali Uthman Taha, 30. Wounded: Muhammad Mahmoud Freij. Escaped: Abdallah Sameer Bdier.

into their heads to ensure their death. How does it measure western civilization, when soldiers of the Israeli border police line up defenseless women, some pregnant, tired, returning home from work, and kill them with cold deliberation?

Samia A. Halaby, born in Jerusalem, Palestine, received a Master of Fine Arts degree from Indiana University in 1963, and taught for 17 years, ten of which were at the Yale School of Art. She has had one-artist shows all over the world, and her works are in many museum collections internationally, including the Guggenheim, The Institute Du Monde Arabe, and the Museum and the Art Institute of Chicago.

As a postscript to Halaby's personal research with the villagers of Kafr Qasem, Shira Robinson's summary of the aftermath of the massacre at Kafr Qasem is of note.

In November 1957, the Israeli government held a "sulha" [ceremony of reconciliation] in Kafr Qasem. Shira Robinson[93] describes it:

"Behind the fanfare of the ceremony – comprised of speeches calling for villagers to move beyond the tragedy for the sake of coexistence, promises

Figure 26. Samia A. Halaby. *The Kafr Qasem Massacre of 1956: The Ninth Wave of Killing, Implosion,* 2012. Charcoal on paper, 30 x 44 ½ in, 76 x 113 cm. Killed: Abdallah Muhammad Sarsour, 14; Aminah Qasem Taha, 50; Bakriyyaa Mahmoud Taha, 14; Fatma Dahoud Sarsour, 30; Fatma Mustafa Easa, 18; Fatma Mahmoud Bdair, 40; Fatma Saleh Sarsour, 14; Hilwa Muhammad Bdier, 65; Khamisa Faraj Amer, 50; Lateefa Dahoud Easa, 14; Mahmoud Habeeb Masarwah, 25; Muhammad Saleem Sarsour, 15; Muhammad Ali Sarsour, 35; Rasheeda Fa'eq Bdier, 14; Safa Muhammad Sarsour, 45; Zaynab Abdal-Rahman Taha, 45; and Zaghloula Ahmad Easa, 45. Wounded: Hana' Amer, 15.

of generous government reparations to the wounded and the families of the victims, and a sumptuous full-course meal – lurked a heavy air of intimidation, anger, and pain."

Robinson further writes:

"For most Palestinian Arab citizens of Israel, who in 1956 [eight years after the Nakba] made up 11 percent of the population, the massacre represented the inevitable (if most brutal) outcome of eight years of what was commonly labeled Israel's 'policies of national oppression' against them. Along with military rule and the deprivation of their civil rights, these policies were expressed in the ongoing confiscation of their land, their consistent portrayal in official discourse as a fifth column, and the cultivation of racist attitudes against them in Jewish schools. Above all, the murders in Kafr Qasem sparked widespread fear that few social, political, or legal safeguards were in place to prevent the repetition of such an assault – a sentiment that won partial confirmation as a result of the government's heavy-handed responses to the crime. These included its seven-week media gag on the 'incidents;' its refusal to hold a public trial despite Arab and Jewish demands to do so; its pardoning of the convicted soldiers and the appointment of the responsible commanders to high government posts; its failure to compensate fully the wounded and bereaved families; and its imposition of the sul`ha. The state's ongoing refusal to acknowledge formal responsibility for the massacre continues to aggravate all of these wounds today."

Questions for Reflection

1. The imprisonment of Abdal Tamam using administrative detentions is another example of Israel's violation of the human rights enshrined in The International Covenant on Civil and Political Rights. From Abdal's narrative, can you find the reason Israel subjected him to Administrative Detention?

2. How can painting about one's lived experiences pose a threat to Israel's security?

3. The author asks: "How does it measure western civilization when soldiers of the Israeli border police line up defenseless women, some pregnant, tired, returning home from work, and kill them with cold deliberation?" How would you answer this question?

4. In examining the three drawings, can you describe the different ways they show the horrors of the massacre and the dignity of the victims?

The Acre District

Two narratives are presented here which differ considerably from each other and show the large disparity between those who ended up in refugee camps and others who were fortunate enough to remain in their villages. The first is that of Rev. Fahed Abu-Akel, who was able to return to his village and later immigrated to the United States, eventually becoming the Moderator of the Presbyterian Church (USA). The second narrative is that of Um Aziz, who fled her village for safety and was not allowed to return.

Twenty-six villages were depopulated and or destroyed by the Yishuv/Israeli forces in the Acre district,[94] which is in northwest Palestine. Kafr Yasif, where Rev Abu-Akel was born, was one of the few fortunate villages that were not destroyed or depopulated. The Carmeli Brigade and the 7th Armored Brigade occupied Kafr Yasif as part of the first stage of Operation Dekel.[95] Inhabitants from three occupied and destroyed nearby villages, al-Birwa, al-Manshiyya, and Kuwaykat,[96] took refuge in Kafr Yasif. On 28 February 1949, most of them were put into trucks and driven to the front lines, where they were forced to cross the frontier border into Lebanon."[97] On March 1, another 250 refugees were deported.[98] Some residents of Kafr Yasif were able to remain in their homes. The village of Umm Aziz is al-Shaykh Dawoud, which is also in the Acre district.

From the Galilee to the American Pulpit
Fahed Abu-Akel

I arrived in America on January 29, 1966, to pursue my college and seminary education and became a naturalized American citizen in 1981. Having lived in the U.S. now for almost half a century, and looking back, I've learned that my Palestinian narrative is unfamiliar to most Americans. My story, like so many Palestinian stories, is one about a people under the colonial power and occupation of England. We experienced war, destruction of our homes and villages, exile, occupation, and oppression by the Israeli military, first in 1947-48, then in 1967, and continuing to this day. Palestinians remain an exiled and occupied people seeking freedom and independence in a state of their own in their historic ancestral land.

I was born in a small Palestinian Arab village called Kafr Yasif, 25 miles northwest of Nazareth in the Galilee area, where Jesus spent his youth. My parents were members of the Eastern Greek Orthodox Church, and our village church, constructed of beautiful Palestinian stone, is now about 800 years old. My father was a farmer and my mother focused on our spiritual journey. She wanted her eight children (five girls and three boys) to understand the faith and believe in Jesus Christ as our Lord. She wanted us to memorize Scripture, focusing on the gospels and Psalms, with special attention to the Lord's Prayer and the Nicene Creed. My mother, Adlah,

Figure 27. Rev. Fahed Abu-Akel holding his Moderator's Cross.

planted the seed of faith in our hearts, cultivating fertile spiritual ground in us for the later arrival of two Scottish Presbyterian Missionaries who rented and lived in the second floor of our home. Dr. Doris Wilson, a Scottish physician, became a key person in my life and strongly influenced my faith and my call to the gospel ministry.

A standout in my memories of Palestine, of course, are the events of 1947-48, which brought about the state of Israel for the Jews who immigrated to Palestine during the previous 40 years. That war is called by the Israeli Jews the War of Independence and is celebrated as a new beginning. By the indigenous Palestinian Arab Christians and Muslims, that war is called The Nakba, or catastrophe.

Here's what I remember about our catastrophe. In the scene in my mind's eye, I was a four-year-old child frantically running in circles around my father, five sisters, and two brothers, looking for my mother. Where was she? When I finally looked up, I saw her standing on the flat roof of our stone home, waiving her hands goodbye. She stayed behind while my father, fearing for our lives and afraid of the violence of war, took us up into the mountains to the East, to Yirka, a small Palestinian Arab village. In Yirka, we were put into a makeshift refugee tent camp. We stayed there several months, and when we could finally go back to our village, we found mother alive and still living in our home.

When I grew up, I asked my father why my mother did not come with us on that fateful day. He answered that she refused to go with him, even as we all left, and said: "Take the children and protect them. I will not leave our home. This is our land, our home, and our church, and if the Jewish soldier wants to kill me, he needs to kill me in my home as a Palestinian Arab Christian woman." She lived to the age of 86, and my father lived to age 96.

When we finally came back to our village, we found that the Israeli soldiers had already destroyed five Palestinian villages near ours. Between 1947-1949, just prior to and after statehood, Israel destroyed more than 500 Palestinian villages and towns and exiled 750,000 Palestinian Arab Christians and Muslims.[99] It is no wonder that Palestinians refer to the 1947-48 Israeli campaign of expulsion of Palestinians as the Nakba; they lost 78 percent of their land, lost their homes, their ancient orchards and olive groves, their livelihoods, and even their places of worship – their churches and Masjids (Mosques).

A way to understand the Palestinian Nakba is to take time and make an effort to understand our stories. I hope that when Americans meet Palestinian Americans who are in their 60s or older, they ask to hear their stories. Palestinians in the diaspora, the West Bank, East Jerusalem, the Gaza Strip, and Israel have their own stories reflecting their differing experiences: exile for those in the diaspora, military occupation for those in the West Bank, discriminatory laws for those in East Jerusalem and Israel, and blockade and siege for those in the Gaza strip.

In my own travels to visit friends and family, I am devastated to see the worsening situation in which these exiles and refugees are surviving. Visiting their olive groves, for example, can take an impossible and arduous effort, due to military checkpoints and separation barriers. Getting from Bethlehem to Jerusalem, a seven-mile journey, can take all day. Getting to work, school, hospital, or worship, is fraught with danger and dehumanization. But Palestinians live a life of *sumud* (steadfastness), and we persevere.

I want to say a word of thanks to God and to our Church and to my adopted country for all the blessings I received since I came to the United States. Each year I celebrate four important dates in my life in thanksgiving and praise to God.

The first date is January 29, 1966, when I came to the United States with one Bible, one dictionary, and one suitcase. Even though I was born in a place of conflict and war, I received the blessing and faith of my mother and Dr. Doris Wilson, and began my journey of faith. I arrived in the United States as an international student to study for my BA at Southeastern University in Lake, Florida. I was lucky enough to continue on to a Master of Divinity at Columbia Theological Seminary in Decatur, Georgia, and then a Doctor of Ministry at McCormick Theological Seminary. My education is a blessing that began on that January day in 1966.

The second date I celebrate is March 10, 1981, when I became an American citizen. It was the most liberating experience of my life in that I now enjoy the many blessings of freedom and liberty.

The third date I celebrate is June 15, 2004, when I was elected as the moderator of the 214th General Assembly of the Presbyterian Church (U.S.A.). What an American Triumph!

And so it follows that the fourth date I celebrate is the Fourth of July. I celebrate that day, thanking God for His goodness and blessing on every step of my journey. And as an American, I promise never to miss a local, city, county, state, or national election.

The Rev. Dr. Fahed Abu-Akel is a Presbyterian Church (USA) minister, member of the Presbytery of Greater Atlanta, Executive Director of the Atlanta Ministry with International Students, Inc. (AMIS), and Moderator of the 214th General Assembly of the Presbyterian Church (USA) 2002-2003.

I Live in a Whirlwind
Amnah Hassan Banat, "Umm Aziz"

This narrative and the pictures below are courtesy of John Halaka,[100] artist and filmmaker. In his words, "one of my objectives in developing this work is to present faces, places, and voices that will haunt the viewer long after they have walked away from my images. . . . I want my artwork to haunt the viewer with its ghosts of memory, ghosts of resistance, and ghosts of desire that characterize the spirit of the Forgotten Survivors."

Amna Bannat, known by her honorific 'Umm Aziz',[101] was born in the Village of al-Shaykh Dawoud in northern Palestine in 1930. As was not uncommon in her culture, she was married at the age of fourteen. In 1948, she was separated from her family while fleeing her village, which came under heavy Israeli mortar fire. Umm Aziz ran out of the village bare-footed carrying her two infant daughters in a metal washtub on her head. The one-month old baby was severely injured by shrapnel during the escape, and tragically both girls died during the arduous journey out of Palestine.

"After the upheavals of the Nakba, most of Umm Aziz's family managed to remain in Palestine and became internally displaced refugees in the newly declared state of Israel, but Umm Aziz could not return to her village or family and joined the columns of displaced Palestinian refugees who made their way into Lebanon. Her husband found her over a year later. They settled in Burj Al Barajneh refugee camp on the outskirts of Beirut, where they had eight more children. Four of her boys were taken from her home and her arms by Lebanese Phalange[102] forces during the Sabra and Shatila massacre in September 1982[103] and were never seen again. Thirty years after they 'disappeared,' she has still not given up hope of their return and listens for their footsteps by her window every night. During the 1985-1987 'War of the Camps,'[104] an artillery shell that fell close to Umm Aziz's home killed her husband in front of her."

Her narrative is from an interview (translated from Arabic) with John Halaka.

Figure 28. Amna Bannat. "Umm Aziz" with a picture of her four missing sons.

"I left Palestine and came here walking. If they told me I could go back to Palestine, I would tell them that I would happily return to Palestine walking. In the same way that I left Palestine and came to Lebanon walking, I would return to Palestine walking, but only after I find out the whereabouts of my children – only after they would tell me what happened to my children. I want to know if they're alive, or dead, or in prison.

"I don't know! I live in a whirlwind.

"In 1982, we were staying in this building. One day, two men entered. They asked, 'What's your religion?' We told them we are Palestinians. My children were eating; it was 8:00 a.m. They were having breakfast. They asked my son, 'What's your nationality?' He replied 'Palestinian.' They said to them all, 'Come with us, come with us, come with us.'

"They took four of my boys along with the superintendent of the building and his son. The superintendent of the building was 70 years old and had a heart operation. The papers for the surgery were still in his pocket. His son was 16 years old.

"One of my sons was 13 years old, another was 22 years old, another was 25 years old, and the oldest was 30 years old. They grabbed them and took them and put them in trucks. There were three trucks standing – waiting. They put them all in these trucks. I went towards them. My son was only in his undershirt; he wasn't even dressed in his clothes but still had his pajamas. My oldest son wasn't even wearing shoes, just flip-flops.

"After they put them in the truck I took his shirt and went towards the truck. My son was sitting with his head pushed down. He heard my footsteps and looked over towards me. One of the men went up to him on the truck and started beating him. He hit him in the face and my son started bleeding from the mouth. As he covered his mouth, the guy hit him in the stomach. My son bent over in pain and the guy pushed him out of the truck and kept on beating him.

"I am a mother. How could I watch this? How could I watch my son being brutally beaten? Not only me. This wasn't only happening to my children.

"They put them in the truck and then would go and bring four more. Then they would go and gather another five. They kept bringing more and more, until they filled all three trucks. They were so full that the men had barely enough room to stand. This went on from 8:00 in the morning until 3:30 in the afternoon. And they were in the hot August sun. The sun baked and burned them. And I was all the time frantically looking for someone to release one or two of the boys. But I couldn't find anyone to help. At 3:30 p.m. they took them and went in the direction of the airport.

"There were Israelis, Lahad Army [South Lebanon Army], and Lebanese forces present. The truck that they placed my sons in had a military insignia of the Lebanese Army on it. Where they took them, to whom they gave them, and where they put them, only God knows.

"From that time until today, I've been searching for them and going to vigils and demonstrations. I must have paved new roads with my feet while looking for them. But all of my efforts have been to no avail.

"I never celebrate a holiday. My sons have been missing for 29 years. These 29 years each had two holidays. I could not celebrate Eid El Adha, or Eid El Fitr, or the New Year or any other holiday. On holidays, those who have relatives celebrate with them. Those who have a dead person in the cemetery can visit their graves. Those who have a relative in prison can go and see them. Who can I visit? I am lost! Who am I to visit!

"I petition my case to God!

"I petition my case to God!

"I petition my case to you my beloved God!

"May God bless your life! [Addressed to John Halaka.] And I pray to God, that all who have loved ones who are prisoners of war, all who have a missing loved one, please, God, return them to their parents. This is what I hope for, even before my sons are returned to me.

"I want them to return before I die, so I can put two by my side and the other two by the other side. So I can smell them and live one week with them. And then I can die.

"Please God! I don't want to die before I see my sons return.

"When I sit to pray, I see them in front of me. When I sit to eat, I see them in front of me. What am I supposed to do? You think I could ever forget them? I can never forget them. I cannot. My husband was killed but he was still a young man. Death is inevitable. When he died we buried him. I know where he is buried. I can offer a drink for the blessing of his soul, but I can't do that for my sons.

"I am lost and don't know if they're dead or alive.

"May God almighty forgive me! May God almighty forgive me!

"If I knew that we would not be able to return if we left, I would not have left even if they destroyed the house on top of me. As long as we are homeless we are called refugees. We are not citizens. We are called refugees. We have no value in society. We are denied our dignity.

"We were better off in our homeland – even if we were beggars there. Our homeland is bountiful and prosperous and full of generosity. When we lived in Palestine, if you [talking to John Halaka] had olive and fig trees, and I didn't have any, I would take a large basket and select the olives that I wanted from your trees. You would come, greet me and say, 'May God give you strength.' I would tell you that I've come to pick some olives for pickling, and you would say, 'Pick what you want and enjoy them in good health. Try that tree over there, it's even better.' If I would come to pick some of your figs, you would tell me, that fig tree over there is a good one; 'Pick what you want, Umm Aziz.'

"We were prosperous. We lived our lives like 'Ba'al' plants. Do you know what is 'Ba'al'? If someone is planting vegetables without water we refer to them as 'Ba'al.' Those vegetables had a distinct flavor because they grew without water. Without irrigation they don't grow well. They don't grow large. Vegetables that are irrigated grow and taste differently. Our lives, now, are like those Ba'al vegetables. We live without irrigation.

"This is how we live. We endure and survive with patience. But the injustices we face are against God's way. Injustices against the human soul are against God's will.

"I raised my children and then they took them away in one day? How long were they in my womb? How much effort did I put in raising them? How much they have grown and worked and suffered in deprivation, until I built them houses and they got married.

"And suddenly I lost them and not only them, but their future wives, their children, and their father. Who can endure this painful load? No one can endure it.

"What can I do?"

Questions for Reflection

1. Palestinian refugees represent an estimated ten per cent of the population of Lebanon. They do not enjoy several important rights; for example, they cannot work in as many as 20 professions. Because they are not formally citizens of another state, Palestinian refugees are unable to claim the same rights as other foreigners living and working in Lebanon. Among the five United Nations Relief and Works Agency (UNRWA) fields, Lebanon has the highest percentage of Palestine refugees living in abject poverty.[105] Contrast the life of Rev. Abu-Akel with that of Umm Aziz and discuss the different opportunities available to each. What are the responsibilities of the international community in regard to Palestinian refugees, particularly the United States and Great Britain, who support Israel in spite of its continued violation of international laws?

2. Under international law, refugees have a right to return to their homes. Umm Aziz expresses the wish to return to Palestine. How would her life be different if she could return to her village and live within the security of her community?

3. The suffering of Umm Aziz and the loss of her four sons is part and parcel of the continued mistreatment of Palestinian refugees. There have been several massacres in Lebanon: Tel al-Zaatar in 1976 and Sabra and Shatila in 1982 are but two examples. The Israeli military (IDF) was implicated in the Sabra and Shatila refugee camps massacres, which killed, it is estimated, between 700 and 3,000 Palestinians. What are the implications of the Right of Return in regards to solving the refugee problem?

III. Art and Culture

Liberation Art of Palestine.

A history of the unique efflorescence of art accompanying the Palestinian uprising of the 1970s and the Intifada of the 1980s.[1]

By Samia A. Halaby

Palestinian artists live the tragedy and heroism of the liberation struggle. Many experienced repeated exile and loss of homes or studios. Many spent decades of their lives in refugee camps. The majority of Palestinians who took refuge in the Arab world, artists among them, live within 100 kilometers of the borders of Mandate Palestine, thus encircling the homeland and hoping for return. Artists who remained under direct Israeli rule after 1948 also experienced severe economic oppression and racist exclusion that harmed their development. Just as artists live the tragedy, they also live the heroism of resistance. They organize schools, nurseries, clinics, museums, galleries, and much more. They serve the multiple roles of art historians, administrators, teachers, or critics as well as artists. Furthermore, many have spent time in prison. The charges leading to imprisonment may have been as absurd as the artist using the colors of the Palestinian flag in a painting, such colors being prohibited by Israeli military order. The Liberation art of Palestine developed simultaneously wherever Palestinians lived, but there were two major centers. One was in the city of Beirut, Lebanon, during the 1970s, and the second period, known as the Intifada, centered in the West Bank and Gaza during the 1980s.

Artists of the Early Twentieth Century

Artists who practiced during the first decades of the twentieth century formed the bedrock on which the Liberation artists built. Many had shops in old city sections where church patronage was available, as in Jerusalem, Nazareth, and Bethlehem. Nicola Sayegh (1888-1942) had such a shop near the Church of the Holy Sepulcher in Jerusalem. Young artists and collectors are known to have frequented the shop, including artist Daoud Zalatimo (1906-1998), whose teaching was important to the Liberation artists.[2]

Participation by women in the arts was substantial during the entire century. They numbered almost one-third of all artists. Women began to participate more actively in the atmosphere of hope prior to the Palestinian revolt of the 1930s against British colonialism. In July 1933, a young Palestinian woman, Zulfa Saadi (1910-1988), held a one-artist show at the Inter-Arab National Fair in Jerusalem – the city which is the heart of the entire Arab world.

Daoud Zalatimo focused on secular subjects and paid special attention to the heroes and events of Arabic history. This focus coincides with the period of the 1930s and the transformation of society, through revolution, to more liberal attitudes. While the Church and tourism supported the icon painters, Zalatimo supported himself by teaching. Jamal Badran (1909-1999) was another important artist who is widely known for his Arabic geometric abstractions and calligraphy.

A towering artist in the area of photography was Hanna Safieh (1910-1979), who was born in Jerusalem. Safieh captured the uprising of the 1930s as well as the 1948 struggle between the civilian population of Palestine and the combined forces of the Zionist and British military. Working for the British colonial government, he had opportunities to document the historic events surrounding him.

Safieh's photograph of 1938, *Searching for Weapons*, reveals his documentary skill and insight.[3] In one of his photographs, a British soldier wearing an army summer uniform of shorts, knee-high socks, and helmet, searches a Palestinian wearing a fez, winter jacket, and long pants. The difference in dress reveals the cultural gap between the two. In a society that values modesty, foreign occupiers in shorts were, at the very least, disrespectful. This incident, which took place in Jerusalem near the Jaffa Gate (Bab Al Khalil), was a typically colonialist scene of oppression. Safieh also photographed the massacre at Dayr Yasin, committed by the Zionist Lehi and Stern Gangs against Palestinian villagers on April 9, 1948, in which over 100 innocent civilians were butchered. He was there on the following day to photograph the scene, before the bodies were removed.[4]

One of Safieh's main subjects was documentation of people at work. Many pictures of shopkeepers, fishermen, and peasant workers date from the 1930s and 1940s. He also documented the religious practice of Palestinians of the Christian, Jewish, and Islamic faiths. Most unusual are the pictures of Palestinian Jews – the Samaritans – celebrating Passover in the city of Nablus. These photographs were taken during the early 1950s, long before the Israeli occupation of 1967. The turbaned and white-robed Jews look natural praying in the streets of Nablus.[5]

Aesthetic Background in Liberation Art of the Twentieth Century

Palestinians have had a long history of cultural development. They live intimately with their ancient monuments, often located within or just outside the borders of their towns or villages.[6] Their sense of being an enduring part of the land of Palestine and its ancient sites is coupled with sincere awe of its beauty. The making of pictorial and sculptural images in many media, such as mural, icons, mosaic, bas-relief, ceramics, weaving, embroidery, and tapestry, existed in Palestine earlier than the 1st millennium BC.[7] Indeed, mural paintings from as early as the 7th millennium BC have been discovered on the eastern shores of the river Jordan. It is also noteworthy that the very first icons of Christianity were most likely made in Palestine; some of them are preserved at the Monastery of St. Catherine in the Negev Desert.[8]

One can discern a sense of aesthetic continuity with the land expressed in the pathways of the city and its public architecture. From the terraced mountains through city doorways, streets, and town squares is a smooth transition and gradual buildup culminating in a mosque's dome. Such is the power of Palestinian Arab aesthetics that television newscasters show the Dome of The Rock as a symbol even when they are talking on behalf of the occupier, Israel. The Dome of The Rock is not only the landmark and center of Jerusalem but also of Palestine.

Aesthetic Boldness

While the two periods of Palestinian Liberation art rely on history and aesthetics, they owe a great debt to revolutionary creativity. In an article published during the days just prior to the first Intifada (1987), leading artists Vera Tamari and Sliman Mansour describe how early exhibitions in Gaza and the West Bank during the 1970s were wildly popular and how poster reproductions of paintings were hallowed possessions in the poorest, remotest villages. People came to group exhibitions full of questions and anxious to converse. Mansour and Tamari write, "To most people this art was the ultimate expression of patriotic commitment. The aesthetic value of the works was secondary."[9] This comment reveals the power of revolutionary creativity, when artists feel that something larger than themselves guides their hand.

Among the Liberation artists of Palestine, an aesthetic attitude developed that to serve their cause they would have to create a new Palestinian art capable of speaking clearly to their own people. They would base this work on the historic forms of Arabic art and on the radical traditions of the Twentieth century. Furthermore, artists sought subjects and symbols directly meaningful to the Palestinian masses.

Subjects and Symbols

Seeking safety from the Israeli aggression of 1948, most Palestinian families locked their homes when they left, expecting to return in a few weeks. As refugees today, they continue to wait and hope for return. In their stubborn resolve to return, most Palestinian families pass the key to their home down from generation to generation. Thus the key became a major symbol of the Right of Return.

Idyllic scenes of pastoral life in Palestine reveal a yearning for the beautiful homeland. These scenes afford escape from the painful reality of life in refugee camps.

Alternately, renditions of the reality of the camps were a cry against displacement and a reason to fight. Artist Ibrahim Ghannam (1930-1984) painted some of the most exquisite scenes of Palestinian pastoral life. The paintings' abundant detail and naïve clarity speak to everyone. He painted these scenes during the 1970s while living in a refugee camp in Beirut and confined to a wheelchair.

Hannoun, the wild Palestinian poppy, represented the blood of fallen fighters. In literature and in painting, where the blood of the fallen heroes touched the ground, tender shoots would grow, symbolizing the birth of new fighters.

An image of the human eye creates an aesthetic shock when first noticed in Palestinian Liberation art. The eye signifies that the artist and the world of the painting are looking back at viewers. Painter Muhamad Al Wahibi (b. 1947) said, "We Palestinians, knowing the world is watching us suffer, let those who watch know that we watch them back – we understand."[10]

The eye also symbolizes awareness and learning. The artist Khalil Rayan (b. 1946), who has lived with Israeli oppression all his life in Palestine 48[11] described the several extra eyes he placed on the face of a woman reading a newspaper. Rayan said, "The eyes represent the need for Palestinians to study many times harder than everyone else in order to gain liberation."[12]

Artist Fayez Sersawi (b. 1961) points out that the Intifada is a confrontation between a military force armed with advanced weapons and a Palestinian population armed only with their will power.[13] Unlike artists of the uprising in Beirut of the 1980s, Intifada artists do not use symbols of armed struggle. They use symbols of lesser confrontation – graffiti and stones. Graffiti, composed of political messages, covered walls in city and village, and to the population, these walls were known as radical newspapers. In scribbling their messages, youth play a dangerous cat-and-

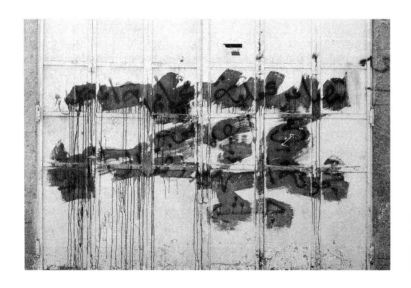

Figure 29. Graffiti on closed shop door inside the old city walls of Jerusalem.

128

mouse game with the occupying Israeli forces. Not able to stop the youth, the Israeli soldiers order any passerby – including senior citizens – to cover the graffiti with paint (Fig. 29) . Yet, overnight, the walls are again covered with messages.

To Palestinians in exile, justice meant their right to return home so as to escape their painful homelessness, while to Palestinians still in Palestine, justice meant their right to live free of oppression on their home soil. In using the sun as a symbol of justice, artists calculated that sunlight lifts the pall of dark injustice cast by Israel. Palestinian men, women, and children experience imprisonment and torture almost universally. Themes of liberation from prison, along with an overwhelming desire for the surcease from torture, are everywhere in Palestinian art. Stock symbols in the art created by prisoners are iron bars, the extended hand, the bared chest, the dove of hope, barbed wire, the lit candle, the tearful eye, and letters from home.

Art of the Uprising from its Beginning in the 1950s to the 1970s in Beirut

Born in Lydd, Ismail Shammout (1931-2006) had the good fortune as a youth to study with Daoud Zalatimo. His training was formal and included perspective and shading, practice in still life, and landscape painting. Zalatimo's influence shows itself in the representational style of Shammout's paintings. The emotional message relies on the facial expressions and body gestures of his subjects. In Shammout's work, thematic content does not rely on symbolism but rather on realism. At age sixteen he persuaded his reluctant father that he could earn a living making art. His father provided him with materials and a space to work. Just one year after this beginning, the Nakba occurred. Shammout organized his first exhibit in 1950 in the refugee camp.

In 1953, after three years of study in Cairo, Shammout returned to Gaza and exhibited sixty paintings at the Workers Club. Because of the exhibition's timing, it seemed to initiate the Liberation art movement. Among the exhibited works was a painting of the massacre at Al-Lydd titled, *Where To?* (Fig. 30), showing a troubled old man with small children walking in the wilderness. Another painting titled, *A sip of Water*, shows the horrific conditions of the enforced march through the wilderness which followed the massacre at Al-Lydd (see Narratives-Al Ramla District, Fig. 16).

Other paintings picture groups carrying bundles and holding tightly to their children. They objectify and socialize a pain that had simmered on a private level. Refugees of Gaza saw themselves mirrored and felt relief. The immense attendance of the general population of Gaza at the exhibition overwhelmed Ismail Shammout, still then a student in Egypt. This stunning response to the show was a hint of the bottled up hope for liberation. In response, Shammout committed his life's work to the art of liberation. The Gaza exhibition marked the beginning of the Liberation movement in its artistic form and was followed by a flood of individual and group shows by a new generation of artists.[14]

Shammout returned to Cairo to finish his schooling. There he took the leading part in an exhibition in which he showed 55 paintings.[15] It was known as the Palestine Exhibition of 1954, and Egyptian president Jamal Abdal Nasser officially opened it. The exhibition was widely attended and received extensive media coverage in the Arab world.[16]

Between Shammout's exhibition in 1953 and the 1967 war, activism and optimism permeated the West Bank and Gaza, and spread to Amman. All these areas were then under Jordanian Arab sovereignty. Artists and revolutionaries traveled freely, spreading their ideas. The iron curtains of Israeli closure were not yet in effect. By the late 1950s a hot center of activity developed in Jerusalem, where young artists began to congregate and study. Art patroness Amineh El Husseini promoted young artists and helped them to organize themselves into a club. Shammout, by then active in Jerusalem, said: "Amineh loved art and artists. She rented a house and created the Association of Painting and Sculpture. Young artists came to talk and to work."[17] These artists exhibited together in Ramallah, Jerusalem, and Amman. The liberal atmosphere is revealed by the large percentage of women who participated. [18]

After study in Egypt and Italy, Shammout returned to the West Bank with his artist wife, Tamam Al Akhal (b. 1935), and lived in the town of Al Bireh. In 1966, when Israel attacked the village of Samooh, Palestinians responded with a mini

Figure 30. Ismail Shammout. *Where To?*, 1953. Oil on canvas. 47 x 37 in, 120 x 95 cm.

Intifada. The Jordanian authority, then in control of the West Bank, responded by jailing members of the resistance movement. Fearing arrest, Shammout and Akhal fled to Beirut and remained there until 1982. They were made refugees yet again when in 1982 the Israeli bombing of Beirut drove them out. They moved to Kuwait. Then the 1991 United States war against Iraq forced them out of Kuwait, and they moved to Amman, where Akhal now lives.

The artistic and life partner of Ismail Sahmmout, Tamam Al Akhal developed her own style and paints in the symbolist manner of the Liberation artists. In *Scent of Return* (Fig. 31), Akhal combines many different views in order to dramatize two realities. In this case, one reality is that of the present painful condition of refugees yearning for return, and the other is a joyful return home. The yearning refugees are a dense crowd in dark-blue monochrome, while the scenes of return are in full color. The refugees rushing home hold peace offerings of roses and olive branches. In the colorful scenes after return, the streets of old Jaffa are full of children playing games wearing their best clothes. Children begin attending school normally. One woman is joyfully ululating at the return. An orange and an olive tree representing two peoples grow next to one another. Beneath the two trees is a family picnicking. Akhal said that early in the 1990s, she was naïve enough to believe that Oslo might bring peace. It was then that she made the painting.[19]

Figure 31. Tamam Al Akhal.
Scent of Return, 1994. Oil on
Canvas. 31 x 39 in, 80 x 100 cm.

Artist-fighter Abdal Rahman al Mozayen (b. 1943) practiced his art during both the movement in Beirut and the Intifada. He believes that Liberation art must be honest and beautiful. He affirms, "We must show all our experiences honestly and we can even show massacre to children, but it must not frighten them. It must be done in a way that informs and gives rest." About the drawings he is completing on the massacre at Jenin of April 2002, he said: "When we draw the tragedies we experience, we must not depress our people. We must help them to recover and renew their resolve to fight for liberation."[20]

During the mid 1980s, Mozayen painted a series of Palestinian women in embroidered dresses – a series that was popular and satisfied the general wish to stress identity. Mozayen wanted to celebrate the beauty of Palestinian women. In *Hope and Return* (Fig. 32), Mozayen paints a typical Palestinian face and places on her head a man and a woman sitting back-to-back playing the flute. The flute recalls the happy days of pastoral life before the Nakba. But Palestinians know that the flute and its tune symbolize the intention to continue the struggle for liberation.

Mustafa Al Hallaj (1938-2003) was born in Salama, near Jaffa, "I was ten at the time of the Nakba in 1948," he said, "and we escaped first to Lydd, then to Ramallah, then Damascus, then Beirut, then Egypt. All in one year!"[21] While studying art in Egypt, Hallaj was deeply affected by ancient Egyptian bas-reliefs. He first became

Figure 32. Abdal Rahman al Mozayen. *Hope and Return*, 1986. Oil on canvas. 31 x 24 in, 80 x 60 cm.

a sculptor, though his favorite and most powerful medium is the Masonite cut. The horse as symbol of the revolution first appeared in his work. He combined the new symbols of the revolution with those of ancient art and popular folklore. In his prints, images of people, animals, and objects are flattened, their contours simplified, and their details removed. Like other early Liberation artists, Hallaj used the dove standing at the mouth of a gun barrel to call for peace through successful liberation (Fig. 33).

Liberation Artist Inside the Green Line Under Direct Israeli Rule

Abed Abdi was born in Palestine in the northern city of Haifa in 1942. He was six years old when the violence of the 1948 Nakba divided his family. While his father remained in Haifa, Abdi's mother wandered with him and his siblings from refugee camp to refugee camp in Lebanon and Syria. Life in refugee camps just after 1948 was extremely painful. After three years of separation and displacement they were able to return to Haifa, where his father had stubbornly remained during the Israeli attacks and massacres. By then Abdi was nine years old. "Maybe four years after my return (to Haifa), I realized that I had a tendency towards art resulting from troubles. I did not live a happy childhood. The socially and politically restricted

Figure 33. Mustafa Al Hallaj. *Battle of Al Karameh*, 1969. Masonite cut. 12 x 16 in, 31 x 41.5 cm.

Figure 34. Abed Abdi and Gershon Knispel. *Nasb al-Tizkari*, memorial sarcophagus for the six martyrs of the Day of the Land, 1978. Cement and aluminum.

environment led me to question why things were as they were, why was my sister in exile, why are there wars, why are there closed borders and as a result I realized that I needed creativity, a spiritual need, and it was perhaps a language of expression available to me."[22]

The sculpture *Nasb al-Tiskari* (Fig. 34) is a memorial sarcophagus for the six martyrs of the massacre of Palestinian demonstrators on March 30, 1976. The massacre started when the Israeli government announced the expropriation of over 5,000 acres of agricultural land near the villages of Sakhnin and Arraba, Israel.[23] It was the time of the first Intifada, a time of high revolutionary spirit. Thus when the Communist Party and Palestinian organizations called for protests, the population responded enthusiastically. During the demonstrations, in addition to the six protesters who were killed, over 100 were wounded and a massive number arrested. The event echoed among Palestinian activists worldwide.

In concert with the high spirits of the time, Abed Abdi, in partnership with his Communist Party comrade Israeli artist Gershon Knispel (b. 1932), completed a monument to be erected in the heart of Sakhnin, the village where most of the demonstrations had taken place. Since this was not allowed by Israel, the monument was erected, instead, in the town's graveyard in 1978. It is sculpted in the form of a sarcophagus as a tomb for the six martyrs. The commemoration of this event as the Palestine Day of the Land is marked internationally; in Galilee it takes place at the graveyard around the memorial.

Liberation Artists of the Intifada in Prison

Hundreds of thousands of Palestinians, including children, have spent time in Israeli prisons, and many have undergone severe torture, isolation, and denial of all rights. There developed a Palestinian genre of art in sympathy with prisoners, and,

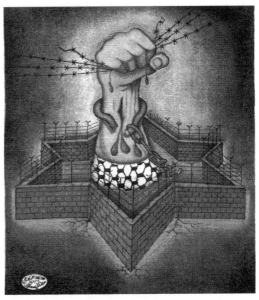

Figure 35. Zuhdi Al Adawi. *Day of the Prisoner*, 1984. Crayons on cloth. 17 x 12 in, 43 x 30.5 cm.

Figure 36. Muhammad Al Rakoui. *Day of the Palestinian Prisoner*, 1984. Crayon on paper. 15 x 13 in, 38 x 32 cm.

more importantly, an art of the Palestinian prisoner. Several prisoner artists were detained at Askalan, where four of them formed an art cell.[24]

Artist Zuhdi Al Adawi was born in 1952 in Nusairat refugee camp in Gaza, where his parents had settled after their forced eviction from Al-Lydd in 1948. He grew up with his parents' memories of the traumatic march through the wilderness forced on them by Zionist soldiers, (see Narratives -Ramla District). With the 1967 war of occupation, Adawi joined the freedom fighters. He was captured and imprisoned at Askalan in 1970 and remained there until 1985.

Self taught, Adawi worked on handkerchiefs using sour milk as medium and any color crayon he could find. When handkerchiefs were unavailable, he cut out pieces of his pillow covers. He said that whenever the guards discovered them, they would place the artists in solitary confinement for one full week.[25] Family members smuggled some supplies in, and pictures folded like small handkerchiefs were smuggled out. These smuggled artworks of Palestinian political prisoners were exhibited widely during the Intifada. One such exhibition took place at the Soviet Cultural Center in Damascus one month before Adawi left prison. After the exhibitions became known, prison authorities began to search visitors thoroughly, and Adawi had to invent new ways to smuggle his art out

In the *Day of the Prisoner* (Fig. 35), Adawi combines symbols of imprisonment and patriotism into a coherent image. Through handcuffs and prison bars there appears a woman whose hair is arranged in the colors of the revolutionary flag.

She wears a red kufiyye, a scarf symbolic of the Palestinian revolution. Arched doorways, a flame, lightning, crowds of people, chains, and the cactus plant, the latter symbolizing patience and endurance, complete the picture.

Muhammad Al Rakoui was born in 1950 in Al Shat refugee camp in Gaza, just 25 kilometers south of the ancient city of Askalan, where his parents had lived until being evicted in 1948. Muhammad studied art in Gaza and afterward began to teach in the Gaza school system. Muhammad channeled his anger at the bitter life of the refugee into organized resistance. He became a fighter at seventeen and successfully carried on until the age of twenty-three, at which time he was captured in Gaza and imprisoned. He remembers the intensity of torture during the first three months. Though it continued throughout his imprisonment, its intensity did diminish. His first three months were spent confined to a 1 x 2 meter cell. This confinement included beating and hanging from one wrist. He remembers the screaming – his own and that of others. He remembers being forced to undress suddenly in winter and having cold water poured over him, followed by scalding hot water.[26]

Rakoui's years in prison, 1973-1985, were the years of revolutionary struggle in Beirut and the pre-Intifada years in Palestine. He said: "My prison mates wanted each painting to be directly about Palestine. The gun, the sun, and liberty, symbolized by the eagle, were important to them. In 1984, they asked me to paint the eight martyrs killed at Al-Aqsa mosque."[27] In 1985, after nearly thirteen years in prison, Rakoui was finally released through a prisoner exchange agreement, on condition that he leave Palestine.

Rakoui gives symbols a sharp clarity by surrounding groups of them with a halo. Handcuffs, the Palestinian flag, the two-finger sign of victory for the revolution, barbed wire, the eagle breaking his chains, the Dome of the Rock, Palestinian village embroidery, the kufiyye, the fisted arm raised in determination (Fig. 36), the peasant dress, the village, prison bars, birds in the colors of the revolutionary flag, the horse as symbol of the revolution, and many other such images are artfully combined to speak the language of Palestinian resistance.

Liberation Artist of the Intifada in the West Bank

Artist Sliman Mansour was born in Birzeit in 1947 and is unusual in that he is as active a painter as he is an organizer. He began painting during the 1960s, wanting to be very Arabic in identity. In the 1970s, he narrowed this goal, seeking to reflect contemporary surroundings in Palestine. He was in effect shifting with the political atmosphere, itself departing from the limitations of Arab nationalism, and growing into working-class uprisings.

In his painting *U.N. Relief* (Fig. 37) Mansour makes a visual allusion to a theme found in both the Bible and the Koran — the flight to Egypt. He paints a Palestinian mother kneeling on the side of a modern highway holding her infant in her arms. A loaf of flat bread on her lap symbolizes the only help she receives from the United

Figure 37. Sliman Mansour. *U. N. Relief*, 1984. Oil on canvas, 31 x 24 in, 80 x 60 cm.

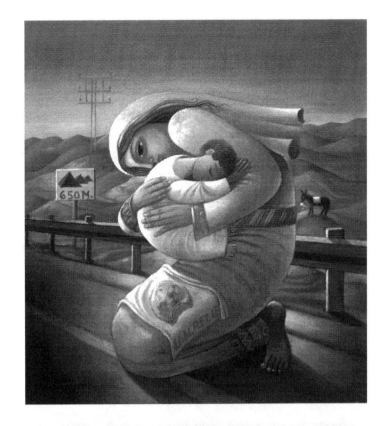

Figure 38. Sliman Mansour. *The Village Awakens*, 1988. Oil on canvas, 35 x 45 in, 90 x 115 cm.

Nations after losing her home, her family, and her country. A road sign next to her records a distance to a destination as a number, which, according to Mansour, might be one more United Nations resolution. The triangles on the sign allude to the pyramids of Egypt, and simultaneously signify the tents of the refugee camps.

Perhaps the archetypal painting of the Intifada is *The Village Awakens* (Fig. 38). In it Mansour depicts a Palestinian woman sitting on the ground in peasant style amidst symbols of the village and resistance.[28] From between her thighs emerges the population, a veritable river of people. Symbols of peasant crafts surround her, while domes and cubes symbolize the peasant village behind her. Variation in scale serves the narrative, along with shifts in time and place.

Questions for Reflection

1. The author tells us that Palestinian artists live the tragedy and heroism of the liberation struggle. Can you give examples from the art exhibited in this chapter of the tragedy of Palestinian life, its heroism, and it steadfastness?

2. When you look at the monument created by Abed Abdi, in partnership with his Communist Party comrade, Israeli artist Gershon Knispel, what do you think created the basis for collaboration between a Palestinian and an Israeli?

3. Look at Figure 36, a picture drawn on a pillowcase by Zuhdi Al Adawi while in an Israeli prison. In your own word summarize what the symbolic images narrate. Similarly look at Figure 37 by Muhammad Al Rakoui, called Day of the Palestinian Prisoner, and discuss the symbolism.

4. Look at Figures 38 and 39, and see how they express through symbolism the pain, hope, and steadfastness of the Palestinian people.

5. As a cross cultural exercise, can you imagine a painting in the style of the Palestinian Intifada using symbols to visually explain a tragedy in your own life or in the lives of victims of racism and elitism?

The Origins of Traditional Palestinian Costume

Hanan Karaman Munayyer[29]

Textile arts have been of unique importance in the Middle East since antiquity. In every age, the crafts of spinning, weaving, dyeing, and embroidery have been held in high esteem, and their traditions have survived over time. This is demonstrated eloquently in Palestinian costume, whose tradition evolved slowly, with the introduction of one component at a time over many centuries.

Around 1500 BC, the land that would later be called Palestine was known as Canaan, the "Land of Purple," famous for the precious purple dye extracted from murex sea snails on its shores. Its inhabitants used this rare extract to dye linen and wool, producing textiles that were prized trade items around the Mediterranean.

Textiles were once central to the economies of the Middle East. The development of highly intricate silk textiles woven in the workshops of the Sassanian[30] kings competed with those from the workshops of the Byzantine emperor. The Byzantine emperors gradually adopted the rich tradition of costume decoration from Mesopotamia and the Levant. Clergy in Jerusalem, a spiritual center of the Byzantine Empire, wore robes heavily woven with metallic thread, a stylistic feature that survives in some Eastern churches to this day.

The period of Muslim Arab rule that followed the Byzantine era in the seventh century witnessed a flourishing of the textile arts. Weavers combined the Byzantine and Persian legacies and elaborated on them. The Arabs introduced a style of ornamentation called tiraz, meaning embroidery, which incorporated Arabic calligraphy into the patterns. Many manuscript illustrations of that era present the costume of both men and women as a long robe with wide bands of embroidered Arabic calligraphy at the upper sleeves. These robes were sometimes inscribed with the name of the ruler (which helps in dating them) and sometimes they were robes of honor that the ruler bestowed on his dignitaries. These robes were made from sumptuous patterned silks, which would limit them to the wealthy and the ruling class. For the average person, robes of linen, not silk, were the norm, and they were decorated with colorful woven patterned bands; in the ninth century, weaving was replaced by embroidery to decorate the fabric.

The medieval Arab world, stretching from Baghdad to Granada, was a leader in the production of textiles, in both volume and magnificence. The weaving and embroidery expertise introduced into Andalusian Spain and Sicily by the Umayyad Arab rulers during the eighth century was subsequently passed on to the rest of Europe, where it was influential in the development of textile centers in Italy and France.

Remnants of finely embroidered ninth-century linen fabrics have been found in Egypt with geometric patterns that recreate the woven designs known from earlier eras. This delicate embroidery became possible because of finer needles, whose appearance coincides with improved steel-manufacturing techniques of the famous Damascus swords. These geometric embroidery motifs from the eighth century are the precursors of those seen on Palestinian dresses from the nineteenth century.

Embroidery using metallic-thread couching is also seen in Arab embroideries from the Fatimid and Mamluk eras (tenth to fifteenth centuries) in Egypt. By the Ottoman period, the fifteenth to early twentieth centuries, couching was a widely used technique, with workshops busy embroidering the annual cover for the Ka'aba in Mecca, costumes for high officials, and bridal dresses in cities all over the Empire. In Palestine, it was used on formal costumes for government officials, on clerical robes, and on dresses of the wives of Ottoman officials. The women of the Bethlehem area incorporated this technique into their traditional dresses, using a combination of colorful silk thread with some metallic thread. The style eventually spread to the surrounding areas of Jerusalem, Jaffa, and beyond.

By the end of the fourteenth century, the main features of a slowly evolving basic traditional style of Palestine had been established. Robes found in Arab-ruled Spain dating from the thirteenth century have the same cut, the same square chest piece, and the same decorated back panel as many Palestinian dresses, implying that a common Arab style had developed in the eastern Mediterranean that was shared with Andalusian Spain. The development of the cut and style of the traditional Palestinian costume is one of two separate elements that defined its origin; the other is the history of the embroidery patterns that are used to decorate it. Both elements are rooted in antiquity.

Though every woman could express her creativity by some choice of patterns, each region of Palestine followed distinctive stylistic rules that were a badge of identity. In festivals or the marketplace, the dress a woman was wearing identified her as being from a specific region and was a great source of pride.

Embroidery of costume and home accessories was done by women who preserved the traditional patterns by copying older dresses and passing them on from mother to daughter for generations. In so doing they created costumes of lasting beauty that have earned a special place among the ethnic folk-dress traditions of the world. More significantly, this tradition of Palestinian needlework has kept alive ancient styles and symbols that give us a unique window to the past.

Development of the Robe

The earliest illustrated record of Eastern Mediterranean costume is found on archaeological ruins. From Egyptian Pharaonic times, images survive of highly decorated Canaanites paying tribute. Their clothing style was distinct from other concurrent communities and even then was used as a badge of identity.

One of the earliest styles recorded is a long A-shaped dress worn by both men and women and known to modern archaeologists as the "Syrian tunic." An ivory engraving dating from 1200 BC, from Megiddo in ancient Palestine, depicts similar tunics decorated at the neckline and hem. This long A-shaped tunic is still the basic shape of most Palestinian costumes.

The tunic worn all around the Mediterranean basin by men and women from the first century AD (or perhaps earlier), called the "dalmatic" by European historians, is the clearest precedent of the Palestinian robe. The dalmatic tunic is also misnamed "Coptic" in current European literature, because many were initially excavated in Egypt; however, their use was not restricted to the Copts in Egypt but was widespread all over the eastern Mediterranean region, as documented in early regional mosaics and frescoes. The dalmatic was worn in Rome in 220 AD by the Syrian-born Emperor Elagabalus and was frequently depicted in Byzantine mosaics and early Christian paintings. It is seen in engravings from Egypt and Syria, and is depicted in ancient mosaics found in Palestine and Jordan. This ancient robe was made from linen woven in one piece, then sewn to form a loose-fitting robe decorated with two purple stripes or woven bands of decoration, called "clavi," and which had a small decorated chest piece.

Toward the eighth century AD, the chest piece became larger. The clavi stripes were usually woven as part of the fabric or tapestry-woven and added to the tunic. That general style is very similar to the twentieth-century Palestinian dress from Majdal.

The two purple lines seen in twentieth-century Palestinian dress of the coastal area of Majdal is a style that survived from the first century AD or before, is also seen in seventh-century dress from Egypt, and is described by a European traveler in 1743. In nineteenth-century Palestine, this fabric was used in several regions. The two stripes were woven vertically into the fabric at its edges and used in the dress as two vertical lines going down the front and back, with added stripes in the side panels.

Starting from the ninth century, counted-stitch embroidery was added to the linen robe instead of the woven patterned bands, as seen on numerous textiles excavated from that era at The Textile Museum in Washington, DC.

The Cut of the Palestinian Robe

According to Max Tilke, an authority on international traditional costume, the cut of a traditional item of clothing is an important indication of its historical origins. The cut of most of the Palestinian robes of the nineteenth and twentieth centuries is identical. They were made of hand-woven linen, sometimes with two colored longitudinal bands at the edge, that was 13 to 17 inches (34 to 44 cm) wide and sold in pieces called maqta, about 9 yards (8 meters) long. The robe was formed of two loom-width pieces of linen running the length of the front and back, with the two bands at the edge and with extra fabric added at the sides to provide more width. The square or rectangular chest piece and added sleeves complete the robe.

This typical traditional cut is seen in Egypt and Syria from the eleventh to the fifteenth centuries during the Ayyubid and Mamluk eras and in Andalusian Spain.

The construction of the Andalusian robe is not only similar to the Palestinian robe with its central panels and side additions but also features a lower back panel woven with an intricate pattern of metallic thread, just like the back panel of the Bethlehem dress in figure 40.

Andalusian tunics from the tenth to the thirteenth century show an intricately woven chest piece, confirming the continuity of the tradition of a chest piece on tunics of the eastern Mediterranean from as far back as the second century AD and earlier. That the tradition continues into the nineteenth and twentieth centuries in Palestine is plain to see in this dress from Beit Dajan (Fig. 41).

The Origins of Palestinian Headdresses

Headdresses are also an important component of Palestinian women's costumes. Some of these headdress styles have survived since antiquity. Canaanite women from antiquity wore a large cloak-like veil. It was later worn over an elevated headdress, very similar to those seen in statues found all over the Roman Empire and on the sarcophagi engravings in Palmyra, Syria, from the sixth to the eighth centuries AD. This style of large veils wrapped over headdresses and long tunics is abundantly

Figure 39. Bethlehem dress. Nineteenth century.

Figure 40. Back of Bethlehem dress. Nineteenth century.

Figure 41. Palestinian dress from Beit Dajan. Nineteenth century.

depicted in Byzantine icons of the Madonna and other women in Biblical scenes and is replicated to this day in Christian iconography. The general profile of the women's attire throughout those centuries was very similar to the nineteenth- and early twentieth-century Palestinian dress, with the long dress and high headdress underneath a large veil.

The headdress of Bethlehem, called shatweh, goes back to antiquity, as seen in several statues, engravings, and mosaics. An ivory bust of a Canaanite woman dating back to the twelfth century BC (Fig. 42) and a third-century AD sarcophagus carving (Fig. 43) have a strong resemblance to the Palestinian shatweh worn by married women in Bethlehem (Figs. 44 and 45) until the early twentieth century. In nineteenth-century Palestine, the shatweh was a wider, lower headdress than that worn in the early twentieth

Figure 42. Ivory bust from Ugarit, Syria. 1200 BC. Courtesy Saudi Aramco World.

Figure 43. Sarcophagus carving of headdress similar to shatweh, Palmyra, Syria. Third century AD. Courtesy of Palmyra Museum, Syria.

Figure 44. Bethlehem woman. 1925. Bethlehem costume with the shatweh. Courtesy of National Geographic.

Figure 45. Tinted studio photo of a Bethlehem bride. Nineteenth century. The shatweh headdress and headscarf. Courtesy Library of Congress.

century, when it became slightly taller and thinner. National Geographic magazines of the 1910s and 1920s refer to the shatweh as a "Crusader hat," mistakenly thinking that it was derived from Crusader styles. Research into European costume from the era of the Crusades (the tenth to twelfth centuries AD) clearly shows, in fact, that the reverse was true: that era saw an influx of styles from the Middle East influencing European fashion.

The wukayeh or smadeh headdress worn in Ramallah, Jerusalem, and other regions of Palestine has a long history recorded in engravings on sarcophagi, mosaics, icons, and statues going back to the second century AD and perhaps earlier. The statue of the woman on the sarcophagus in Palmyra, Syria, (Fig. 46) displays the same headdress style as that worn by Palestinian women in several regions in the early twentieth century (Fig. 47).

Figure 46. Statue of woman from Palmyra. Second century AD. Headdress with a style similar to the wukayeh headdress of the Ramallah and Jerusalem areas. Courtesy of Palmyra Museum, Syria.

Figure 47. Woman from Ramallah. 1920s. Headdress covered with large headscarf. Courtesy of National Geographic.

The bridal headdress of Al-Khalil and the northern Gaza region is quite unique. The headdress, called wikayat-el-darahem, was very ornately decorated with Ottoman silver coins and was worn only by a bride on her wedding day. It was shared by all the brides within the clan. It was also decorated with semi-precious stones such as carnelian and turquoise and with coral beads. This headdress was another mistakenly described in the nineteenth century as of "Crusader influence," although no such style was found in Europe during that period. The effect of the densely layered small Ottoman coins is unique, but headdresses decorated with silver coins and precious stones are common in the Middle East; some headdresses from Afghanistan have an abundance of coins and precious stones, probably harking back to an ancient widespread Middle Eastern custom.

The construction of the top of this headdress is similar to the Bethlehem shatweh and was made by professional women in Bethlehem for customers from the Al-Khalil hills and northern Gaza.

The Development of the Bethlehem Chest Piece

Many of the Bethlehem dresses from the nineteenth century have a chest piece with a traditional design of four main floral branches coming out of a small vase, surrounding a central flower (Fig. 48). The same pattern of four branches coming out of an amphora is seen in mosaics in a fifth-century Byzantine church and in the Dome of the Rock in Jerusalem (Fig. 49). This vase-and-branches pattern, a religious symbol, was also carved in stone above the entrances to homes in Palestine, a form of blessing or prayer.

Figure 48. Bethlehem chest piece. Nineteenth century. Four branches come out of a small vase and surround a central medallion with a cross. Courtesy of Widad Kawar.

Figure 49. Mosaic in the Dome of the Rock, Jerusalem, seventh century AD, with four branches coming out of an amphora.

Figure 50. Syrian gospel-book cover. Twentieth century. With iconic representations of Jesus Christ in the middle and the four evangelists Matthew, Mark, Luke, and John in the corners.

In some of the Bethlehem chest pieces, the central flower or medallion encloses a cross, reflecting the Christian faith of the wearer. (As the birthplace of Jesus, Bethlehem has always had a large Christian Arab community.) Often the embroidery on the sides of the dress also has several crosses. In addition, the chest piece has a continuous scroll pattern going all around it, which may itself be another religious symbol.

In the early twentieth century, the embroidery of the chest piece from the Bethlehem area became more dense, and the four curling branches were transformed into circles in the corners of the square surrounding the central medallion, which often contained a cross. This arrangement has a striking similarity to the iconic composition seen on the cover of most Middle Eastern gospel books, which feature an icon of Jesus Christ in the central medallion and four icons of the Evangelists Matthew, Mark, Luke, and John in the corners (Fig. 50).

One wonders, then, whether this is the real significance of the chest-piece patterns, and both the earlier (four branches surrounding a central medallion) and the later (four circles surrounding a central medallion) versions represent Jesus and the four Evangelists, especially since the cross on the chest piece is always found in the central medallion, corresponding to the icon of Jesus in the center of the gospel cover.

The continuous-scroll pattern used on the periphery of the Bethlehem chest piece might also be seen as part of Christian iconography, symbolizing the vine. But scroll patterns have been a popular motif since antiquity. The scroll-and-vine pattern was associated with the pagan tree of life, and although it evolved later into a Christian symbol in Byzantine art, it had been popular in ancient Greek and Roman decoration throughout the Middle East and Europe, and can be seen, among other places, on first-century AD stone engravings on a Nabataean pagan altar near Petra and on the seventh-century mosaics of the Dome of the Rock Mosque in Jerusalem.

The Roots of Palestinian Embroidery Patterns

The repertoire of Palestinian embroidery motifs from the nineteenth century can be traced to some very ancient motifs that have survived for centuries in Palestine and the surrounding region. Some have roots in antiquity and can be seen on ivory carvings, mosaics, or engravings; others are found in geometric tapestry decoration of tunics from Egypt and Syria from the fourth and fifth centuries. A Large collection of patterns is seen in embroideries from the Arab world starting from the ninth to the sixteenth centuries AD, and these patterns were passed on through to the early twentieth century. These embroideries are documented in publications from several museums worldwide. An important source of information about the collection of Arab textiles at the Ashmolean Museum is Marianne Ellis' *Embroideries and Samplers from Islamic Egypt*. The textile pieces range from the Tulunid (868–905 AD), Fatimid (969–1171 AD), Ayyubid (1172–1249 AD), and Mamluk (1249-1517 AD) periods. Other valuable published sources are from the Textile Museum in Washington, DC, and the Museum of Islamic Art in Cairo.

These patterns have survived with remarkable consistency from one era to another, and some are later seen in sixteenth-century European pattern books. The continuity of transfer of these ancient patterns is also seen in nineteenth-century embroideries from several areas of the Arab world, like Palestine, Syria, and Morocco, attesting to their widespread use and popularity. A few of these patterns will be demonstrated here.

Motifs from Antiquity

Palmette and "Tall Palms"

In Palestinian embroidery, the palmette pattern appears on dresses from the Gaza area, arranged one above the other (Fig. 51). The palmette is a stylized version of fruiting branches of the palm and is a common motif in Canaanite and Phoenician art that symbolizes nutrition and good health (Fig. 52). Archaeological ruins from the tenth to the eighth centuries BC in Palestine frequently have palmettes on the capitals of columns, called Proto-Aeolic by archaeologists. The palm and palmette designs are found on ancient ivory, stone, and metal carvings, and also in the mosaics of the Dome of the Rock in Jerusalem. The palm was considered an important tree in antiquity because of its highly nutritious fruit, the date.

Stair and Crowstep

A stair-like pattern embroidered on the dresses and scarves from Asdud and other Gaza-area towns is similar to chevron-pattern decoration painted on mud houses in the Gaza area in the early twentieth century. This house decoration is similar to the ancient wall carvings in Petra and Mada'in Saleh, called "crowsteps" by archaeologists.

Acanthus Leaves and Cup

A recurrent embroidery pattern in Palestinian dress (Fig. 53) is derived from the ancient "acanthus leaves and cup" pattern, carved in ancient ruins in several areas of the Middle East, which symbolizes prosperity. It is seen in a marble relief found in Syria from 727 AD (Fig. 54). A related pattern is found in the mosaics of the Dome of the Rock Mosque in Jerusalem.

Figure 51. Palestinian embroidery palmette pattern on Gaza dress.

Figure 52 Palmette – a common motif in Canaanite and Phoenician art.

Figure 53. Acanthus leaves with cup pattern seen on numerous Palestinian dresses.

Figure 54. Marble engraving in Qasr el-Kheir al Gharbi, Syria. 727 AD.

Embroidery Patterns from the Fatimid and Ayyubid Eras

Several museums around the world possess pieces of textiles with embroidery from the Arab world. Two of the earliest examples showing geometrical embroidered patterns similar to Palestinian patterns are found at the Textile Museum in Washington, DC. One dates from 885 AD from Egypt and the other from 926–928 AD. The very fine counted-stitch embroidery of geometric patterns in multicolored silk thread on linen is similar to Palestinian cross-stitch embroidery.

Average people wore robes made of linen rather than silk; the average woman's robes were embroidered at home with geometrical patterns that included flowers, animals, and birds. Silk-thread embroidery decorated every item worn, from robes to trousers, headscarves, belts, and handkerchiefs, and some home furnishings. It is this average person's style that shows a strong similarity to the Palestinian style of the twentieth century: in the linen fabric, in the cut of the robe, in the silk counted-stitch embroidery, and in the patterns employed.

S-Shape or Alaq (Leeches)

One striking example of a pattern that has survived for centuries is the S-shaped pattern (Fig. 55), which is seen frequently in Arab Fatimid and Ayyubid embroideries. It appears in a sampler radiocarbon dated to about 1155 AD. This pattern is frequently used in Palestinian embroideries, where it is called alak (leeches). In Palestinian folklore, leeches symbolize good health and longevity, as they were used by medieval doctors to treat high blood pressure.

Figure 55. S-shape pattern on Ramallah scarf.

149

Birds

In Palestinian embroidery of the 19th and 20th centuries, innumerable examples of bird patterns – small birds, roosters, and peacocks – exist on dresses, headscarves, pillows, and bags from Ramallah, Jaffa, Hebron, Bethlehem, and Upper Galilee. These birds are part of the repertoire of motifs prevalent in the Arab world and are seen on an Ayyubid sampler featuring bird patterns done in counted stitch, arranged in pairs. Paired birds are also seen on an earlier embroidered textile from the Fatimid era, 969 - 1171 AD, and also woven on a silk brocade. Actually, the paired-birds motif goes back in the Middle East to much earlier periods and is found in Egyptian knitting samples from 600 - 800 AD.

Arab Embroidery in the Mamluk Era

After the Ayyubid era drew to a close in 1250, strong trade contacts between Europe and the Arabs under Mamluk rule provided economic growth that enabled the patronage of the arts, including textiles, embroidery, carpets, glass, metalwork, and woodcarving. Workshops produced wares for the embellishment of the court and for export to Europe. Textiles, embroidered in silk or brocaded with metallic thread, were an important export to Venice and the rest of Europe.

The arts in the Mamluk era were actually indigenous Arab arts and crafts that were patronized by the Mamluks and later formed the foundation of the arts and crafts of the Ottoman Empire that would follow. After the Ottomans defeated the Mamluks in the sixteenth century, many of these artists from Egypt, Syria, and Palestine were moved to the Ottoman capital to work in workshops for the new court and thus participated in establishing the arts that flourished under Ottoman rule.

Couching-Stitch Embroidery

The motifs used in Mamluk times were a continuation with variations of patterns used earlier, with improvements, such as the use of metallic thread for couching-stitch embroidery. The Mamluk-era embroideries are very similar to the couching-stitch embroideries of the Bethlehem, Jerusalem, and Jaffa areas done on silks, linens, and velvets.

Patchwork Appliqué

Many clothing items, bags, and banners in the Mamluk era were also decorated by patchworks of colorful small pieces of silk. In Palestinian costume, similar patchwork is seen on the fronts of dresses, Al-Khalil pillows, and Galilee coats.

Samplers

Samplers used by embroiderers in medieval Egypt preserved collections of patterns for future use. These samplers have proven to be a valuable documentation of the repertoire of patterns used in that era and include patterns frequently found in Palestinian embroideries from the nineteenth century, like the S-shape, the diamond patterns, and the "paired birds and trees" found frequently in Greek-Island embroideries in later centuries.

Eight-Pointed Star

The ancient eight-pointed star pattern, found in the Middle East on stone, metal, and woodwork in many crafts since antiquity, is also found on Egyptian tapestry decoration of tunics from the fourth century, Arab embroidery samplers from the Fatimid era, and embroideries of the Mamluk era, where it appears frequently on samplers and on clothes. In the Mamluk era, it was usually incorporated into composite patterns that appear remarkably similar to Palestinian embroideries (Fig. 56).

Reesh (Feather)

Another popular Palestinian embroidery motif called reesh (feather) has roots in embroideries from the Mamluk era (Fig.57).

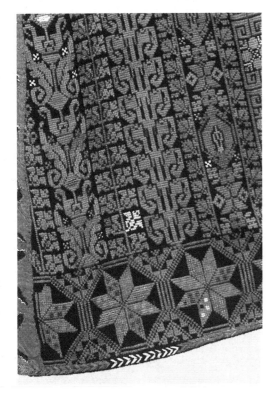

Figure 56. Eight-pointed star pattern on Palestinian dress from Al-Khalil. Silk on linen. Twentieth century.

Figure 57. Reesh (feather) pattern from Palestine. Early twentieth century.

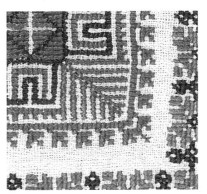

Tareeq Masr (Road to Egypt)

A Mamluk-era pattern seen on an Egyptian knitted-woolen sample has survived to the present in the cross-stitch embroidery of Palestinian dresses (Fig. 58), where it is called tareeq Masr (road to Egypt) or kibrit (matches).

Figure 58. The Tareeq Masr (road to Egypt) pattern in a Palestinian dress. Early twentieth century.

Zahra (Flower)

Another Palestinian pattern (Fig. 59), the zahra (flower), popular in Ramallah, is usually used in a vertical row. This same configuration of the pattern is found on a printed fabric from Mamluk Egypt, from the fifteenth century AD.

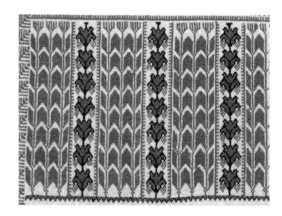

As demonstrated here, the patterns in Arab embroideries were a culmination of motifs from all the previous centuries and were preserved as part of the traditional costume styles of the region that were

Figure 59. Zahra pattern on a Ramallah headscarf. Nineteenth century.

perpetuated from generation to generation, copied from one textile to another. By the time Ottoman rule was established in the region in the sixteenth century, the style of traditional dress in the various regions of the Arab world was well defined.

The Dissemination of Palestinian Embroidery Patterns in Europe

The flourishing trade route between medieval Europe and the Arab world included textiles as an important component. One of the main venues was Italy, especially Venice, which sold a large quantity of Arab textiles to the rest of Europe. This trade accounts for the familiarity of European craftsmen with Arab design and the transmission to Europe of Arab-style embroidery for decorating clothing, as seen in portraits from the late-fifteenth and early-sixteenth centuries. In 1523, a German printer by the name of Johann Schonsperger printed the first European pattern book containing "mooresque" and "arabesque" (as he called them) patterns, and the following years saw the widespread use of the patterns through constant re-printing of these books.

Another major route of transmission of these Arab embroidery patterns was through European pilgrims to Jerusalem and the Holy Land. In his *History of Folk*

Cross Stitch, Kiewe concludes that the similarity of some patterns in the embroidery of White Russia to Palestinian embroidery confirms his "belief in the common, Palestinian source of these designs." He describes the patterns used in Palestine as religiously significant to European pilgrims visiting Palestine, quoting copied patterns with European names such as the "Holy Star of Bethlehem," "Holy Keys of Jerusalem," and "Guardian Angels." In the fifth edition of his book in 1964, he added "75 Ancient Charts from the Holy Land," exploring the ancient origins of these patterns and stressing the transfer over many centuries of Palestinian patterns into Europe by pilgrims visiting the Holy Land.

Although the influences on Palestinian costume have been many, the result is uniquely and distinctly Palestinian. The ancient embroidered patterns were symbols of hope, prosperity, good health, and protection, with traditional names that reflect nature: the moon, the cypress tree, the tree of life, and the bird of paradise. Today, Palestinian embroidered costume has transcended its role as a symbol of tradition to become a symbol of Palestinian identity.

Questions for Reflection

1. The Zionist narrative would have us believe that the Palestinian people are intruders into Palestine coming from the desert to the East, and therefore they should not enjoy the same rights as the large wave of twentieth-century Jewish immigrants to Palestine. How does this chapter demonstrate the connection of today's Palestinians to their ancient land of Canaan and Palestine?

2. Consider the strong similarly between the nineteenth- and twentieth-century Palestinian costumes and stone sculptures from the first and second centuries BC and AD found in lands of the original Canaanites. What do you think is the significance of these similarities?

Epilogue

In conclusion, two voices: One from the Palestinian diaspora and the other from occupied Palestine.

A voice from the Palestinian diaspora.

I am old enough to remember Palestine before its partition. Through the eyes of a child, I remember the sweetness of Palestine – the abundance and beauty of its land and above all the friends and acquaintances: Christian, Jewish, and Muslim. As an adult I have learned of the history of Palestine and have understood the tumultuous stage upon which I was born.

Memories of Palestine, nevertheless, live and provide an anchor for life. Life in Palestine was a rich blend of three faiths and many cultures. One of the most pleasant memories I have is the sound of Jerusalem waking up in the morning. Waking up gently in a warm bed at my grandmother's home, I remember the distant Muslim call to prayer before dawn, followed by a the sound of a lone motor car passing in the street outside, the cooing of the mourning dove, then of a cacophony of motor cars and people passing outside my window, culminating in the full sound of a wide-awake Jerusalem. Other sounds live in my memory. The first time I heard the sad toll of Jerusalem's church bells on Good Friday, I was puzzled, but then the look on my Grandmother's face told me that this was a very solemn occasion indeed. Someone close and beloved to my Grandmother had died. It was the day of the Funeral Mass for Jesus in many Jerusalem churches. But on Sunday, the glorious toll of the Church bells rang out in celebration of the Resurrection and of life.

The tragedy of Palestine is that powerful outside forces shaped our lives and the lives of its new Jewish immigrants. These outside forces continue to shape the Palestine-Israel conflict, frequently more for ill than good.

If one were to visit Palestine and speak to its people today, one would find that by far the majority of Palestinians seek peace and yearn for a time when they will be free to enjoy life in its fullest without restrictions on their movements, to build a life for themselves and children, and to have their own nationality so that they can move freely as full citizens in the world. They only wish for the freedoms enjoyed by us here in the United States.

However, it is sad to see the daily reality of the occupation in the Palestinian Territories. Life contains uncertainties and fear: the fear of having one's house demolished, fear of deportation, fear of the inability to have sufficient food to feed one's family, fear of not being able to reach a hospital in case of an emergency, fear of arrest, and fear of sudden death due to violence. These are some of the daily fears experienced by Christian and Muslim Palestinians. The people of Israel, understandably, have their own fears, partly from tragic and sad memories of their past and partly from the inflated fear of retaliatory actions from Palestinians in response to the daily trials, humiliations, and repressions of living under occupation.

The Christian presence in Palestine is dwindling. There are many causes, but the main cause is the difficulties and uncertainties of life under the Israeli occupation in the Palestinian territories and to a somewhat lesser extent in Israel. The proportion of Christians is dwindling to a precariously low level, and estimates as low as 1.2 percent of the population are frequently cited. The land where Jesus was born, lived, taught, and witnessed to God is in danger of losing its entire population of Christians. This is a reality that saddens me; it is as if I can hear the sad toll of Jerusalem's church bells on Good Friday from my childhood. But, as I now embody the Easter Faith of my grandmother, I know that this is not the end – as I pray that I will hear the glorious toll of the Church bells ringing out in celebration of the Resurrection in my lifetime.

It is this abundance of life that flows from the Resurrection that inspires us to help bring justice to Palestine/Israel. This is not a justice where one party or the other triumphs, but is a justice built upon truth telling, repentance, and forgiveness. The involvement of our Church in making recommendations can only further our testimony to the truth, though the painful reality from my Palestinian-American perspective is that these recommendations fall short of acknowledging the full truth and of speaking truth to power. There are powerful governmental forces that contribute to the conflict, and Church recommendations have not made a difference for the past 66 years and will probably not make any difference in the future unless the people demand change from their governments.

A Christian Palestinian voice from Occupied Palestine.

It saddens me deeply to watch the Christian values and ideals, which were inculcated in me ever since my early years rendered invalid. My family's involvement in the Church has taught me that being a Christian is not merely professing the act of faith and going to church every Sunday. My grandfather was one of the earliest Anglican pastors in Palestine and my father was a church elder, an educator, and an idealist who sought until the last years of his life to offer a moral solution to the Palestinian problem. I was raised to believe that being a Christian meant being responsible, compassionate, courageous, and fearless in speaking truth to power, regardless of consequences. I was raised to believe that the Church is the conscience of the world and that it never shies away from taking the side of justice and the oppressed.

Unfortunately, as I was getting older and wiser, I realized that politics is often anathema to God's love that Jesus of Nazareth revealed. However, I continued to hope that Christian churches would be effective if they would emulate the example of the Master and stand fearless and united before the powerful political structures that seem to be wreaking havoc in our beleaguered world. For several years, the World Council of Churches and several individual churches ushered a light of hope to our people as they courageously advocated justice and human rights for the Palestinians. Unfortunately, growing pressures of various lobbies seem to have blunted the edge of their voices. They fell into the trap of addressing the conflict as one between two equal parties and not as one between an occupier and an occupied, and they overlooked that the roots of the conflict are embedded in the dispossession of the Palestinians and the continued denial of their national and human rights.

In 1948, as a result of the establishment of the state of Israel, almost a million Palestinians were displaced from their homes. Despite the myriad United Nations resolutions calling for their return, the Palestinians were never allowed to do so. Instead of respecting and abiding by United Nations resolutions which gave it legitimacy, the nascent state embarked on a policy of fait accompli, demolishing Palestinian villages and settling Jews from all over the world in Palestinian homes. This policy remains the backbone of Israeli policy up until the present. Unfortunately, Israel was never sanctioned or obliged to comply with international law. The moral, financial, and military support of the United States government has allowed it to flout international law and conventions as a fledgling state, as a formidable occupying power, and as a perpetrator of grievous violations of human rights and war crimes.

As long as the root causes of the conflict are not addressed, peace in the region will remain a mirage and an unattainable dream. The human spirit yearning for equality, justice, and freedom will not be quelled and cannot be overcome by military might. The only path to peace is justice and the recognition of the humanity of the other.

We both remind our readers that before the 20th century, Palestinian Jews, Muslims, and Christians lived peacefully together. It can happen again if we support non-violence and peacemaking in Israel and Palestine rather than continually providing weapons. The hope of Palestine/Israel lies with Jews, Muslims, and Christians who speak out for truth, justice, and reconciliation and make their voices heard by people in power.

Nahida Halaby Gordon, Ph.D., a life-long Presbyterian and currently a church Elder, is a Palestinian-American who experienced, first hand, the 1948 Palestinian Nakba. Professor Gordon was a member of the Middle East Study Committee of the Presbyterian Church (U.S.A.) and currently sits on several Presbyterian Church (U.S.A.) committees.

Rima Tarazi is a musician, social activist, co-founder and chairperson of the Supervisory Board of the Edward Said National Conservatory of Music, and Board member of Birzeit University. She also served as President of the Administrative Board of the General Union of Palestinian Women, National President of the YWCA of Palestine, and Board member of the Society of Ina'sh El Usra.

Questions for Reflection

1. Review and discuss your group's stand on the predicament in which Palestinians find themselves. What further actions can your group take?

2. The Kairos Palestine document begins with a prayer: "We, a group of Christian Palestinians, after prayer, reflection and an exchange of opinion, cry out from within the suffering in our country, under the Israeli occupation, with a cry of hope in the absence of all hope, a cry full of prayer and faith in a God ever vigilant, in God's divine providence for all the inhabitants of this land." Do you think that this hope and faith are realistic in view of current world politics?

Leader's Guide

Palestine is Our Home has thirteen sections of varying length. Ideally conducting thirteen sessions would be a comfortable pace to read and discuss the book; however your group may not be able to devote thirteen sessions. Below are two suggested timetables – one long and the other somewhat shorter.

Table 1. Sections taken in order of appearance in the text.

Session	Book Sections/Activity	Preparation Before the Session
1	Discuss the scope of the Study/ view the video by Nur Masalha	Obtain a copy of the book and watch the video, The Land Speaks Arabic
2	Introduction and Brief Historical Background	Read the Introduction and Chapter 1
3	Jerusalem District Narratives	Read assigned sections
4	Jaffa District Narratives	Read assigned sections
5	Al-Ramla District Narratives	Read assigned sections
6	Gaza District Narratives	Read assigned sections and view the Video
7	Ramallah District Narratives	Read assigned sections
8	Nablus District Narrative	Read assigned sections and view the Video
9	Tulkarem District - Kafer Qasem Massacre	Read assigned sections
10	Acre District Narratives	Read assigned sections and view the Video
11	Liberation Art of Palestine	Read assigned chapter
12	The Origins of Palestinian Costume	Read assigned chapter
13	Epilogue and Conclusions	Read assigned sections

Taken chronologically, the Jerusalem, Jaffa, Al-Ramla, and Acre districts all have narratives originating from the 1947-48 Nakba and your group may want to consider these first. Next, the Tulkarem District section deals with a 1956 massacre in Kafir Qasem; the Ramallah section deals with the 1967 expulsion and the aftermath. And finally, the Nablus and Gaza sections deal with more recent events.

If you feel that the reading assignments for each week are too long, perhaps, you may find it helpful to make reading assignments for each week of narratives to various members of the group and ask them to report back to the group.

Table 2. Alternate timetable.

Session	Book Sections/Activity	Preparation Before the Session
1	Discuss the scope of the Study/ view the video by Nur Masalha	Obtain a copy of the book
2	Introduction and Brief Historical Background	Read the Introduction and Chapter 1
3	Jerusalem District Narratives	Read assigned sections and/or narratives
4	Jaffa, Al-Ramla Districts Narratives	Read assigned sections and/or narratives
5	Acre and Tulkarem District - Kafer Qasem Massacre	Read assigned sections and/or narratives and watch the video
6	Ramallah District Narratives	Read assigned sections and/or narratives
7	Gaza and Nablus District Narratives	Read assigned sections and/or narratives and watch the video
8	Liberation Art of Palestine	Read assigned chapter
9	The Origins of Palestinian Costume	Read assigned chapter
10	Epilogue and Conclusions	Read assigned sections

Table 3. Online Video Resources

Book Sections/Activity	Video Resource
First Session	The Land Speaks Arabic https://www.youtube.com/watch?v=JfF-N8gw1jSI
Gaza District	One Family in Gaza, Jen Marlowe's award-winning short documentary film featuring the Awajah family. This documentary can be viewed on Vimeo (https://vimeo.com/18384109) and The Awajah Family in 2014 Vimeo (https://vimeo.com/111795152).
Ramallah District	https://electronicintifada.net/blogs/ali-abunimah/video-israe-li-night-raids-sleeping-palestin-ian-children
Nablus District	Video of Majeda Akram Fida www.addameer.org/evideo.php?id=109

Further references to up to date resources (both online videos and short films) can be found at www.palestinebooks.com.

Notes

Introduction

1. Tubb, Jonathan N. *People of the Past: Canaanites*. Norman, Oklahoma: University of Oklahoma Press, 1998. Print.
2. Ibid. 14.
3. Hafiz, Yasmine. "Israeli Police Wouldn't Let This Boy Go To Al-Aqsa Mosque -- Here's The Amazing Way He Responded." *The Huffington Post* April 7, 2014. Web. 15 Oct. 2015.

I. Brief Contemporary History of Palestine

1. The Avalon Project – Yale Law School. "The Palestine Mandate." http://avalon.law.yale.edu/20th_century/palmanda.asp. Web. 15 Oct. 2015.
2. Quigley, John. *The Statehood of Palestine: International Law in the Middle East Conflict*. New York, NY: Cambridge University Press, 2010. Print.
3. The Avalon Project – Yale Law School. "The Covenant of the League of Nations." http://avalon.law.yale.edu/20th_century/leagcov.asp. Web. 15 Oct. 2015.
4. Ibid. Paragraph four.
5. BBC News. "The Balfour Declaration." Letter dated November 2, 1917, from Arthur James Balfour, the British Foreign Secretary, addressed to Lord Rothschild, a leader of the Jewish community in Britain, which became known as the Balfour Declaration, http://news.bbc.co.uk/2/hi/in_depth/middle_east/israel_and_the_palestinians/key_documents/1682961.stm. Web. 15 Oct. 2015.
6. Khalidi, Rashid. *The Iron Cage: The Story of the Palestinian Struggle for Statehood*. Boston, MA: Beacon Press, Boston, 2006. 32. Print.
7. McCarthy, Justin. Israel Palestine ProCon. "Population Statistics." Table 4. http://israelipalestinian.procon.org/viewresource.asp?resourceID=000636. Web. 15 Oct. 2015.
8. Khalidi, Rashid. *The Iron Cage: The Story of the Palestinian Struggle for Statehood*. Boston, MA: Beacon Press, Boston, 2006. 33. Print.
9. The Avalon Project – Yale Law School. "President Woodrow Wilson's Fourteen Points." http://avalon.law.yale.edu/20th_century/wilson14.asp. Web. 15 Oct. 2015.
10. Khalidi, Rashid. *The Iron Cage: The Story of the Palestinian Struggle for Statehood*. Boston, MA: Beacon Press, Boston, 2006. 33. Print.
11. Population of Ottoman and Mandate Palestine, Statistical and Demographic Considerations. Table 3. http://www.mideastweb.org/palpop.htm. Web. 15 Oct. 2015.
12. Haim Levenberg. *Military Preparations of the Arab Community in Palestine: 1945–1948*. London: UK: Routledge, 1993. 74–76. Print.
13. Baruch Kimmerling and Joel S. Migdal. *Palestinians: The Making of a People*. New York, New York: Free Press, 1993. 123. Cited by Jonathan Schanzer in "Palestinian Uprisings Compared." *Middle East Quarterly*, Summer 2002, 7-37. Web. 15 Oct. 2015.

14. Khalidi, Rashid. *The Iron Cage: The Story of the Palestinian Struggle for Statehood.* Boston, MA: Beacon Press, 2006. 35. Print.

15. Lilienthal, Alfred. *What Price Israel?* Chicago, Ill: Henry Regenery Co, 1953. 48-73. Print.

16. Ibid. 48-73.

17. Charter of the United Nations. "Chapter XI: Declaration Regarding Non-self Governing Territories, Article 73" http://www.un.org/en/documents/charter/chapter11.shtml. Web. 15 Oct. 21015. Members of the United Nations which have or assume responsibilities for the administration of territories whose peoples have not yet attained a full measure of self-government recognize the principle that the interests of the inhabitants of these territories are paramount, and accept as a sacred trust the obligation to promote to the utmost, within the system of international peace and security established by the present Charter, the well-being of the inhabitants of these territories, and, to this end: ensure, with due respect for the culture of the peoples concerned, their political, economic, social, and educational advancement, their just treatment, and their protection against abuses.

18. UN Documents: Gathering a body of global agreements. "2625 (XXV). Declaration on the Principles of International Law concerning the Friendly Relations and Co-operation among States in accordance with the Charter of the United Nations. ." : The principle of equal rights and self-determination of people. http://www.un-documents.net/a25r2625.htm. Web. 15 Oct. 2015. By virtue of the principle of equal rights and self-determination of peoples enshrined in the Charter of the United Nations, all peoples have the right freely to determine, without external interference, their political status and to pursue their economic, social and cultural development, and every State has the duty to respect this right in accordance with the provisions of the Charter.

19. Doebbler, Curtis. "Palestine's right to statehood and what it means." *Ma'an News Agency.* 22 November 2009 http://www.maannews.com/Content.aspx?id=241245. Web. 19 Oct. 2015.

20. The Avalon Project – Yale Law School. United Nations General Assembly Resolutions 181, November 19, 1947. http://avalon.law.yale.edu/20th_century/res181.asp. Web. 15 Oct. 2015.

21. Ibid.

22. Lilienthal, Alfred. *What Price Israel?* Chicago, Ill: Henry Regenery Co, 1953. 48-73. Print.

23. Esber, R M. *Under the Cover of War: The Zionist Expulsion of the Palestinians.* Alexandria, VA: Arabicus Books & Media, 2009. Print.

24. "Expulsions Denied by Mr. Ben-Gurion" during a Knesset speech, May 17, 1961. The Times, May 18, 1961, p12. Web. 15 Oct. 2015.

25. Middle East Research and Information Project. "Primer on Palestine, Israel and the Arab-Israeli Conflict." http://www.merip.org/palestine-israel_primer/un-partition-plan-pal-isr.html. Web. 15 Oct. 2015. See also

    • Esber, R M. *Under the Cover of War: The Zionist Expulsion of the Palestinians.* Alexandria, VA: Arabicus Books & Media, 2009. Print.

    • Khalidi, Rashid. *The Iron Cage: The Story of the Palestinian Struggle for Statehood.* Boston, MA: Beacon Press, 2006, Print.

    • Masalha, Nur. *A Land without a People: Israel, Transfer and the Palestinians 1949-96.* Faber and Faber, 1997. Print.

    • Quigley, John. *Palestine and Israel: A Challenge to Justice..* Durham and London: Duke University Press, 1990. 82-86. Print.

    • Pappe, Ilan. *The Ethnic Cleansing of Palestine.* Oxford, UK: Oneworld, 2006. Print.

26. Pappe, Ilan. *The Ethnic Cleansing of Palestine*. Oxford, UK: Oneworld, 2006: 287. Print.

27. Ibid. p 287.

28. Pappe, Ilan. *A History of Modern Palestine: One Land, Two Peoples*. Cambridge, UK: Cambridge University Press, 2004: 139. Print.

29. Abu Sitta, Salman. *Atlas of Palestine, 1917-1966*. London, UK: Palestine Land Society, London, UK: 2010: 92-97.Print.

30. Ibid. 121.

31. Ibid. 97.

32. Ibid. 121.

33. Ibid. 122.

34. Masalha, Nur. *The Politics of Denial: Israel and the Palestinian Refugee Problem*. London, UK: Pluto Press. 2003. Print.

35. Ibid. 12.

36. Ibid. 17.

37. Ibid. 17 - 41.

38. The Avalon Project – Yale Law School. "United Nations Security Council Resolution 242". http://www.yale.edu/lawweb/avalon/un/un242.htm. WEB. 15 OCT. 2015.

39. Segev, Tom & Weinstein, A N. The *First Israelis*. New York: Henry Holt, 1986: 80-81. Print.

40. Palestinian Central Bureau of Statistics. "Palestine in Figures 2007". Ramallah – Palestine. http://www.pcbs.gov.ps/Downloads/book1432.pdf. Web. 15 Oct. 2015.

41. United Nations Relief and Works Agency. http://www.unrwa.org/palestine-refugees. Web. 15 Oct. 2015.

42. Leviticus 25:13, New International Version.

43. United Nations. "The Universal Declaration of Human Rights." can retrieved from: http://www.un.org/en/documents/udhr. Web. 15 Oct. 2015.

44. United Nations General Assembly. "Resolution 194(III)-Progress Report of the United Nations Mediator". http://unispal.un.org/UNISPAL.NSF/0/C758572B78D1CD0085256BCF0077E51A. Web. 15 Oct. 2015.

45. United Nations Human Rights Office of the United Nations High Commissioner for Human Rights. "International Covenant on Civil and Political Rights." http://www.ohchr.org/en/professionalinterest/pages/ccpr.aspx. Web. 15 Oct. 2015.

46. Abu Sitta, Salman. "The Implementation of the Right of Return". *Palestine - Israel Journal of Politics, Economics & Culture*, Vol. 15/16 Issue 4/1, (2008):23-30, (AN 42842708). Web. 15 Oct. 2015.

47. Quigley, John. "Displaced Palestinians and a Right of Return." *Harvard International Law Journal*, Winter 1998: 39. WEB. 15 OCT 2015.

48. United Nations. "Progress Report of the United Nations Mediator on Palestine." http://unispal.un.org/UNISPAL.NSF/0/AB14D4AAFC4E1BB985256204004F55FA. Web. 15 Oct. 2015.

49. Halaby, Samia. *Liberation Art of Palestine: Palestinian Painting and Sculpture in the Second Half of the Twentieth Century*. New York, New York: H. T. T. B. Publications, 2001. The event was sponsored by Museum Artystow, The Artists' Museum, International Provisional Artists' Community, Lods, Poland.

50. Ibid.

II. The Narratives

Jerusalem District.

1. Khalidi, Walid (ed). *All that Remains: The Palestinian Villages Occupied and Depopulated by Israel in 1948*. Washington DC: The Institute of Palestine Studies, 1992: 264. Print.
2. Ibid. 289.
3. Ibid. 290.
4. McGowan, Daniel A. & Ellis, Mark H. *Remembering Dayr Yasin*, Olive Branch Press. Brooklyn, New York: 35. cited in Esber, R M. *Under the Cover of War: The Zionist Expulsion of the Palestinians*. Alexandria, VA: Arabicus Books & Media, 2009: 187. Print.
5. Morris, Benny. *The Birth of the Palestinian Refugee Problem-1947-1949*. Cambridge University Press, 1987: 38 as cited in Salim Tamarai, (ed). *Jerusalem 1948: The Arab Neighbourhoods and their Fate in the War*. Jerusalem, Palestine: The Institute of Jerusalem Studies and Badil Resource Center, 2002, p 96. Print.
6. IZL commander Mordechai Ranaan; cited in *Uri Milstein, History of Israel's war of Independence, vol 4, Out of Decision Came Crisis,* trans. and ed. Alan I Sacks (Lanham, Md.: University Press of America, 1998), 269 and in turn cited in Esber, R M. *Under the Cover of War: The Zionist Expulsion of the Palestinians.* Alexandria, VA: Arabicus Books & Media, 2009. Print.191.
7. Khalidi, Walid. *Deir Yassin: 9 April 1948*. Beirut, Lebanon: Institute for Palestine Studies, 1999. Print.
8. Tamari, Salim (ed). Jerusalem 1948: The Arab Neighbourhoods and their Fate in the War. Jerusalem: The Institute of Jerusalem Studies and Badil Resource Center, 2002. pp 96-100. Print.
9. Collins, Larry & Lapiere, Dominique. *O Jeruslaem*. New York: Simon & Schuster Paperbacks, 1972. p 279. Cited in Tamari, Salim (ed). *Jerusalem 1948: The Arab Neighbourhoods and their Fate in the War.* Jerusalem: The Institute of Jerusalem Studies and Badil Resource Center, 2002. p 99. Print.
10. Banks, Lynne R. *Torn Country*. New York: Franklin Watts, 1982 p. 57. Cited in Tamari, Salim (ed). *Jerusalem 1948: The Arab Neighbourhoods and their Fate in the War.* Jerusalem: The Institute of Jerusalem Studies and Badil Resource Center, 2002. p 99. Print.
11. Collins, Larry & Lapiere, Dominique. (1972). *O Jeruslaem*. New York: Simon & Schuster Paperbacks, p 279. Cited in Tamari, Salim (ed). *Jerusalem 1948: The Arab Neighbourhoods and their Fate in the War.* Jerusalem: The Institute of Jerusalem Studies and Badil Resource Center, 2002, p 99. Print.
12. Ibid. 280.
13. Benny, Morris. *The Birth of the Palestinian Refugee Problem-1947-1949*. Cambridge University Press, 1987. p38. Cited in Tamari, Salim (ed). *Jerusalem 1948: The Arab Neighbourhoods and their Fate in the War.* Jerusalem: The Institute of Jerusalem Studies and Badil Resource Center, 2002. p 99. Print.
14. Churchil, Winston. *The World Crisis: The Aftermath*. London, UK: Bloomsbury Academic, 1929, p 157. Cited in Fisk, Robert. *The Great War for Civilization: The Conquest of the Middle East*. New York: Vintage Books, 2005. p1045. Print.

15. This narrative is based on an article by Halaby, Raouf J. "You Can Never Go Home Again." *Counterpunch*, 23 January 2013. Web. 15 Oct. 2015.

16. McCullers, Carson. *The Ballad of the Sad Cafe.* New York, NY: First Mariner Books, 1951. Print.

17. Halaby, Raouf J. "Palestinians Recall Another Wall that Fell." *Counterpunch*, 24 Dec. 2014. Web. 15 Oct 2015.

18. Palestine was part of the Byzantine Empire until the conquest of Jerusalem by the Caliph Umar's in 683.

19. Masalha, Nur. "Expulsion of the Palestinians: The Concept of 'Transfer' in Zionist Political Thought, 1982-1948." Beirut: *Institute of Palestine Studies*,1992, p 117. Print.

20. The German colony was founded at the end of the 19th Century by Christian Germans, members of the Templar movement.

21. Chofshi, Nathan. *Jewish Newsletter*. New York, NY, 9 February 1959. Cited in Erskine Childers. "The Other Exodus." *Spectator Magazine*, London, UK 12 May 1962. Web. 19 Oct. 2015.

22. For example, Gold Meir is quoted in the *Sunday Times*, London, 15 June, 1969 saying, "There were no such things as Palestinians. When was there an independent Palestinian people with a Palestinian State? It was not as though there was a Palestinian people in Palestine considering itself as a Palestinian people and we came and threw them out and took their country away from them. They did not exist."

23. Muir, Diana. "A Land without a People for a People without a Land". *Middle East Quarterly* (Spring 2008) 55-62. Ms. Muir discuses the many sources for the phrase. In addition to many Zionist sources, the phrase has also been used by nineteenth century Christian writers.

Jaffa District

24. Khalidi, Walid (ed). *All that Remains: The Palestinian Villages Occupied and Depopulated by Israel in 1948.* Washington DC: The Institute of Palestine Studies, 1992, 230. Print.

25. For further information about Jaffa before and after its surrender see article "Jaffa: from eminence to ethnic cleansing" by Sami Abu Shehadeh and Fadi Shbaytah which appeared in the *Electronic Intifada*, 26 Feb. 2009. Web. 10 Oct. 2015.

26. Esber, R M. *Under the Cover of War: The Zionist Expulsion of the Palestinians.* Alexandria, VA: Arabicus Books & Media, 2009. Print.

27. The Avalon Project – Yale Law School. United Nations General Assembly Resolutions 181, November 19, 1947. http://avalon.law.yale.edu/20th_century/res181.asp. Web. 15 Oct. 2015.

28. Ibid. 274.

29. The National Archives of the United Kingdom, (TNA) Abdul Rahman Azzam to Brigadier L. N. Clayton, British Middle East Office, Cairo, 28 Feb. 28, 1948 as referred to in Esber, R M. *Under the Cover of War: The Zionist Expulsion of the Palestinians.* Alexandria, VA: Arabicus Books & Media, 2009. p 275. Print.

30. Ibid. 293.

31. TNA War Office Papers 275/66: cited in Palumbo M (1987). "Palestinian Catastrophe: The 1948 Expulsion of a people from their Homeland." London, UK: Faber and Faber, 1987. p 86. Cited in Esber, R M *Und.er the Cover of War: The Zionist Expulsion of the Palestinians.* Alexandria, VA: Arabicus Books & Media, 2009, 276. Print.

32. Ibid.

33. 'Abd al-Ghani Nair, interviewed in Zarka, Jordan , 22 Sep. 22, 2001 by the author Esber, R M. and cited in Esber, R M. *Under the Cover of War: The Zionist Expulsion of the Palestinians.* Alexandria, VA: Arabicus Books & Media, 2009. Print.

34. Lazar, Haim. "Kubush Yaffo [Conquest of Jaffa]", 1981 cited in Moris B. *The Birth of the Palestinian Refugee Problem-1947-1949.* Cambridge University Press, 1987, p 96, in turn cited in Esber, R M. *Under the Cover of War: The Zionist Expulsion of the Palestinians.* Alexandria, VA: Arabicus Books & Media, 2009, 277. Print.

35. The National Archives of the United Kingdom, War Office papers 275/66; cited in Palumbo, Michael. *Palestinian Catastrophe: The 1948 Expulsion of a People From Their Homeland.* Lonon Quartet Books, 1989, p 90, and cited in Esber, R M Under the Cover of War: The Zionist Expulsion of the Palestinians. Alexandria, VA: Arabicus Books & Media, 2009. p 284. Print.

36. Esber, R M. *Under the Cover of War: The Zionist Expulsion of the Palestinians.* Alexandria, VA: Arabicus Books & Media, 2009. p 284. Print.

37. Ibid, 284.

38. Halaby, Samia A. *Liberation Art of Palestine: Palestinian Painting and Sculpture in the Second Half of the 20th Century,* Ramallah and New York: H. T. T. B. Publications, Ramallah and New York, 2001. Print.

39. Pesonal papers of Asaad S Halaby, resident and businessman of Jaffa, May 14, 1948.

40. Pappe, Ilan. *The Ethnic Cleansing of Palestine.* Oxford, UK: Oneworld, 2006, p 204. Print.

41. Israeli State Archives (ISA) Foreign Ministry (Israel) 2406/2 second memorandum submitted by the Emergency Committee of Jaffa protesting against the irregular activities of the Jewish Forces in Jaffa Area May 28, 1948; ISA Foreign Ministry 2564/9, Chizik, Minutes of a Meeting Held on the 31.548 between Military Governor of Jaffa and Mr. Robert Gee [sic] of the International Red Cross; Israeli Defense Forces and Defense Ministry Archives 321/48/97. Military Governor's Office, Jaffa, Summary 15.5.48; cited in Morris, Birth Revisited, 22nn3 97-98. Source: Esber, R M. *Under the Cover of War: The Zionist Expulsion of the Palestinians.* Alexandria, VA: Arabicus Books & Media, 2009. Print.

42. LeBor, Adam. *The City of Oranges: An Intimate History of Arabs and Jews in Jaffa.* New York: W W Norton & Co, 2007. Print.

43. Ibid.

44. Pappe, Ilan. *The Ethnic Cleansing of Palestine.* Oxford, UK: Oneworld, 2006. Print.

45. LeBor, Adam. *The City of Oranges: An Intimate History of Arabs and Jews in Jaffa.* New York: W W Norton & Co, 2007. Print.

46. Esber, R M. *Under the Cover of War: The Zionist Expulsion of the Palestinians.* Alexandria, VA: Arabicus Books & Media, 2009. Print.

Al-Ramla District

47. Khalidi, Walid (ed.). (1992). *All that Remains: The Palestinian Villages Occupied and Depopulated by Israel in 1948.* Washington DC: The Institute of Palestine Studies, 1992, 354-425. Print.

48. Morris, Benny. "Operation Dani and the Palestinian Exodus from Al-Lydda and Al-Ramla in 1948." *Middle East Journal* 40, no. 1 (Winter 1986), p. 91, as reported in Masalha, Nur. (2003) *The Politics of Denial: Israel and the Palestinian Refugee Problem.* London, UK: Pluto Press, 29. Print.

49. Morris, Benny. *1948 and After,* Oxford University Press, p. 2, as reported in Masalha, Nur. *The Politics of Denial: Israel and the Palestinian Refugee Problem.* London: Pluto Press, 1997, 30. Print.

50. Halaby, Samia A. *Liberation Art of Palestine: Palestinian Painting and Sculpture in the Second Half of the 20th Century.* Ramallah and New York: H. T. T. B. Publications, 2001. p 47. Print.

51. Ibid. Samia Halaby personal communication with Ismail Shammout.

52. Rantisi, Audeh G., and Beebe, Ralph K. *Blessed are the Peacemakers: A Palestinian Christian in the Occupied West Bank.* Grand Rapids, Michigan: Zondervan Books, Zondervan Publishing House, 1990. Print. The narrative is reprinted here with the permission of Ralph K. Beebe and Patricia Rantisi, Rev. Rantisi's wife.

53. Abdal Qader el-Husseini is a national hero who led the Palestinian uprising against the British in 1936-1939 and then against the Zionists in 1948. He was killed in the battle at Qastal, Palestine on April 8, 1948 while fighting the Zionist takeover of Palestine. He and the movement had widespread popular support to the extent that the resistance became known at the "hallowed struggle."

54. Pappe, Ilan. *The Ethnic Cleansing of Palestine.* Oxford, UK: Oneworld, 2006. Print.

Gaza District

55. Khalidi, Walid (ed.). *All that Remains: The Palestinian Villages Occupied and Depopulated by Israel in 1948.* Washington DC: The Institute of Palestine Studies, 1992, 78-13. Print.

56. Ibid.

57. Ibid.

58. Esber, R M. *Under the Cover of War: The Zionist Expulsion of the Palestinians.* Alexandria, VA: Arabicus Books & Media, 2009. Print.

59. Ibid. 311.

60. UN Office for the Coordination of Humanitarian Affairs – occupied Palestinian territory. 'The Gaza Strip: The Humanitarian impact of movement restrictions on people and good.' July 2013. Web. 16 Oct. 2015. http://www.ochaopt.org/documents/ocha_opt_gaza_blockade_factsheet_july_2013_english.pdf.

61. These Statistics can be retrieved from www.btselem.org/statistics. Web. 19 Oct. 2015.

62. Data presented by Institute for Middle East Understanding. 50 Days of Death and Destruction: Israel's "Operation Protective Edge," September 12, 2014, and the Al Mean Center for Human Rights. The article can be accessed at http://imeu.org/article/50-days-of-death-destruction-israels-operation-protective-edge.

63. The Palestinian Ministry of Health.

64. United Nations Conference on Trade and Development. "Occupation of Palestinian territory jeopardizes economic viability of two-state solution," Web. 16 Oct. 2015. http://unctad.org/en/pages/PressRelease.aspx?OriginalVersionID=204. Also see Institute for Middle East Understanding. "50 Days of Death & Destruction: Israel's 'Operation Protective Edge'." Published 20 Sep. 2014. Web. 16 Oct. 2015.

65. B'Tselem – The Israeli Information Center for Human Rights in the Occupied Territories. These statistics can be accessed at http://www.btselem.org/statistics/fatalities/before-cast-lead/by-date-of-event. Web. 10 Oct. 2015.

66. This article first appeared December 7, 2014, in TomDispatch.com.

67. Jen Marlowe is a human rights activist, author, documentary filmmaker, and founder of donkeysaddle projects.

68. One Family in Gaza, Jen Marlowe's award-winning short documentary film featuring the Awajah family. This documentary can be viewed on Vimeo (https://vimeo.com/18384109).

69. A documentary video by Jen Marlowe of the Awajah family in 2014 can be viewed on Vimeo (https://vimeo.com/111795152).

70. Weir, Alison. " Missing Headlines from Israel-Palestine." www.ifamericansknew.org/cur_sit/missingheadlines.html. Web. 16 Oct. 2015.

Ramallah District

71. Qumsiyeh, Mazin B. *Palestinian Popular Resistance in Palestine: A History of Hope and Empowerment*. New York: Pluto Press, 2011, p 100. Print.

72. Jiries, Sabri. *The Arabs in Israel*. Palestine Liberation Organization Research Center, 14, 1967,143-5, as cited by Qumsiyeh, Mazin B. *Palestinian Popular Resistance in Palestine: A History of Hope and Empowerment*. New York: Pluto Press, 2011, p 100. Print.

73. Ibid.

74. Qumsiyeh, Mazin B. *Palestinian Popular Resistance in Palestine: A History of Hope and Empowerment*. New York: Pluto Press, 2011, p98. Print.

75. Palestinian Central Bureau of Statistics 2007 census. 114.

76. Budrus and Kharbata are both in the Ramallah and al-Bireh Governorate, located 31 kilometers and 17 kilometers, respectively, northwest of Ramallah.

77. Baramki, Gabi. *Peaceful Resistance, Building a Palestinian University under Occupation*, London: Pluto Press. 2010. Print.

78. The articles can be retrieved at: http://www.thelancet.com/series/health-in-the-occupied-palestinian-territory, and are freely accessible with registration.

Nablus District

79. Palestinian Academic Society for the Study of International Affairs, 'Government and Administration' can be accessed at the PASSIA web site, http://www.passia.org/images/meetings/2015/Material%20for%20the%20Website/Government%20(2015).pdf. Web. 19 Oct. 2015.

80. Addameer (Arabic for conscience) Prisoners Support and Human Rights Association is a Palestinian non-governmental, civil institution that focuses on human rights issues. The report cited can be retrieved from http://www.addameer.org/the_prisoners/plc_member. Web. 19 Oct. 2015.

81. http://www.addameer.org/prisoner/majeda-akram-nimer-fidda. Web. 19 Oct. 2015.

82. See the Addameer website at www.addameer.org.

83. Refer to the Addameer web site at: http://www.addameer.org/the_prisoners/children. Web. 19 Oct. 2015.

84. Ibid.

85. See UNICEF: Children in Israeli Military Detention: Observations and Recommendations (2013), http://www.unicef.org/oPt/UNICEF_oPt_Children_in_Israeli_Military_Detention_Observations_and_Recommendations_-_6_March_2013.pdf; Defense for

Children International-Palestine: Bound, Blindfolded and Convicted Children held in military detention (2012), http://www.dci-palestine.org/sites/default/files/report_0.pdf; The Special Rapporteur on the situation of human rights in the Palestinian territories occupied since 1967, Report of the Special Rapporteur on the situation of human rights in the Palestinian territories occupied since 1967, U.N. Doc. A/HRC/25/67 (Jan. 13, 2014), http://daccess-dds-ny.un.org/doc/UNDOC/GEN/G14/101/98/PDF/G1410198.pdf; and U. S. Department of State, Country Reports on Human Rights Practices for 2013: Israel and the Occupied Territories (2014), http://www.state.gov/documents/organization/220568.pdf.

86. See Defense of Children International-Palestine, Palestinian Children Detained in the Israeli Military Court System (2013),   https://d3n8a8pro7vhmx.cloudfront.net/dcipalestine/pages/339/attachments/original/1437406651/solitary_confinement_report_2013_DCIP_final_29apr2014.pdf?1437406651.

87. Refer to the Addameer web site at: http://www.addameer.org/israeli_military_judicial_system/administrative_detention. Web. 10 Oct. 2015.

88. International Covenant on Civil and Political Rights, http://www.ohchr.org/en/professionalinterest/pages/ccpr.aspx. Web. 19 Oct. 2015.

89. International Convention on the Suppression and Punishment of the Crime of Apartheid. Adopted by the General Assembly of the United Nations on 30 November 1973. The full text of the convention can be accessed at https://treaties.un.org/doc/Publication/UNTS/Volume%201015/volume-1015-I-14861-English.pdf. Web. 19 Oct. 2015.

90. Racial group is defined by the Rome Statute of the International Criminal Court: The U.N. defines "racial discrimination" as "any distinct exclusion, restriction, or preference based on race, color, descent, or national or ethnic origin."

Tulkarem District

91. Esber, R M. *Under the Cover of War: The Zionist Expulsion of the Palestinians.* Alexandria, Virginia: Arabicus Books & Media, LLC, 2009, p 296. Print.

92. Ibid.

93. Robinson, S. "Local Struggle, National Struggle: Palestinian Responses to the Kafr Qasem Massacre and its Aftermath 1956-66." *International Journal of Middle East Studies*, Vol. 35, No. 3, 2003, pp393-416.

Acre District

94. Khalidi, Walid (ed.). *All that Remains: The Palestinian Villages Occupied and Depopulated by Israel in 1948.* Washington DC: The Institute of Palestine Studies, 1992, p 2. Print.

95. Morris, Benny. *Birth of the Palestinian Refugee Problem Revisited.* Cambridge University Press. 2004, p 416. Print.

96. Khalidi, Walid (ed.). *All that Remains: The Palestinian Villages Occupied and Depopulated by Israel in 1948.* Washington DC: The Institute of Palestine Studies, 1992, pp 9-24. Print.

97. Freeman, Charles. *Evacuation of Refugees from Kafr Yasif.* 1949, as cited by Morris, Benny. *Righteous Victims: A History of the Zioist-Arab Conflict 1881-1998.* Knopf Doubleday Publishing Group. 2011.

98. Morris, Benny. *Birth of the Palestinian Refugee Problem Revisited.* Cabridge University Press, 2004, p 515. Print.

99. Pappe, Ilan. *History of Modern Palestine: One Land, Two Peoples.* Cambrfidge, UK: Cambridge University Press, 2004, p39. Print.

100. John Halaka's web site can be accessed at http://www.sittingcrowproductions.com.

101. "Umm Aziz" means "mother of Aziz" following an Arabic custom of referring to the mother as the mother of her oldest son. Similarly, her husband would be called "Abu Aziz".

102. The Lebanese Phalange is a Maronite Christian militia founded by Pierre Jumayyil. Throughout the Lebanese civil war, the Phalange party was a formidable fighting force. Abukhalil, As'ad. Encyclopedia of the Modern Middle East and North Africa, 2004.

103. During the Lebanese civil war, Israel invaded Lebanon in June 1982 with the ostensible intention of destroying the Palestine Liberation Organization, which was operating in Lebanon and was involved in the Lebanese civil war.

104. The War of the Camps refers to the attacks on Palestinian refugee camps by the Shi'ite Amal militia, one of many operating during the Lebanese civil war Refer to http://www.unrwa.org/where-we-work/lebanon for more information.

III Art and Culture

Liberation Art of Palestine

1.   This chapter, with the permission of the author, Samia Halaby, is excerpted from her book, *Liberation Art of Palestine: Palestinian Painting and Sculpture in the Second Half of the Twentieth Century.* H. T. T. B. Publications, Ramallah and New York, 2001.

2.   Ismail Shammout. *Fan Tashkili Fi Filastine* (*The Visual Arts in Palestine*). Kuwait: Qabas Printers, 1989. 31. Print.

3.   Issam Nassar, *A Man and his Camera,* Hanna Safieh. Jerusalem: Raffi Safieh, 1999. Print.

4.   Ibid. We do not have these photographs because the British colonial government never shared its documentation with Palestinians, choosing to pass them to their Zionists heirs, and because Safieh's negatives were vandalized.

5.   It is a little-known fact that there are Palestinian Arab Jews who live among the Palestinians. There is also a community of ancient Jews that lives in the West Bank and has existed there since ancient times. These ancient Jews live on one of the two mountaintops between which the City of Nablus is located. Their mountaintop is called Gerizim and the opposite one is called Ebal, and today on Ebal is a very threatening Israeli military installation. The Jews of Gerizim refuse association with Israel.

6.   For example, Palestinians living in the village of Sabastia are aware of their connection to the land not only by their own crafting of the land, but also through the Roman and Christian ruins within their village. Their care of this heritage through the centuries is noteworthy. After the 1967 occupation of the West Bank, Israel confiscated all archeological sites in Palestine.

7.   For an excellent pictorial record of ancient mosaics in Palestine and Jordan see Michele Piccarello, The Mosaics of Jordan. Amman, Jordan: American Center of Oriental Research, plate 129. Print.

8.   Kurt Weitzmann, Manoles Chatzidakis, Svetozar Radojcic. *Icons.* New Yorkm NY: Alpine Fine Arts, 1980, 13-60. Print.

9.   Vera Tamari and Sliman Mansour. "Art in Occupied Palestine," *Naura Cultura*: (Summer 1990), 17.

10. Muhamad Al Wahibi, personal interview, 14 November 2000.

11. "Palestine 48" refers to the original land of Palestine.

12. Khalil Rayan, personal interview, 1999.

13. Fayez Sirsawi, personal interview, 21 June 2000.

14. Shammout, Ismail. *Fan Tashkili Fi Filastine* (*The Visual Arts in Palestine*). Kuwait: Qabas Printers, 1989, 78. Print. In his book, Shammout lists over 150 exhibitions, and he states that many small exhibitions took place in schools and refugee camps throughout Palestine that are not accounted for.

15. Artists Tamam Al Akhal and Nihad Sabasi exhibited in this show with Ismail Shammout.

16. Shammout, Ismail. *Fan Tashkili Fi Filastine* (*The Visual Arts in Palestine*). Kuwait: Qabas Printers, 1989, 54.

17. Ismail Shammout, personal interview, 31 May 2000.

18. Zaru, Samia Taktak. Tents and Stones. New York, NY: Palestine Week, United Nations, 238. Artists Kamal Boullata, Sari Khouri, Ismail Shammout, Vladimir Tamari, and Samia Taktak are all known to have participated in the Association. Two other young women known to be practicing artists in Jerusalem at the time were Afaf Arafat and Rihab Al Nammari.

19. Tamam Al Akhal, personal interview, 2001.

20. Abdal Rahman Al Mozayen, personal interview, July 2002.

21. Mustafa Al Hallaj, personal interview, 13 July 2000.

22. Abed Abdi, personal interview, 30 October 2012.

23. In early March of 1976, Israel published plans to expropriate about 20,000 dunums (2,000 hectares) of land around the Palestinian villages of Sakhnin and Arraba, which would later be used to establish new Jewish settlements and a military training camp. These plans were part of an official state policy to Judaize the Galilee following the creation of the state of Israel. In a collective response on March 30, 1976 - marking one of the first displays of mass coordinated action by Palestinians inside Israel - Palestinians demonstrated from across Galilee in the north all the way to the Negev in the south. Six Palestinians were shot dead by Israeli forces and more than 100 were injured. Accessed 10/16/2015 at http://www.aljazeera.com/indepth/inpictures/2015/03/land-day-palestinians-walk-memories-150329121424807.html.

24. Mahmoud Jadda, personal interview, 21 June 2002.

25. Zuhdie Al Adawi, personal interview, April 2002.

26. Muhammad Al Rakoui, personal interviews, 1997 and 2000.

27. Muhammad Al Rakoui, personal interviews, 1997 and 2000.

28. To sit in peasant style is to bend the knees deeply without resting any part of the body on the ground except the feet.

The Origins of Traditional Palestinian Costume

29. This chapter on the Origins of Traditional Palestinian Costume is excerpted by Hanan Munayyer from a stunningly beautiful 554-page book, *Traditional Palestinian Costume: Origins and Evolution,* by Hanan Karaman Munayyer. The reference for this book is: Munayyer, Hanan Karaman. *Traditional Palestinian Costume: Origins and Evolution.* Northampton, Massachusetts: Olive Branch Press, 2011. Print.

30. The last Iranian empire before the rise of Islam.

Nahida Halaby Gordon, Ph. D., Professor Emerita in Probability and Statistics at Case Western Reserve University, has a deep interest in Palestine which motivated her to serve as a Fulbright Senior Scholar at Birzeit University, Palestine. In addition, she was granted a US Congress, Fulbright-Hayes Senior Scholar Program to engage in an exchange program with faculty at the Institute of Community and Public Health at Birzeit University.

During Professor Gordon's teaching career, she served on many university and departmental committees and mentored students as thesis advisor at the master's and doctoral level in biostatistics. She authored 97 peer reviewed articles both solo and in collaboration with others in the fields of biostatistics, epidemiology, nursing and medicine; and presented research papers at scientific meetings nationally and internationally. In support of her research, she received grants from the American Cancer Society, National Institutes of Health, and Fulbright-Hayes Senior Scholar Program. She served as scientific reviewer for these organizations as well as the American Institute of Biological Sciences, and also served on the editorial board of the Journal of Immigrant Health, and editorial reviewer for various journals in biostatistics and epidemiology.

For years, Nahida Gordon, has been engaged in advocacy for peace and justice for Palestine. Currently, she is a member of the steering committees of the Israel Palestine Mission Network and the Advocacy Committee for Racial Ethnic Concerns both of the Presbyterian Church (U.S.A.). She is also a member of the Interfaith Council for Peace in the Middle East and is a past president and currently serves on its leadership board. A life-long Presbyterian and a church Elder, Professor Gordon, is a Palestinian-American who experienced, first hand, the 1948 Palestinian Nakba.

This book, *Palestine is Our Home: Voices of Loss, Courage, and Steadfastness,* is an expression of her passion for peace and justice for the people of Palestine.

Made in the USA
Middletown, DE
11 May 2016